BATMAN
DETECTIVE COMICS

VOL. 1:
MYTHOLOGY

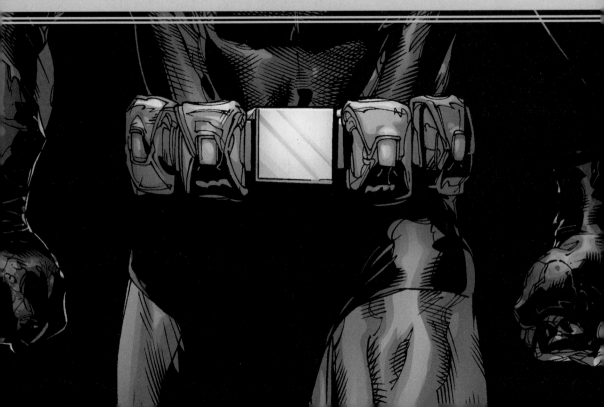

BATMAN
DETECTIVE COMICS

VOL. 1:
MYTHOLOGY

PETER J. TOMASI
WRITER

DOUG MAHNKE
PENCILLER

DAVID BARON
COLORIST

ROB LEIGH
LETTERER

JAIME MENDOZA
MARK IRWIN
CHRISTIAN ALAMY
KEITH CHAMPAGNE
INKERS

DOUG MAHNKE
JAIME MENDOZA
and **DAVID BARON**
COLLECTION COVER ARTISTS

BATMAN CREATED BY **BOB KANE** WITH **BILL FINGER**

CHRIS CONROY Editor – Original Series
DAVE WIELGOSZ Assistant Editor – Original Series
JEB WOODARD Group Editor – Collected Editions
ROBIN WILDMAN Editor – Collected Edition
STEVE COOK Design Director – Books
DAMIAN RYLAND Publication Design
CHRISTY SAWYER Publication Production

BOB HARRAS Senior VP – Editor-in-Chief, DC Comics
PAT McCALLUM Executive Editor, DC Comics

DAN DiDIO Publisher
JIM LEE Publisher & Chief Creative Officer
BOBBIE CHASE VP – New Publishing Initiatives & Talent Development
DON FALLETTI VP – Manufacturing Operations & Workflow Management
LAWRENCE GANEM VP – Talent Services
ALISON GILL Senior VP – Manufacturing & Operations
HANK KANALZ Senior VP – Publishing Strategy & Support Services
DAN MIRON VP – Publishing Operations
NICK J. NAPOLITANO VP – Manufacturing Administration & Design
NANCY SPEARS VP – Sales
MICHELE R. WELLS VP & Executive Editor, Young Reader

BATMAN: DETECTIVE COMICS VOL. 1: MYTHOLOGY

DC Comics, 2900 West Alameda Ave., Burbank, CA 91505
Printed by LSC Communications, Owensville, MO, USA. 1/17/20.
First Printing.
ISBN: 978-1-77950-172-1

Library of Congress Cataloging-in-Publication Data is available.

PEFC Certified

This product is from
sustainably managed
forests and controlled
sources

PEFC/29-31-337   www.pefc.org

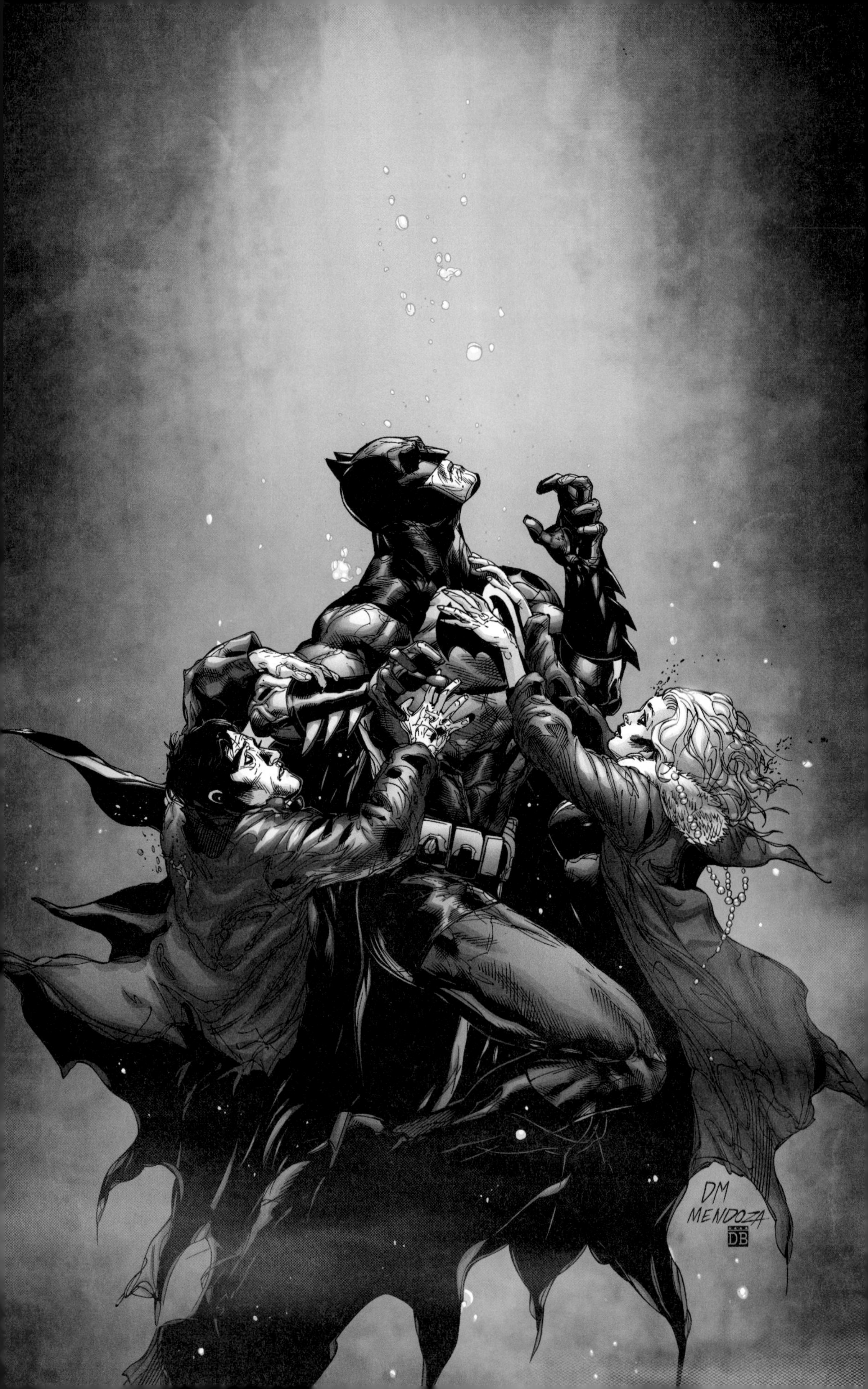
DM
MENDOZA
DB

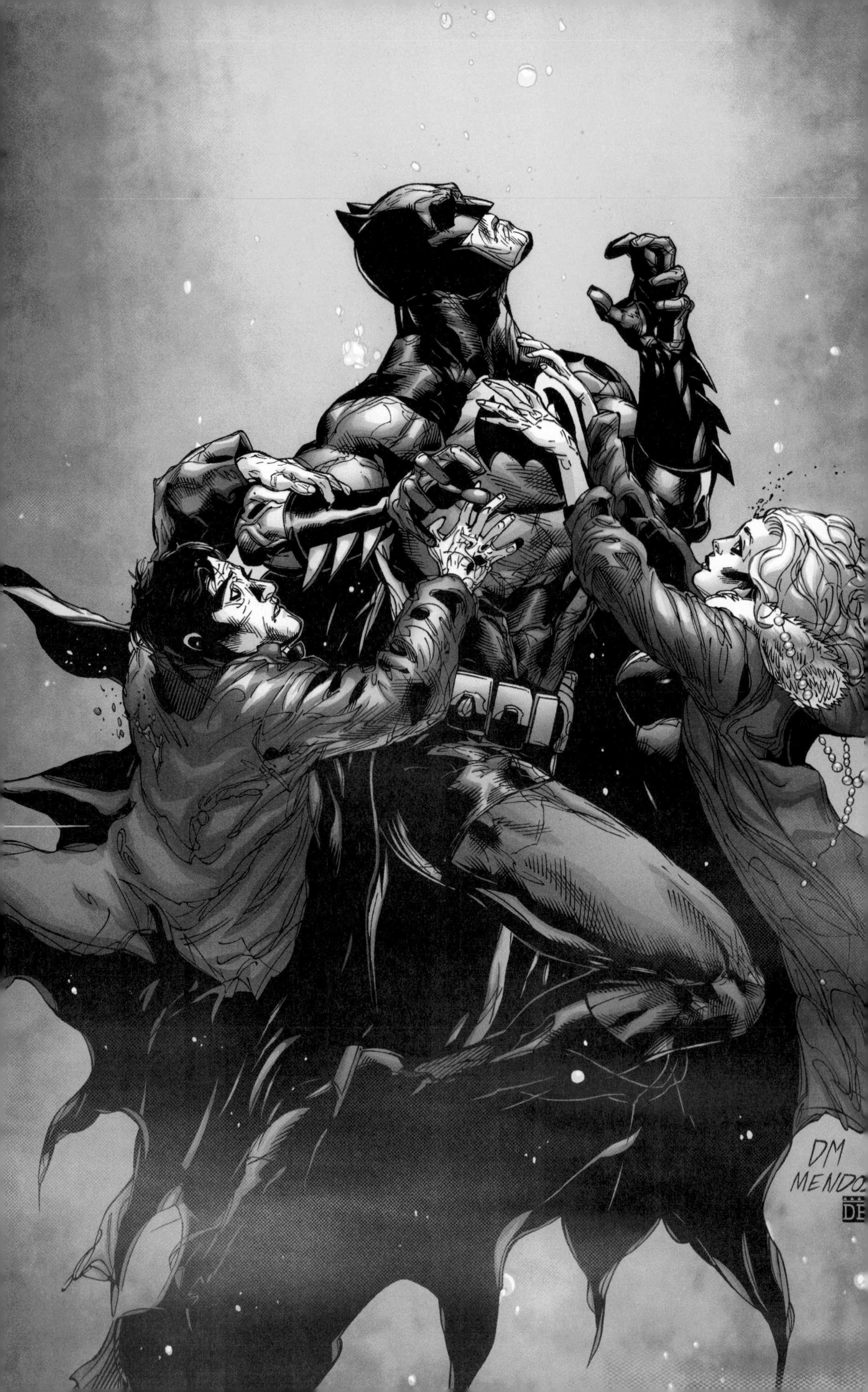
DM
MENDO

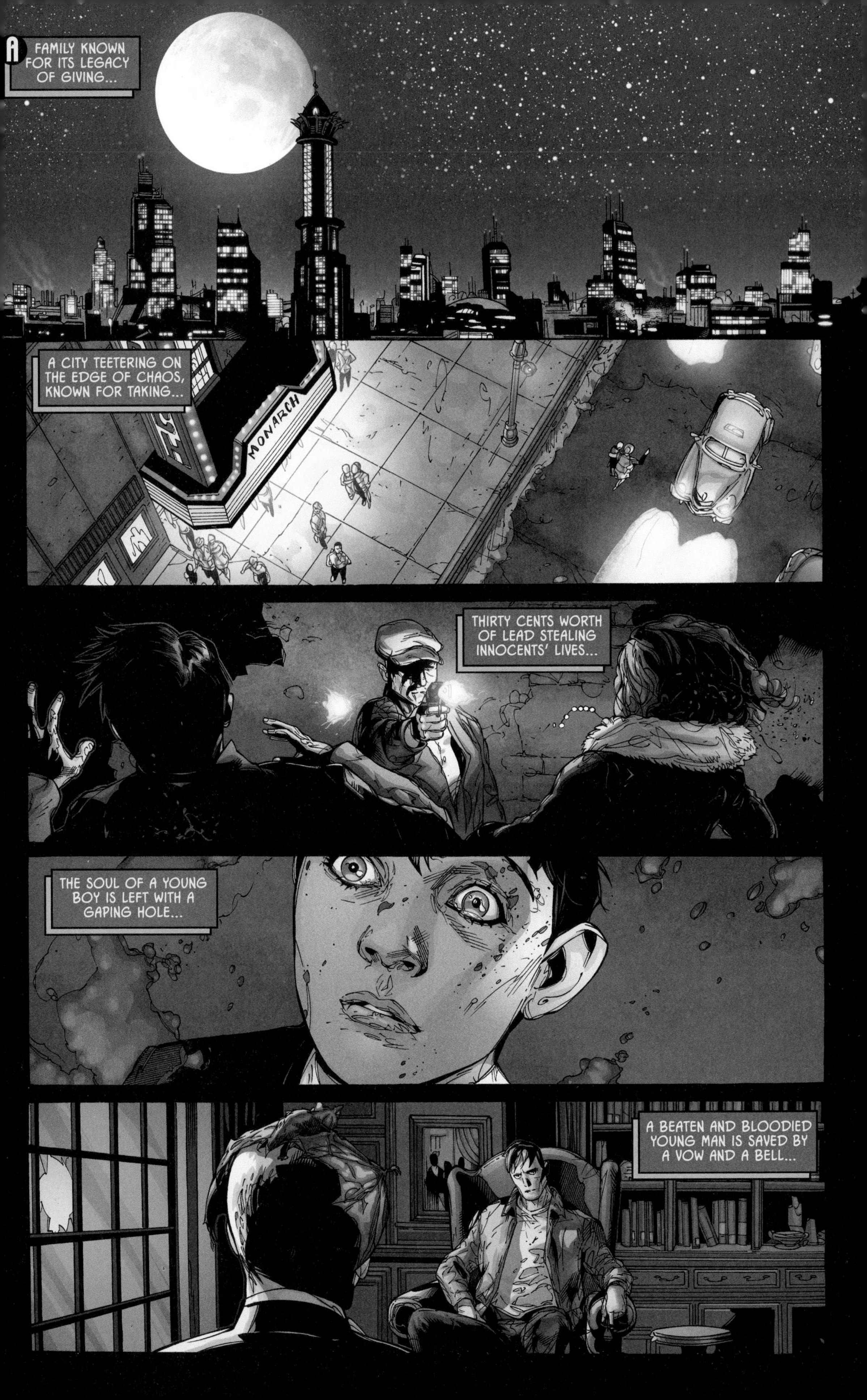
A FAMILY KNOWN FOR ITS LEGACY OF GIVING...
A CITY TEETERING ON THE EDGE OF CHAOS, KNOWN FOR TAKING...
MONARCH
THIRTY CENTS WORTH OF LEAD STEALING INNOCENTS' LIVES...
THE SOUL OF A YOUNG BOY IS LEFT WITH A GAPING HOLE...
A BEATEN AND BLOODIED YOUNG MAN IS SAVED BY A VOW AND A BELL...

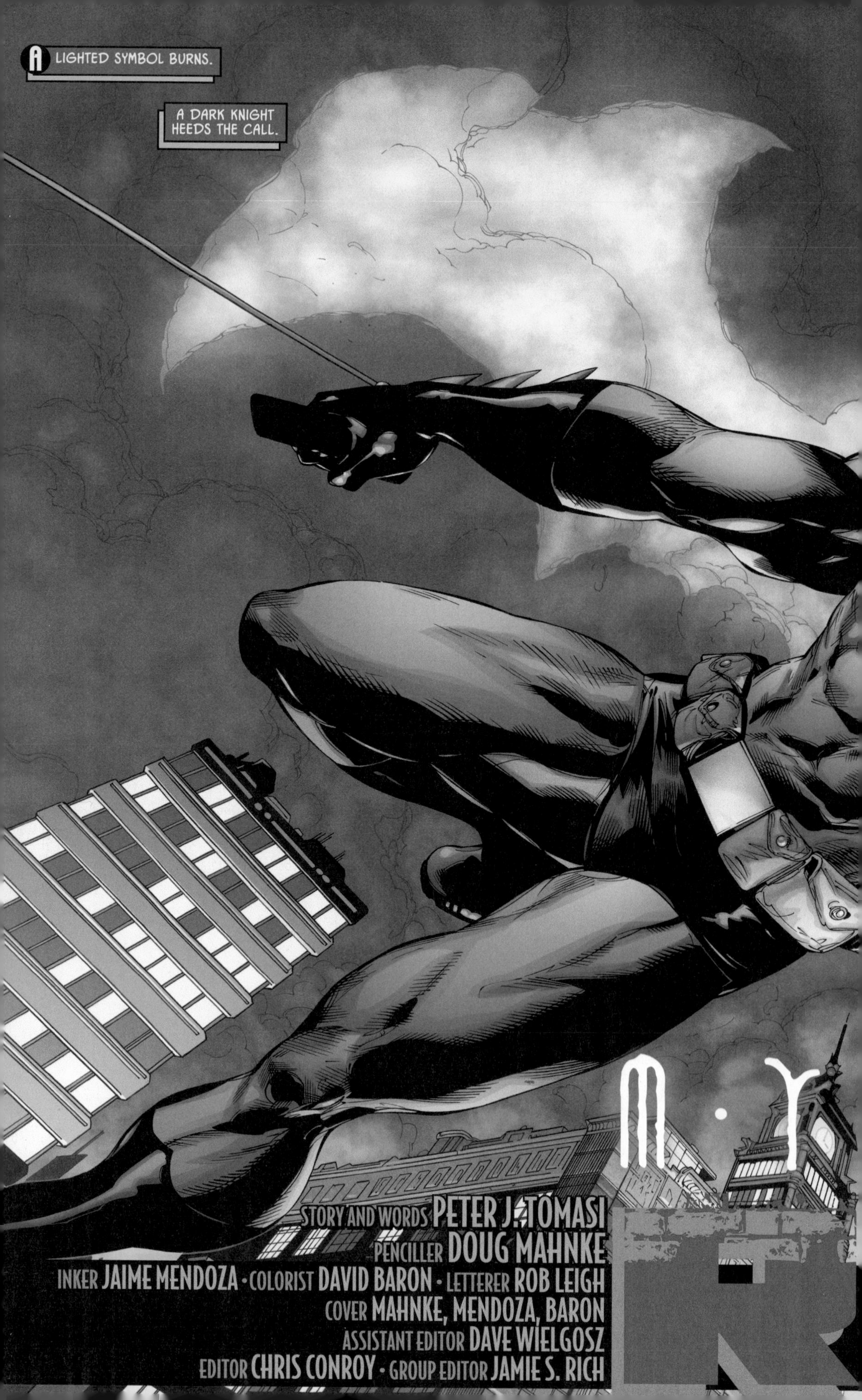
A LIGHTED SYMBOL BURNS.
A DARK KNIGHT HEEDS THE CALL.
STORY AND WORDS PETER J. TOMASI
PENCILLER DOUG MAHNKE
INKER JAIME MENDOZA · COLORIST DAVID BARON · LETTERER ROB LEIGH
COVER MAHNKE, MENDOZA, BARON
ASSISTANT EDITOR DAVE WIELGOSZ
EDITOR CHRIS CONROY · GROUP EDITOR JAMIE S. RICH

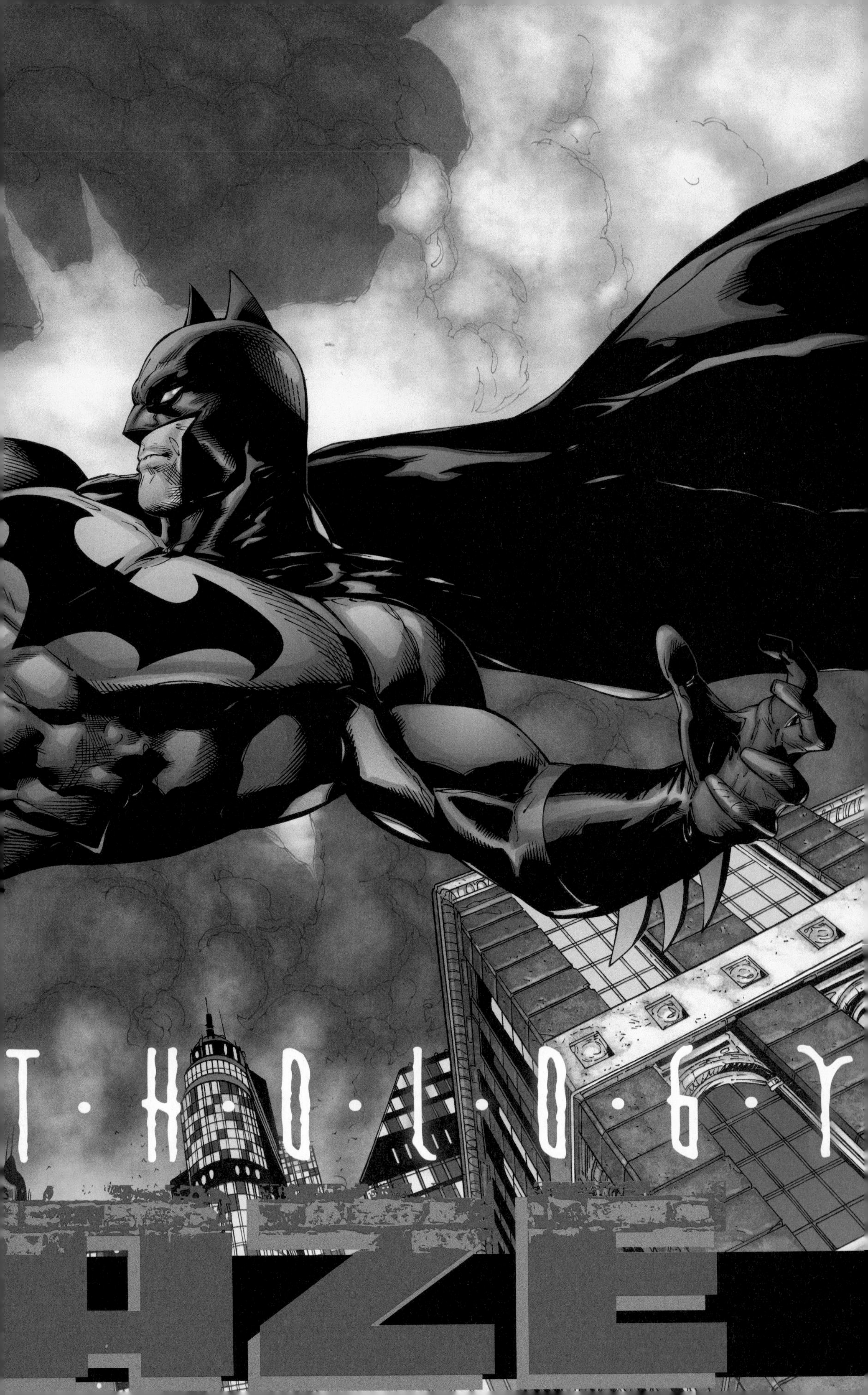
T · H · O · L · O · G · Y

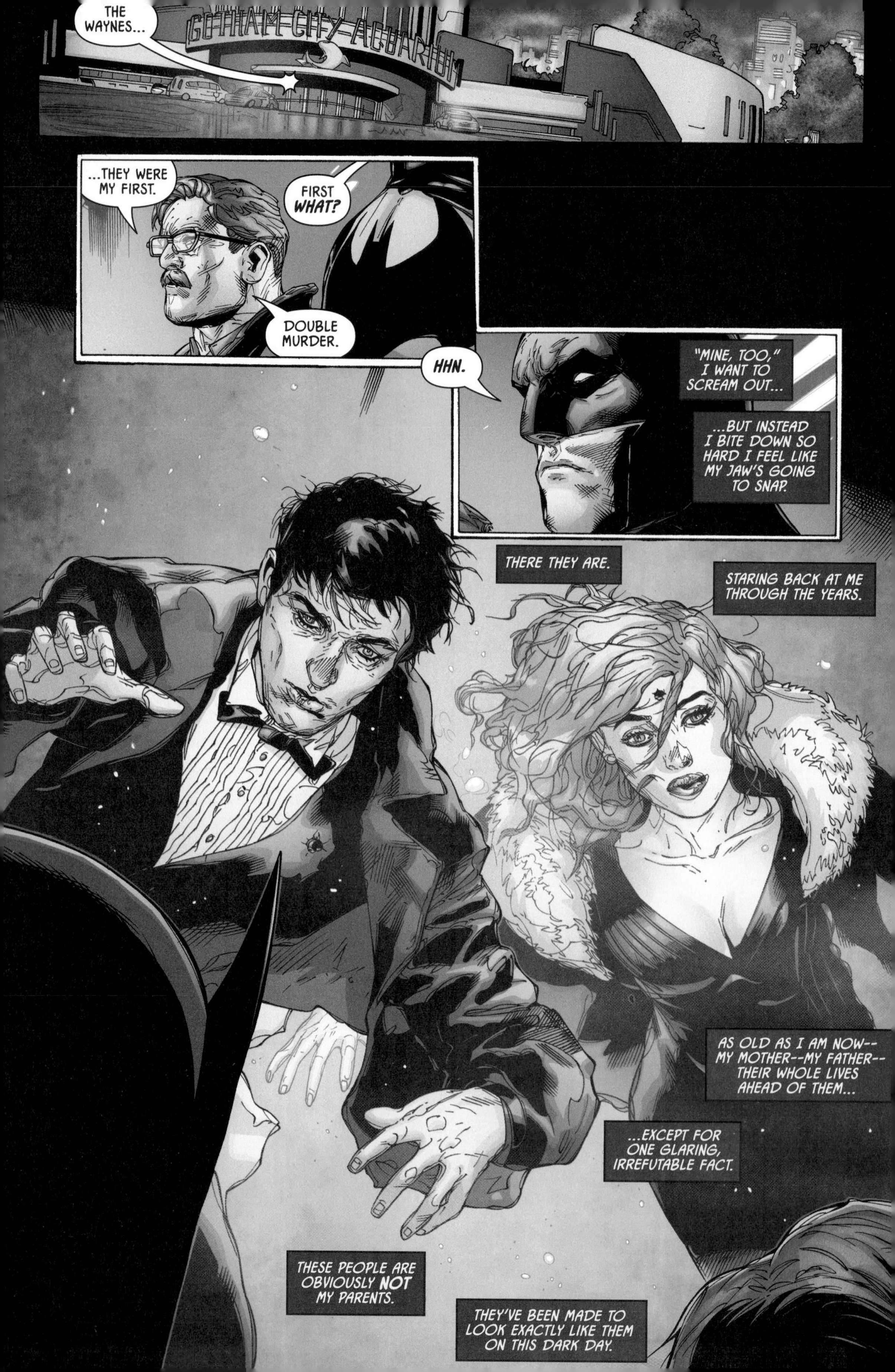
GOTHAM CITY AQUARIUM
THE WAYNES...
...THEY WERE MY FIRST.
FIRST WHAT?
DOUBLE MURDER.
HHN.
"MINE, TOO," I WANT TO SCREAM OUT...
...BUT INSTEAD I BITE DOWN SO HARD I FEEL LIKE MY JAW'S GOING TO SNAP.
THERE THEY ARE.
STARING BACK AT ME THROUGH THE YEARS.
AS OLD AS I AM NOW-- MY MOTHER--MY FATHER-- THEIR WHOLE LIVES AHEAD OF THEM...
...EXCEPT FOR ONE GLARING, IRREFUTABLE FACT.
THESE PEOPLE ARE OBVIOUSLY NOT MY PARENTS.
THEY'VE BEEN MADE TO LOOK EXACTLY LIKE THEM ON THIS DARK DAY.

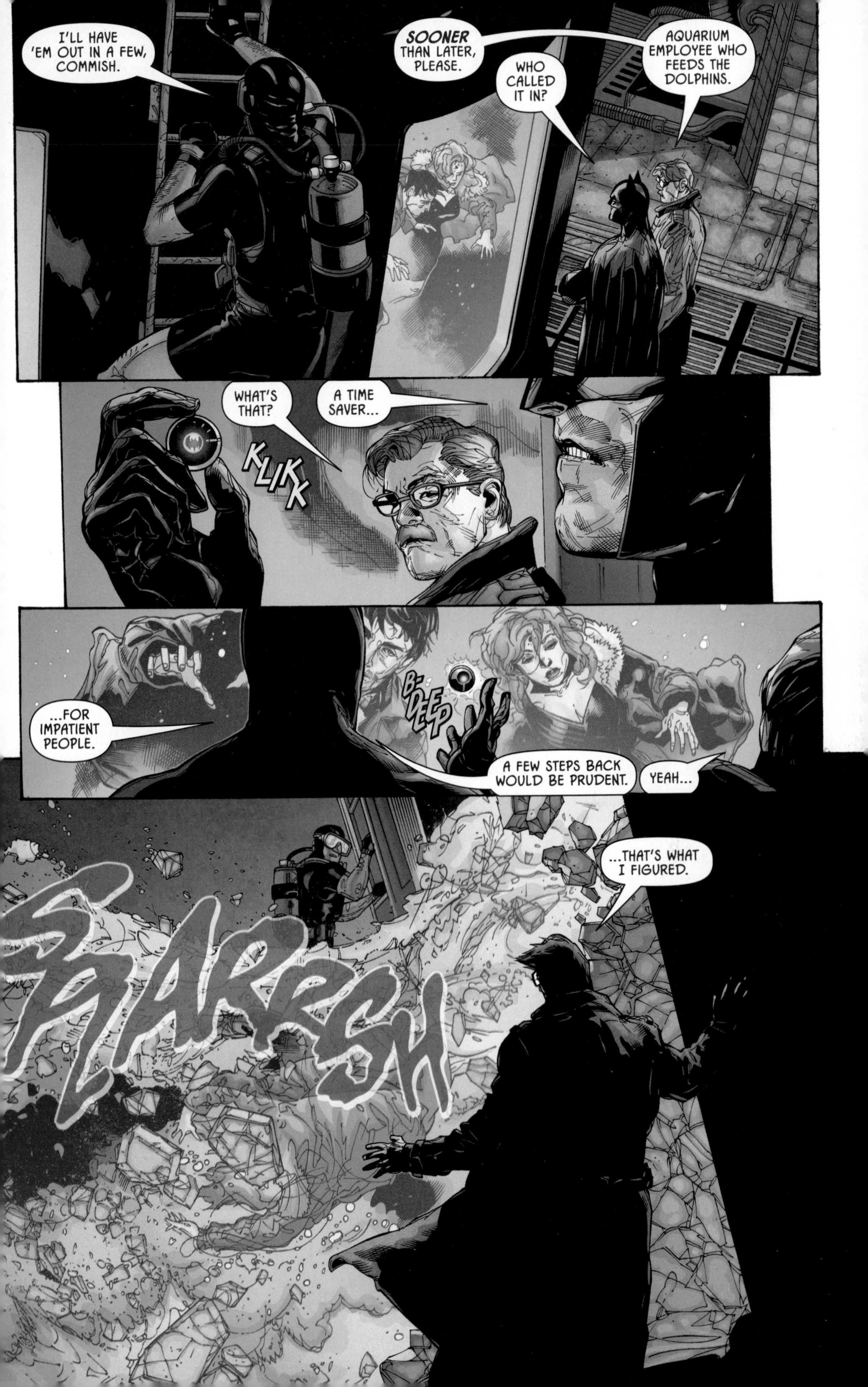
I'LL HAVE 'EM OUT IN A FEW, COMMISH.
SOONER THAN LATER, PLEASE.
WHO CALLED IT IN?
AQUARIUM EMPLOYEE WHO FEEDS THE DOLPHINS.
WHAT'S THAT?
A TIME SAVER...
KLIKK
...FOR IMPATIENT PEOPLE.
B-DEEP
A FEW STEPS BACK WOULD BE PRUDENT.
YEAH...
...THAT'S WHAT I FIGURED.
SHARRSH

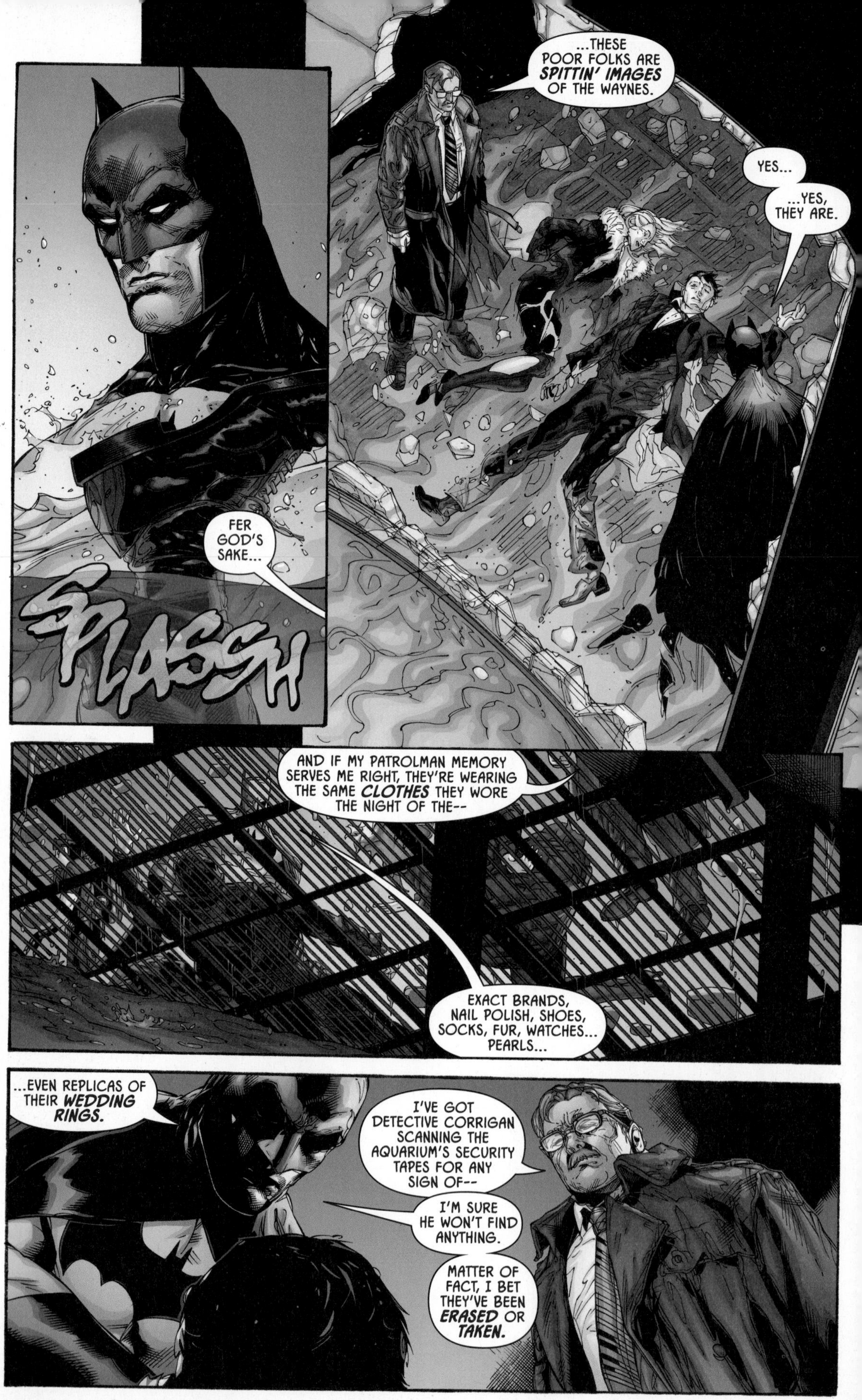
...THESE POOR FOLKS ARE SPITTIN' IMAGES OF THE WAYNES.
YES...
...YES, THEY ARE.
FER GOD'S SAKE...
SPLASSH
AND IF MY PATROLMAN MEMORY SERVES ME RIGHT, THEY'RE WEARING THE SAME CLOTHES THEY WORE THE NIGHT OF THE--
EXACT BRANDS, NAIL POLISH, SHOES, SOCKS, FUR, WATCHES... PEARLS...
...EVEN REPLICAS OF THEIR WEDDING RINGS.
I'VE GOT DETECTIVE CORRIGAN SCANNING THE AQUARIUM'S SECURITY TAPES FOR ANY SIGN OF--
I'M SURE HE WON'T FIND ANYTHING.
MATTER OF FACT, I BET THEY'VE BEEN ERASED OR TAKEN.

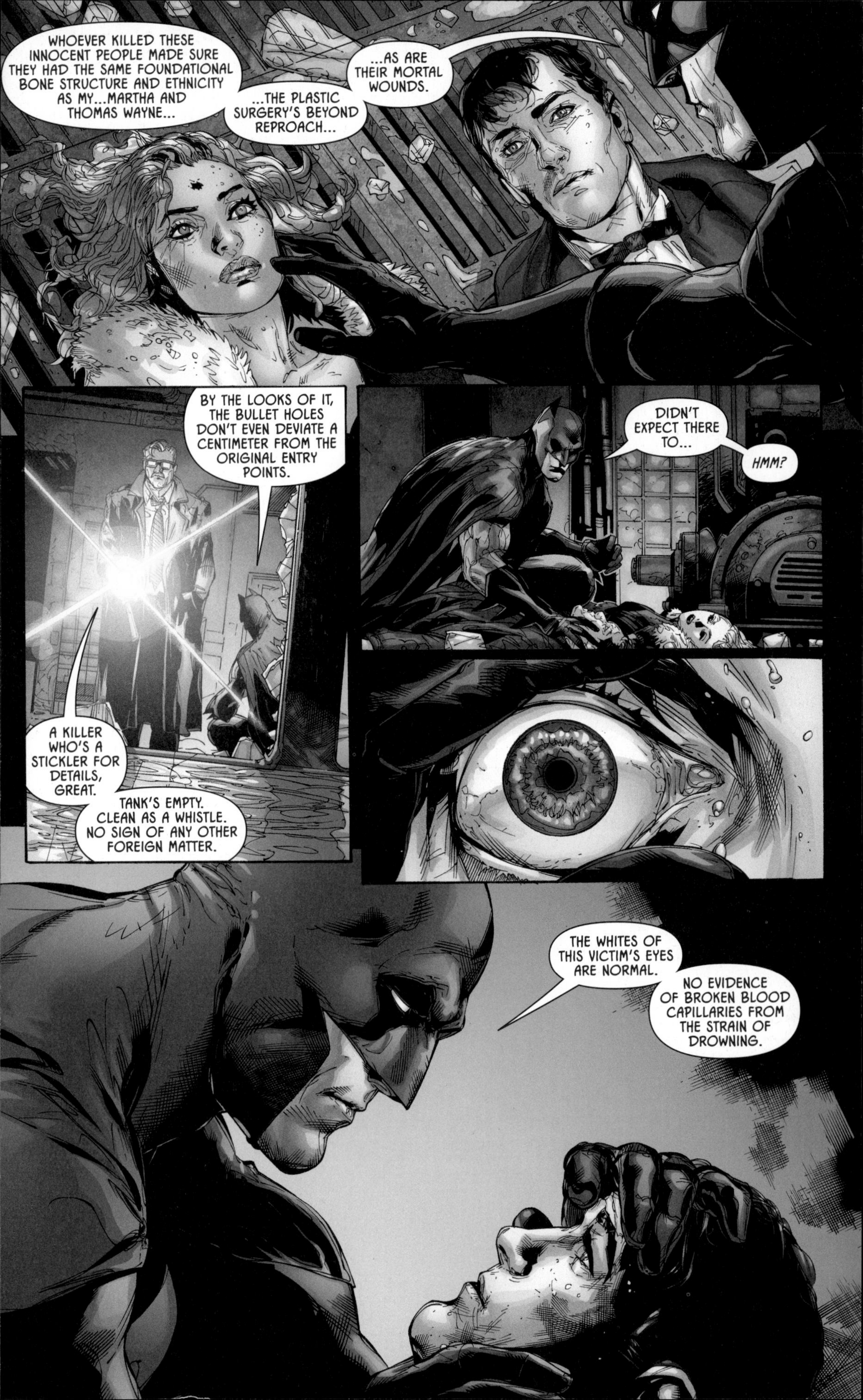
WHOEVER KILLED THESE INNOCENT PEOPLE MADE SURE THEY HAD THE SAME FOUNDATIONAL BONE STRUCTURE AND ETHNICITY AS MY...MARTHA AND THOMAS WAYNE...
...THE PLASTIC SURGERY'S BEYOND REPROACH...
...AS ARE THEIR MORTAL WOUNDS.
BY THE LOOKS OF IT, THE BULLET HOLES DON'T EVEN DEVIATE A CENTIMETER FROM THE ORIGINAL ENTRY POINTS.
A KILLER WHO'S A STICKLER FOR DETAILS, GREAT.
TANK'S EMPTY. CLEAN AS A WHISTLE. NO SIGN OF ANY OTHER FOREIGN MATTER.
DIDN'T EXPECT THERE TO...
HMM?
THE WHITES OF THIS VICTIM'S EYES ARE NORMAL.
NO EVIDENCE OF BROKEN BLOOD CAPILLARIES FROM THE STRAIN OF DROWNING.

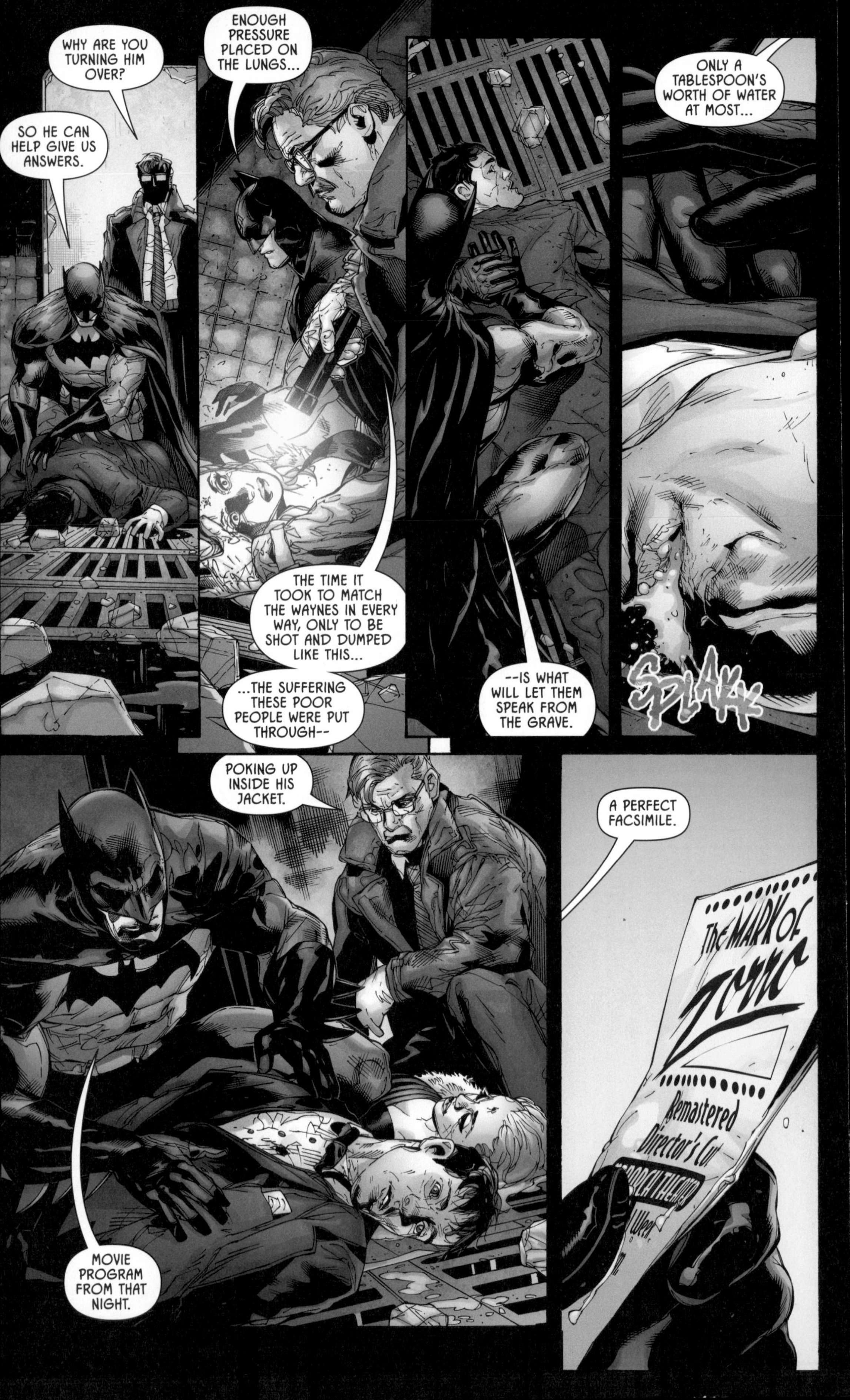
WHY ARE YOU TURNING HIM OVER?
SO HE CAN HELP GIVE US ANSWERS.
ENOUGH PRESSURE PLACED ON THE LUNGS...
THE TIME IT TOOK TO MATCH THE WAYNES IN EVERY WAY, ONLY TO BE SHOT AND DUMPED LIKE THIS...
...THE SUFFERING THESE POOR PEOPLE WERE PUT THROUGH--
--IS WHAT WILL LET THEM SPEAK FROM THE GRAVE.
ONLY A TABLESPOON'S WORTH OF WATER AT MOST...
SPLAKK
POKING UP INSIDE HIS JACKET.
MOVIE PROGRAM FROM THAT NIGHT.
A PERFECT FACSIMILE.
The MARK OF ZORRO
Remastered Director's Cut

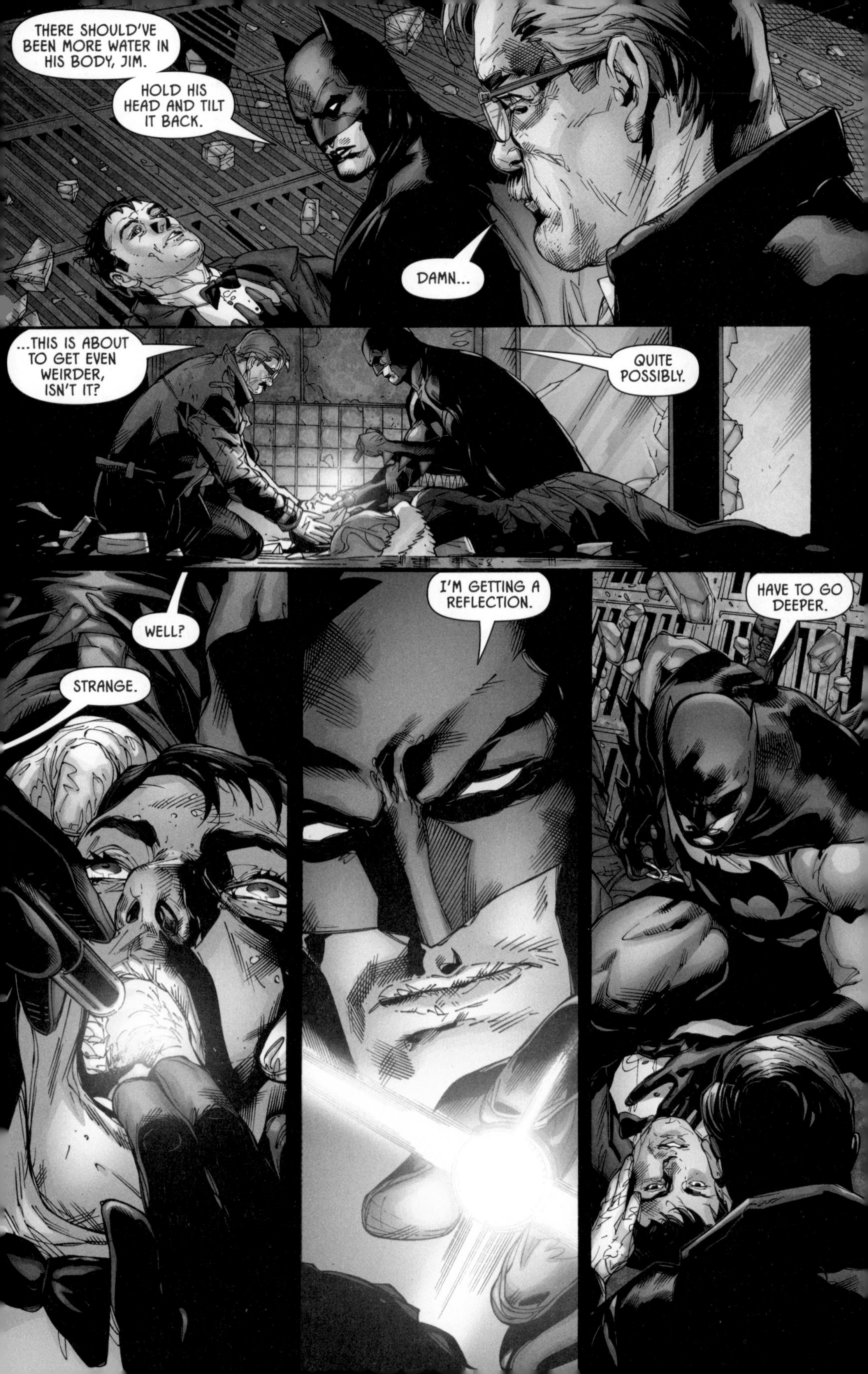
THERE SHOULD'VE BEEN MORE WATER IN HIS BODY, JIM.
HOLD HIS HEAD AND TILT IT BACK.
DAMN...
...THIS IS ABOUT TO GET EVEN WEIRDER, ISN'T IT?
QUITE POSSIBLY.
WELL?
STRANGE.
I'M GETTING A REFLECTION.
HAVE TO GO DEEPER.

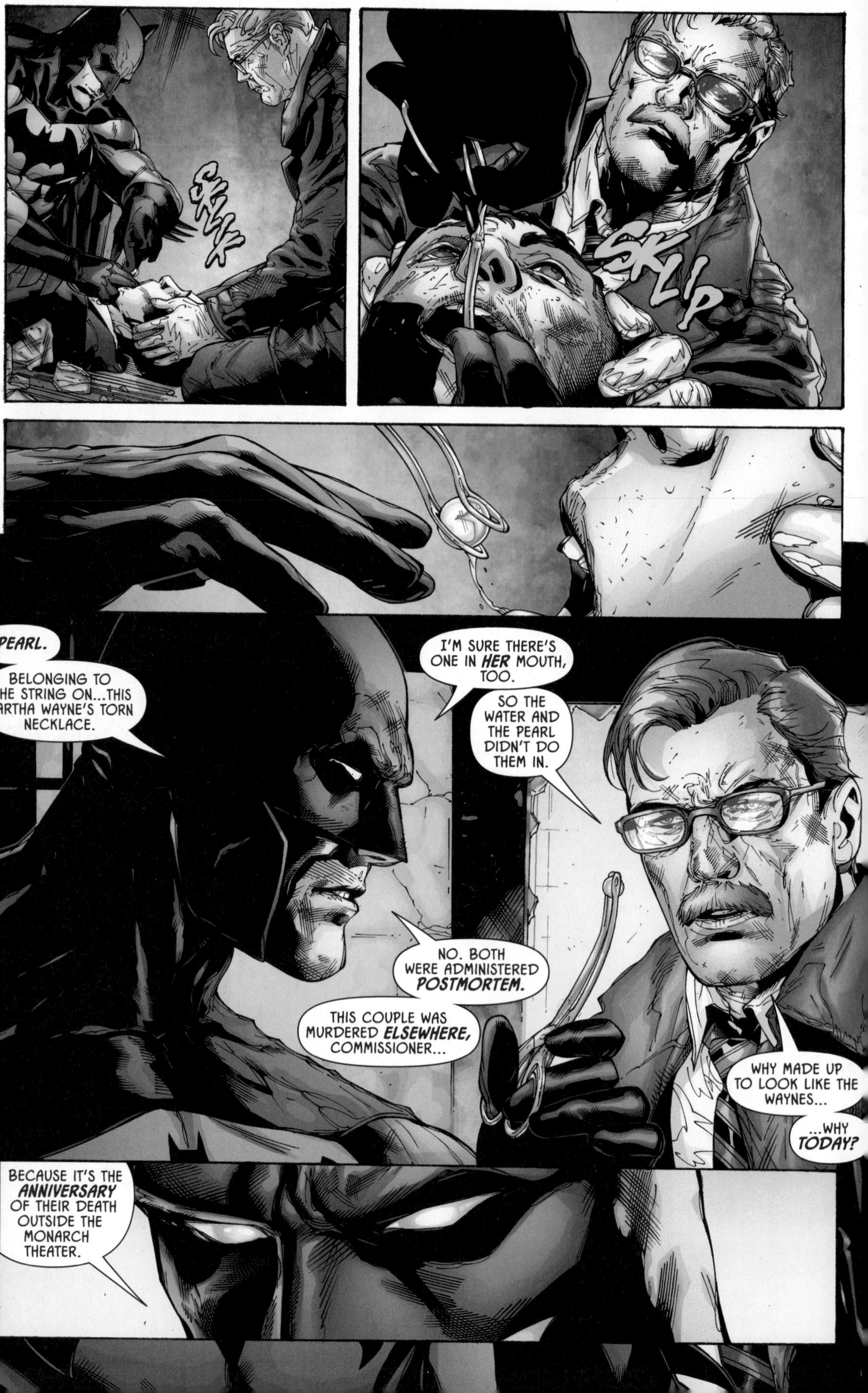
SKLK
SKLIP
A PEARL.
BELONGING TO THE STRING ON...THIS MARTHA WAYNE'S TORN NECKLACE.
I'M SURE THERE'S ONE IN HER MOUTH, TOO.
SO THE WATER AND THE PEARL DIDN'T DO THEM IN.
NO. BOTH WERE ADMINISTERED POSTMORTEM.
THIS COUPLE WAS MURDERED ELSEWHERE, COMMISSIONER...
WHY MADE UP TO LOOK LIKE THE WAYNES...
...WHY TODAY?
BECAUSE IT'S THE ANNIVERSARY OF THEIR DEATH OUTSIDE THE MONARCH THEATER.

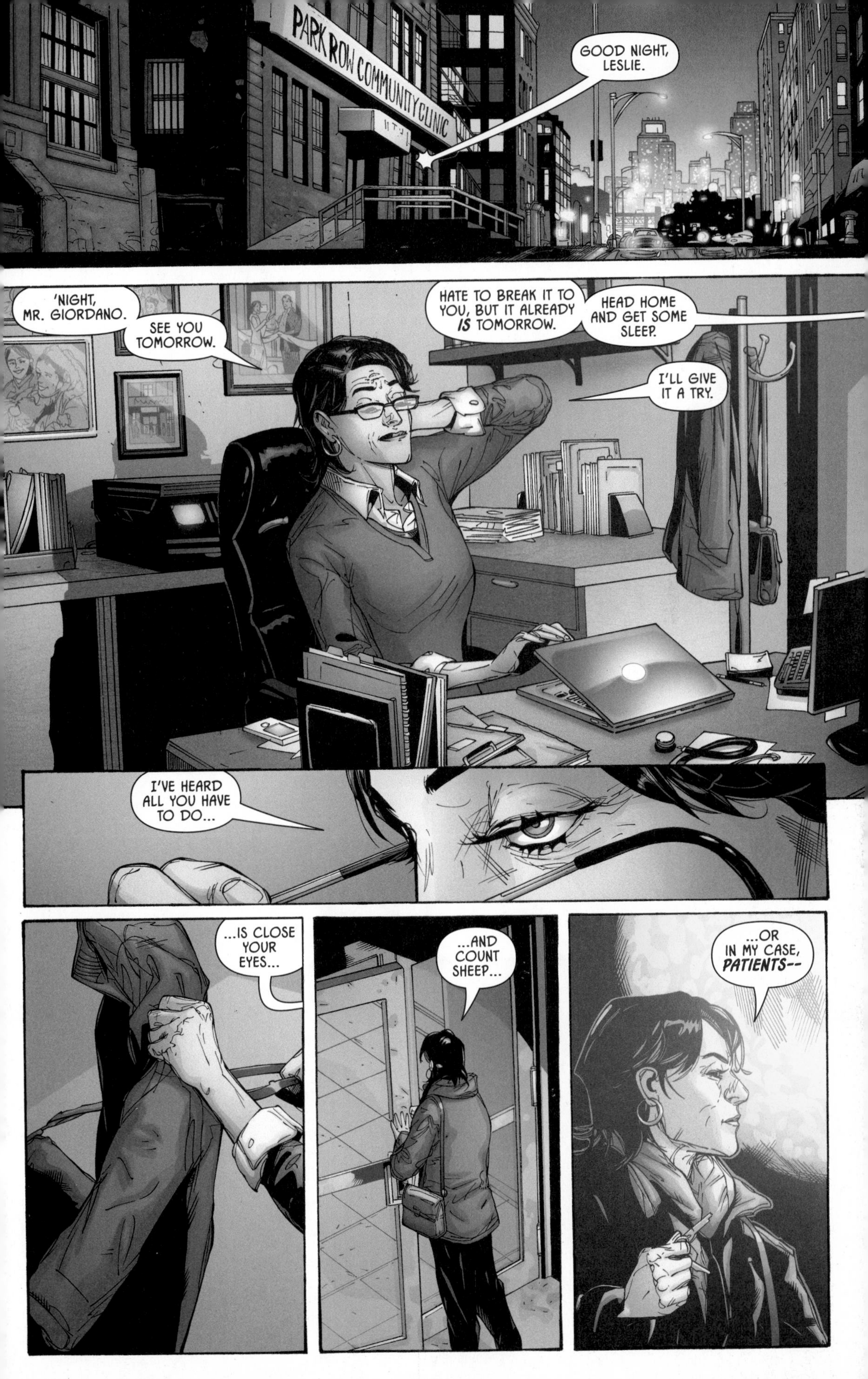
PARK ROW COMMUNITY CLINIC
GOOD NIGHT, LESLIE.
'NIGHT, MR. GIORDANO.
SEE YOU TOMORROW.
HATE TO BREAK IT TO YOU, BUT IT ALREADY *IS* TOMORROW.
HEAD HOME AND GET SOME SLEEP.
I'LL GIVE IT A TRY.
I'VE HEARD ALL YOU HAVE TO DO...
...IS CLOSE YOUR EYES...
...AND COUNT SHEEP...
...OR IN MY CASE, ***PATIENTS--***

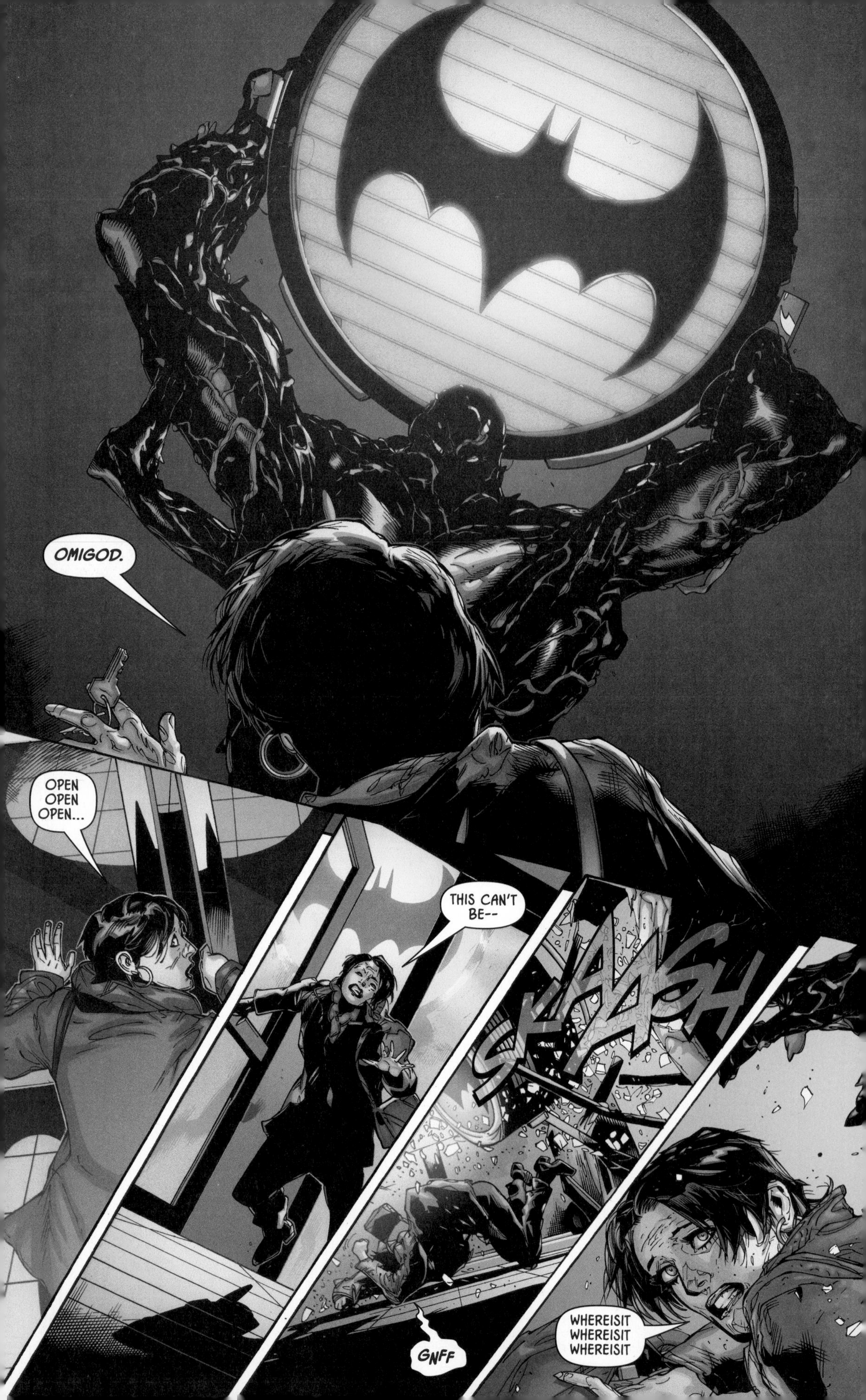
OMIGOD.
OPEN OPEN OPEN...
THIS CAN'T BE--
GNFF
WHEREISIT WHEREISIT WHEREISIT

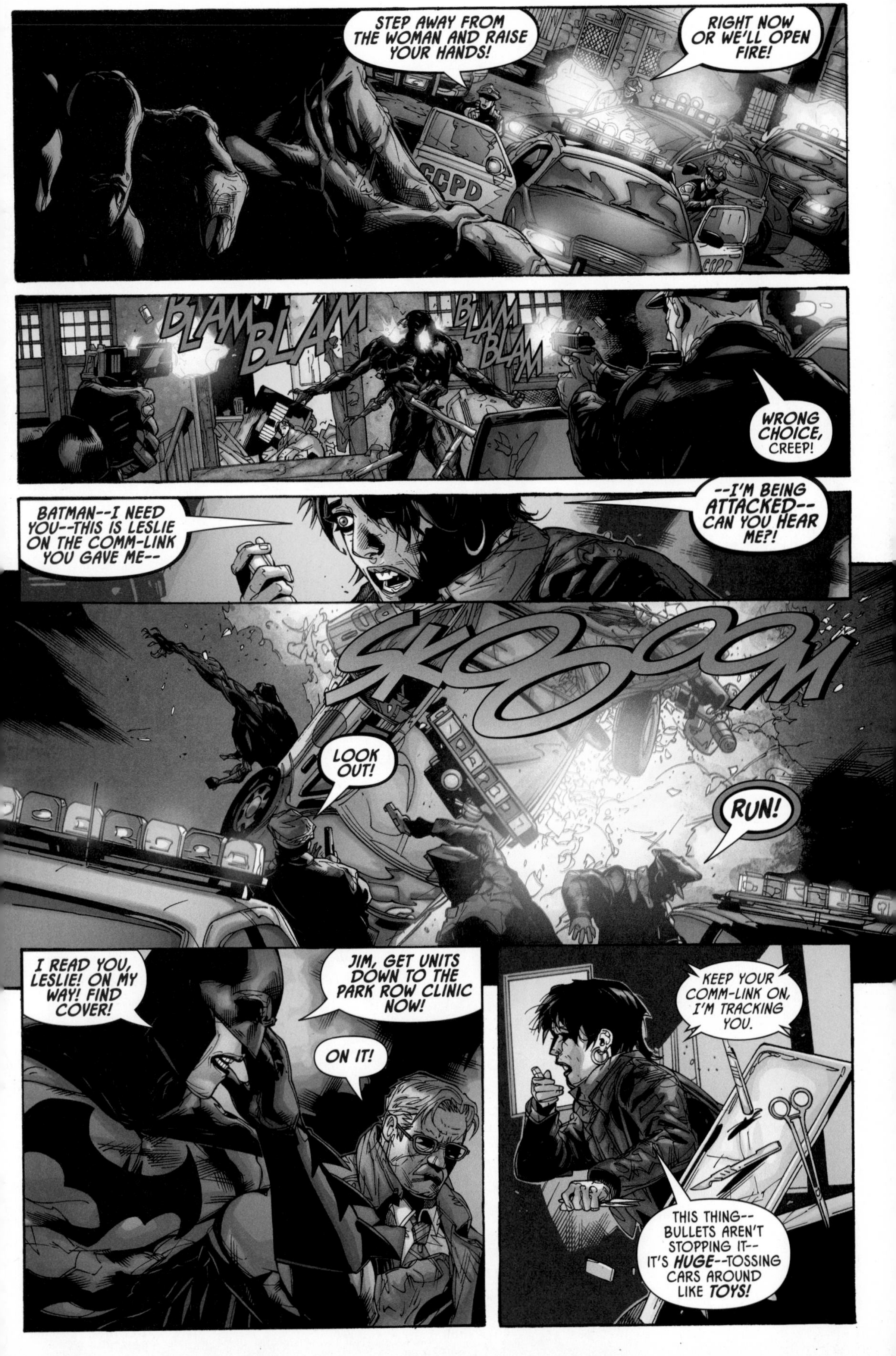
STEP AWAY FROM THE WOMAN AND RAISE YOUR HANDS!
RIGHT NOW OR WE'LL OPEN FIRE!
GCPD
BLAM BLAM
BLAM BLAM
WRONG CHOICE, CREEP!
BATMAN--I NEED YOU--THIS IS LESLIE ON THE COMM-LINK YOU GAVE ME--
--I'M BEING ATTACKED--CAN YOU HEAR ME?!
SKOOOM
LOOK OUT!
RUN!
I READ YOU, LESLIE! ON MY WAY! FIND COVER!
JIM, GET UNITS DOWN TO THE PARK ROW CLINIC NOW!
ON IT!
KEEP YOUR COMM-LINK ON, I'M TRACKING YOU.
THIS THING--BULLETS AREN'T STOPPING IT--IT'S HUGE--TOSSING CARS AROUND LIKE TOYS!

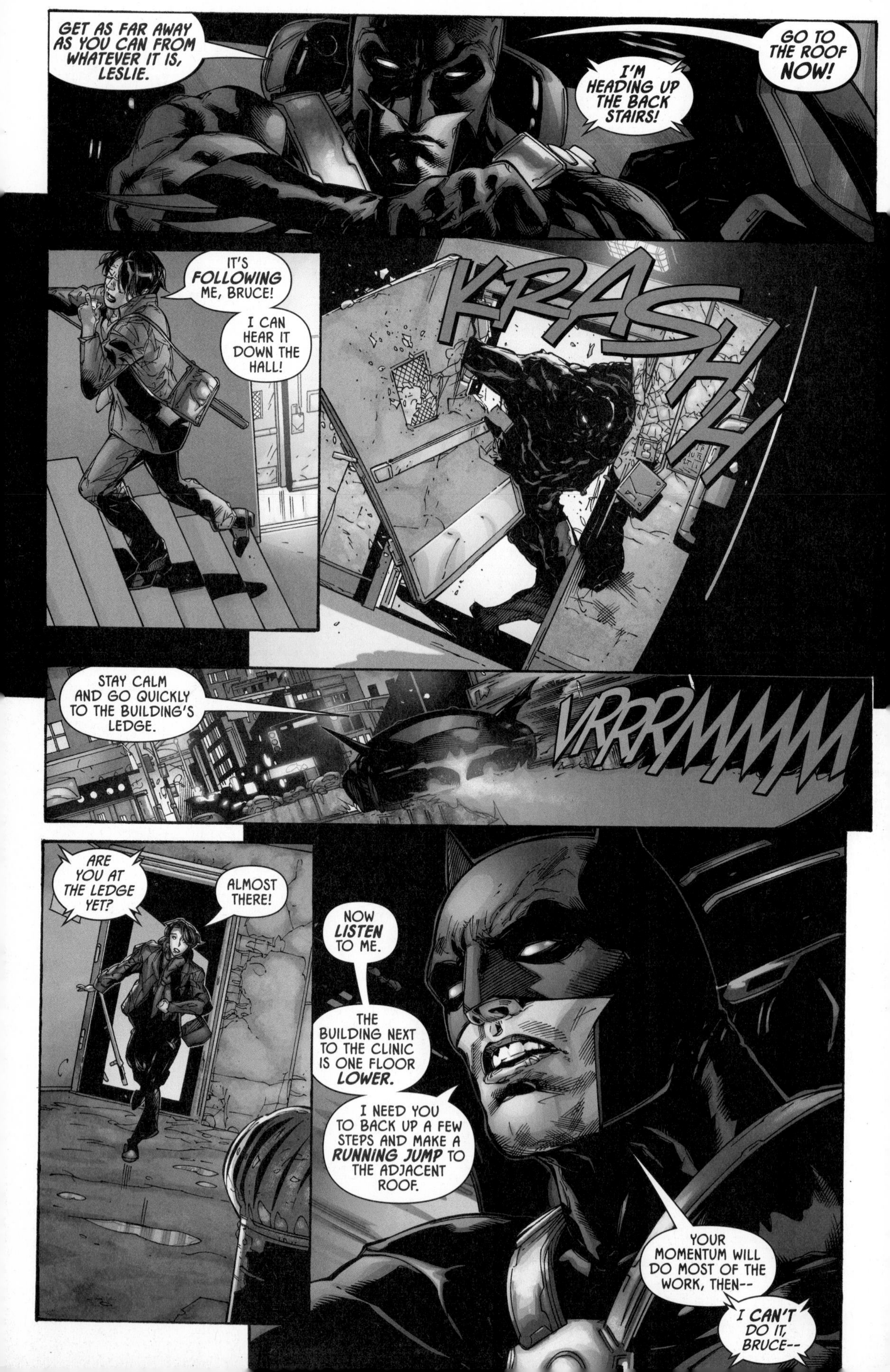
GET AS FAR AWAY AS YOU CAN FROM WHATEVER IT IS, LESLIE.
I'M HEADING UP THE BACK STAIRS!
GO TO THE ROOF NOW!
IT'S FOLLOWING ME, BRUCE!
I CAN HEAR IT DOWN THE HALL!
KRASHH
STAY CALM AND GO QUICKLY TO THE BUILDING'S LEDGE.
VRRRMMMM
ARE YOU AT THE LEDGE YET?
ALMOST THERE!
NOW LISTEN TO ME.
THE BUILDING NEXT TO THE CLINIC IS ONE FLOOR LOWER.
I NEED YOU TO BACK UP A FEW STEPS AND MAKE A RUNNING JUMP TO THE ADJACENT ROOF.
YOUR MOMENTUM WILL DO MOST OF THE WORK, THEN--
I CAN'T DO IT, BRUCE--

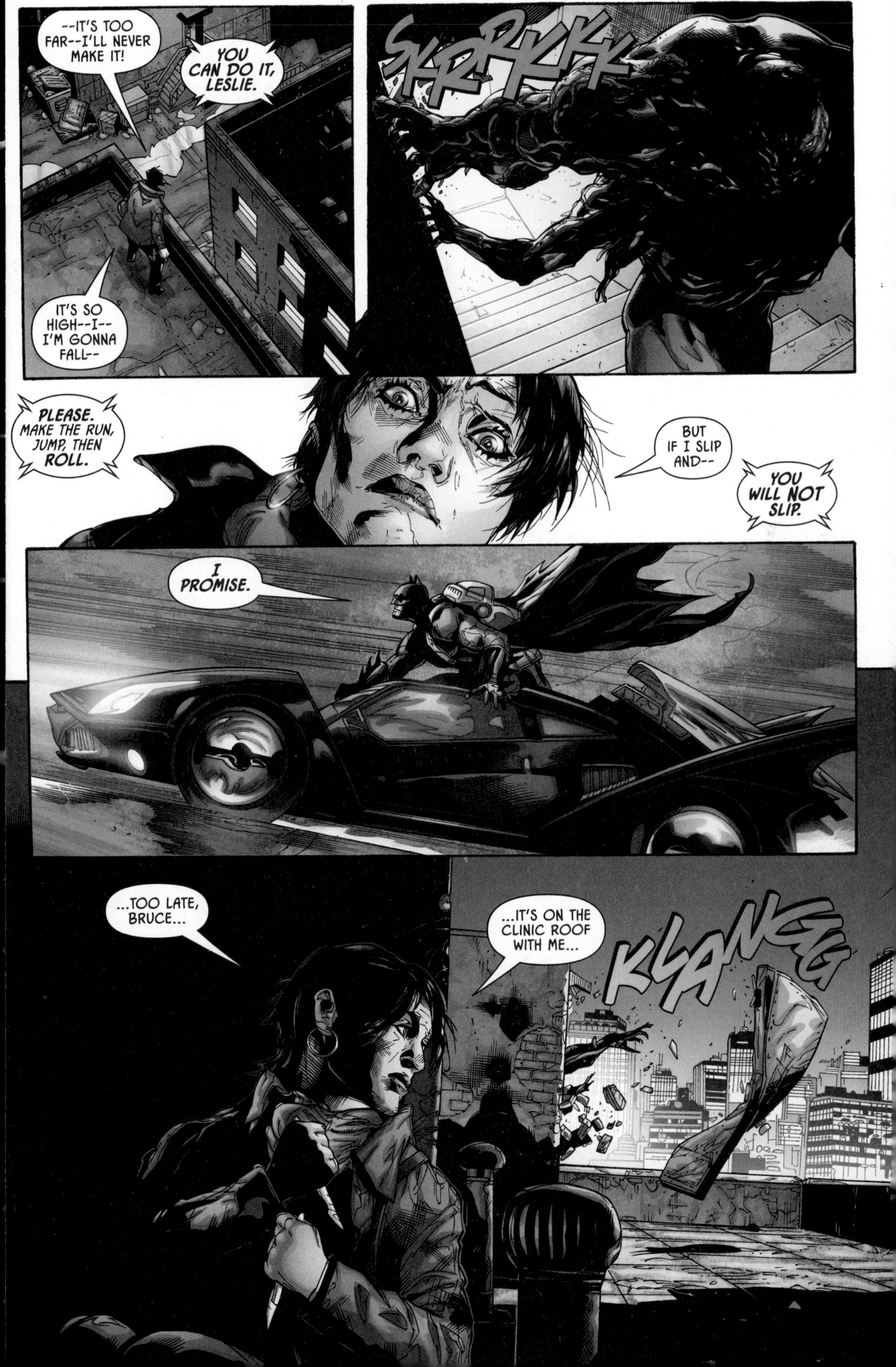
--IT'S TOO FAR--I'LL NEVER MAKE IT!
YOU CAN DO IT, LESLIE.
IT'S SO HIGH--I--I'M GONNA FALL--
SKRKKK
PLEASE. MAKE THE RUN, JUMP, THEN ROLL.
BUT IF I SLIP AND--
YOU WILL NOT SLIP.
I PROMISE.
...TOO LATE, BRUCE...
...IT'S ON THE CLINIC ROOF WITH ME...
KLANGG

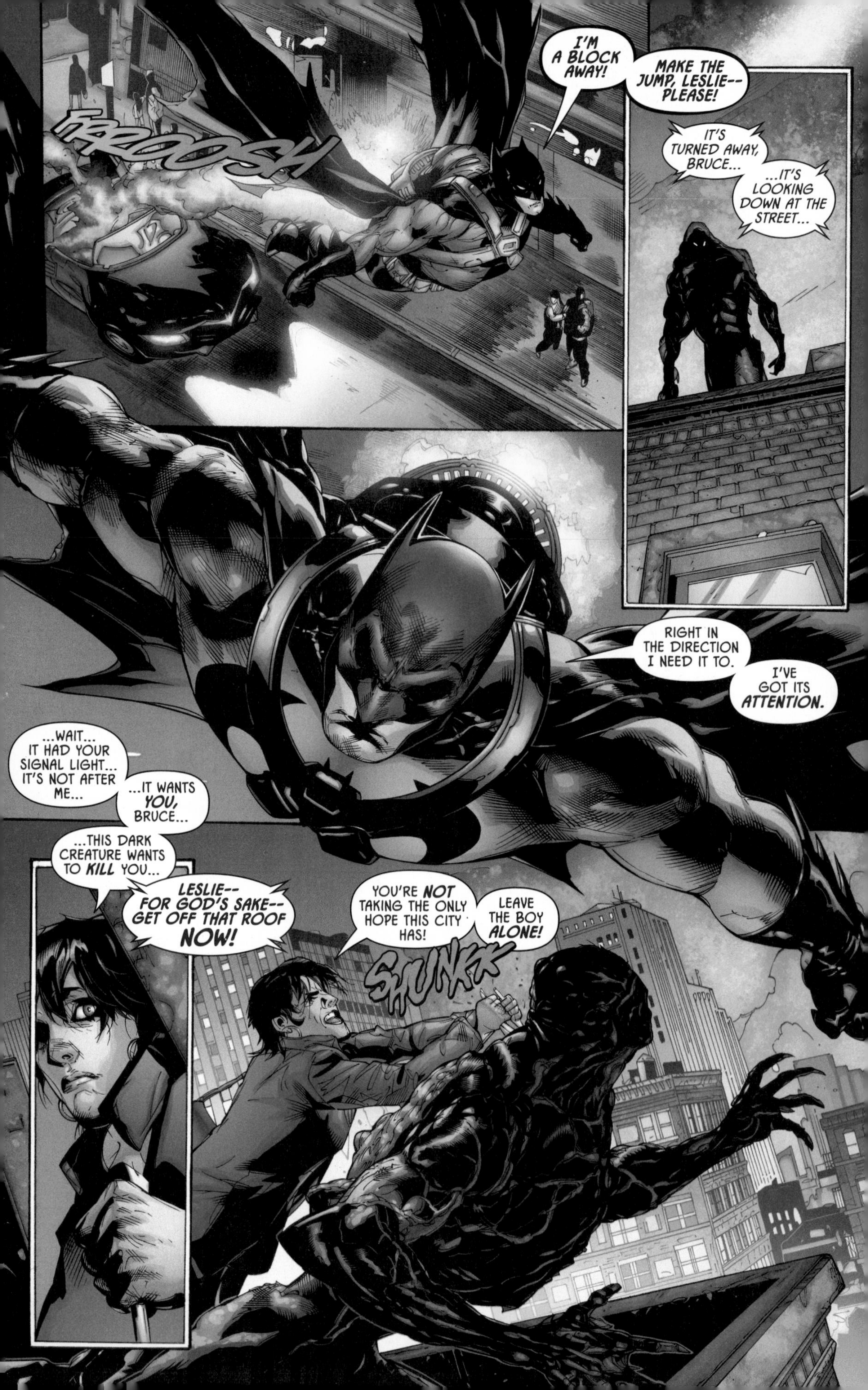

FRROOSH
I'M A BLOCK AWAY!
MAKE THE JUMP, LESLIE-- PLEASE!
IT'S TURNED AWAY, BRUCE...
...IT'S LOOKING DOWN AT THE STREET...
RIGHT IN THE DIRECTION I NEED IT TO.
I'VE GOT ITS ATTENTION.
...WAIT... IT HAD YOUR SIGNAL LIGHT... IT'S NOT AFTER ME...
...IT WANTS YOU, BRUCE...
...THIS DARK CREATURE WANTS TO KILL YOU...
LESLIE-- FOR GOD'S SAKE-- GET OFF THAT ROOF NOW!
YOU'RE NOT TAKING THE ONLY HOPE THIS CITY HAS!
LEAVE THE BOY ALONE!
SHUNKK

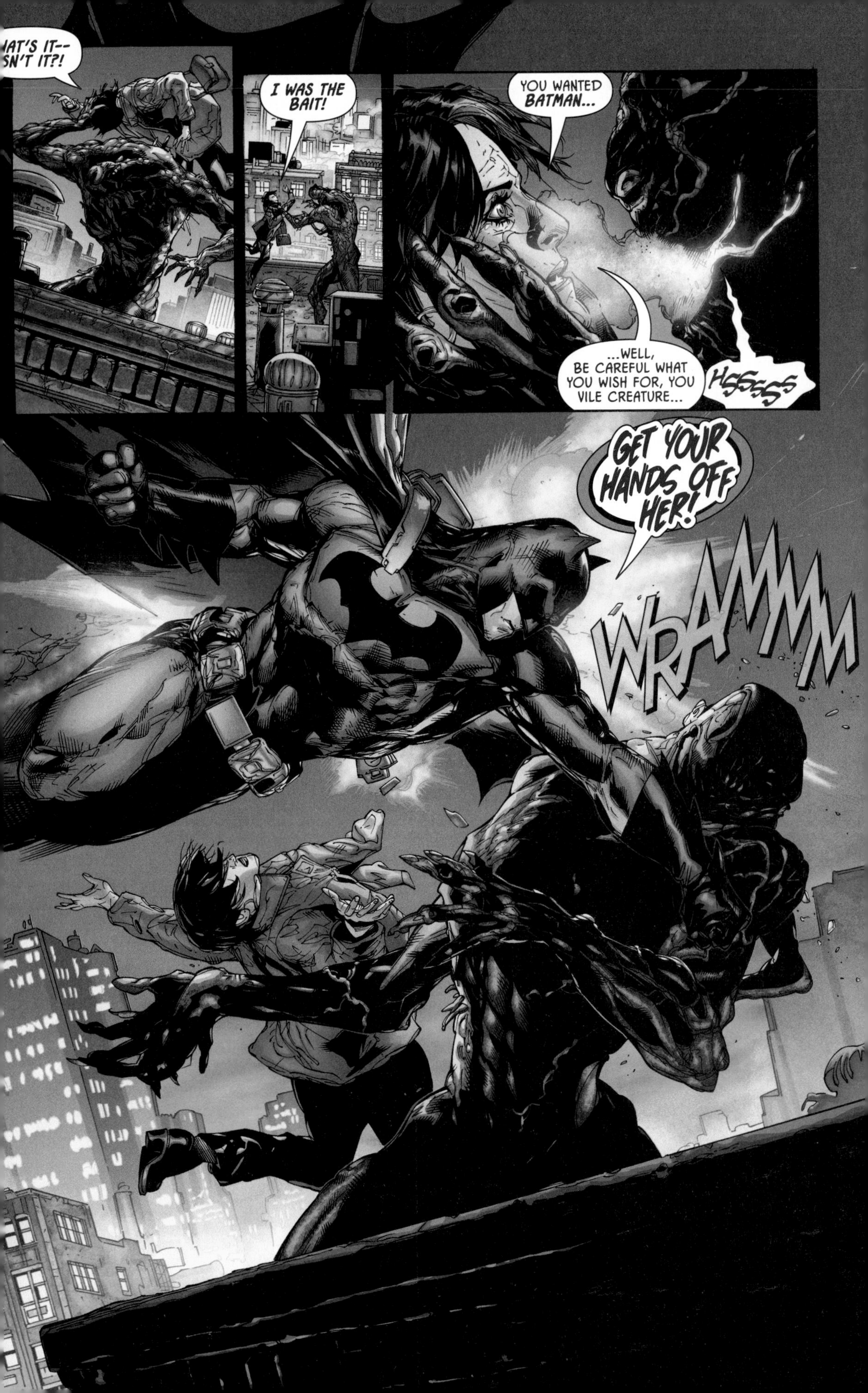

HAT'S IT--
SN'T IT?!
I WAS THE BAIT!
YOU WANTED BATMAN...
...WELL, BE CAREFUL WHAT YOU WISH FOR, YOU VILE CREATURE...
HSSSSS
GET YOUR HANDS OFF HER!
WRAMMM

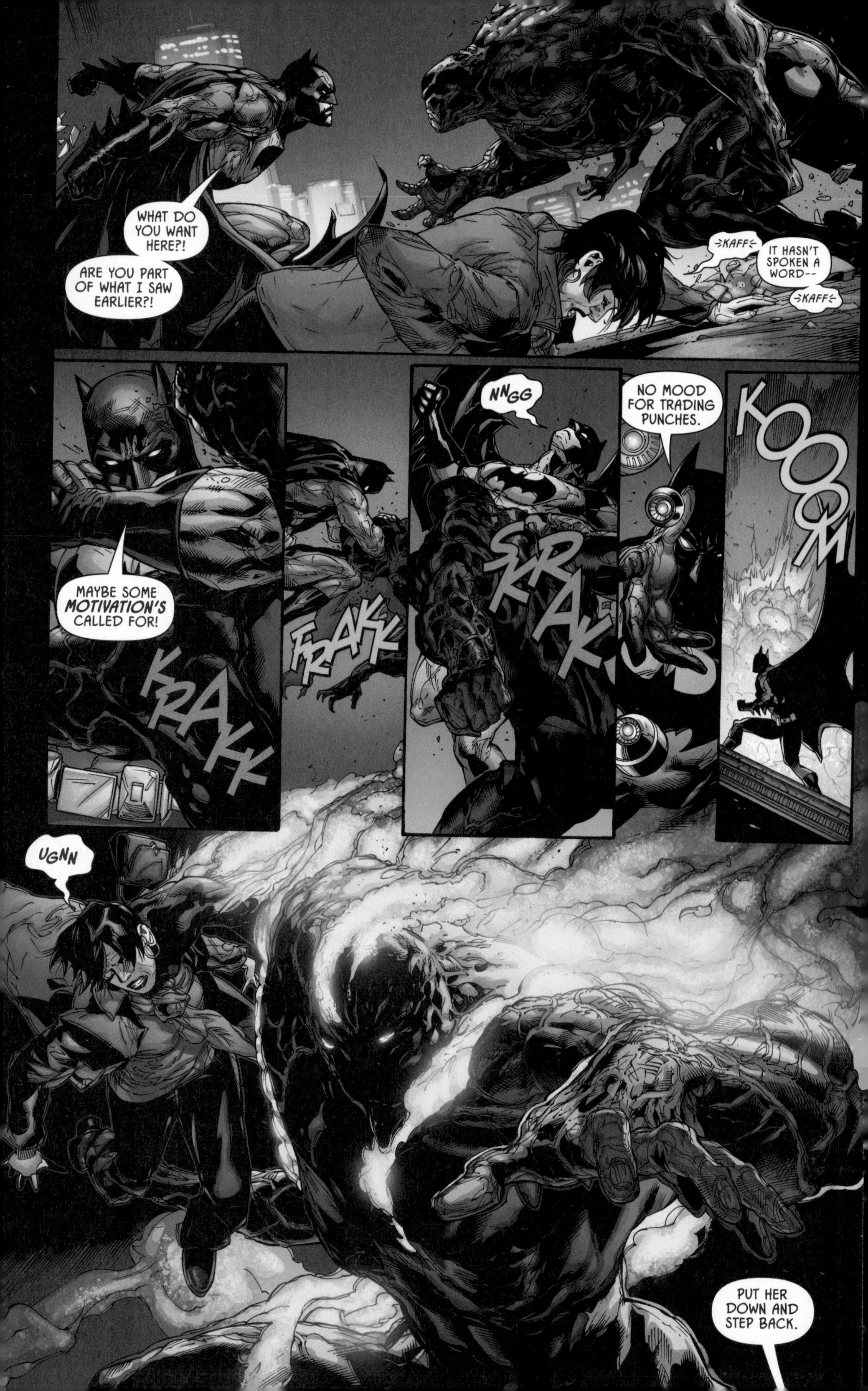
WHAT DO YOU WANT HERE?!
ARE YOU PART OF WHAT I SAW EARLIER?!
KAFF
IT HASN'T SPOKEN A WORD--
KAFF
MAYBE SOME MOTIVATION'S CALLED FOR!
KRAKK
FRAKK
NNGG
SKRAKK
NO MOOD FOR TRADING PUNCHES.
KOOOM
UGNN
PUT HER DOWN AND STEP BACK.

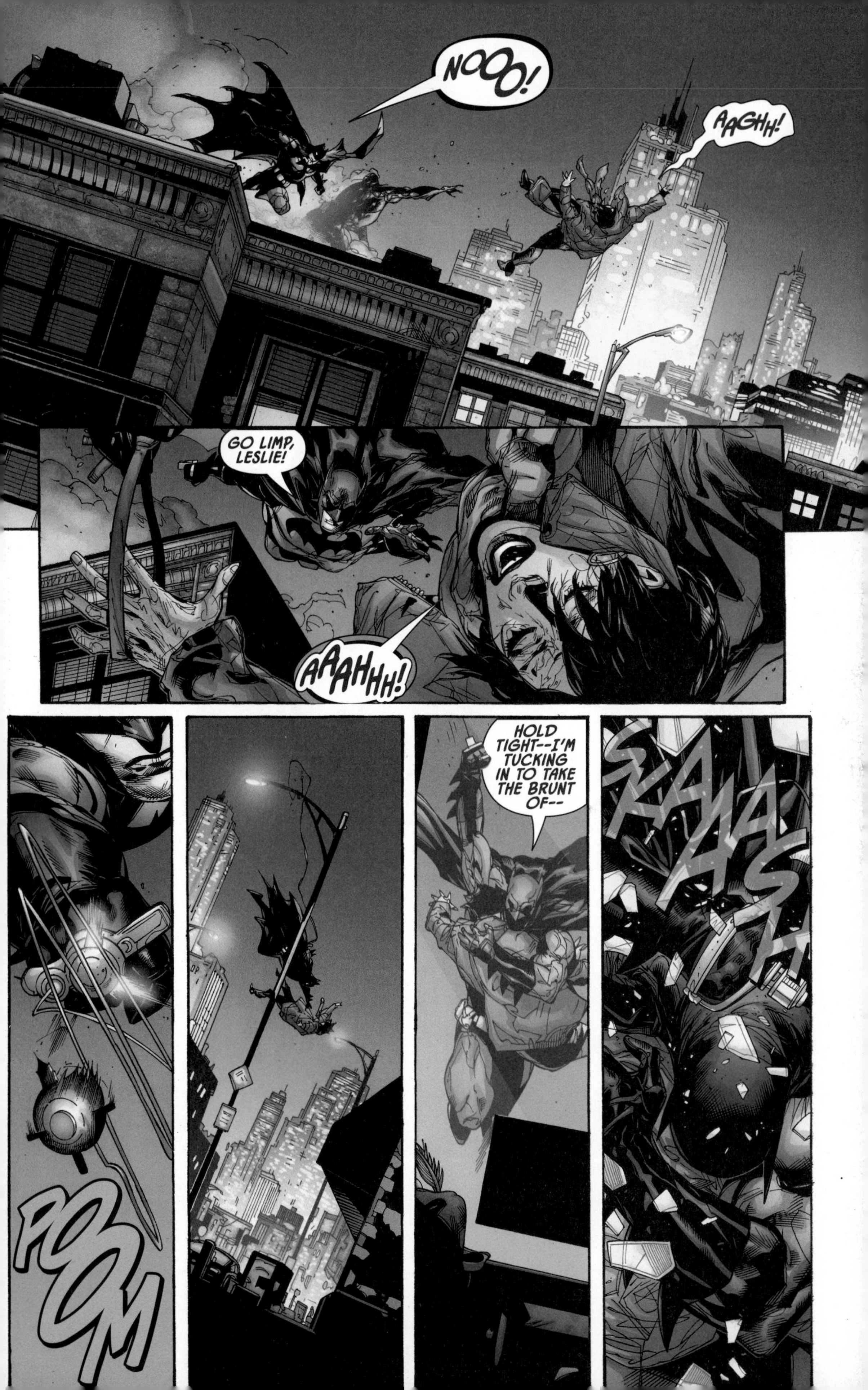
NOOO!
AAGHH!
GO LIMP, LESLIE!
AAAHHH!
POOM
HOLD TIGHT--I'M TUCKING IN TO TAKE THE BRUNT OF--
SKAAASH

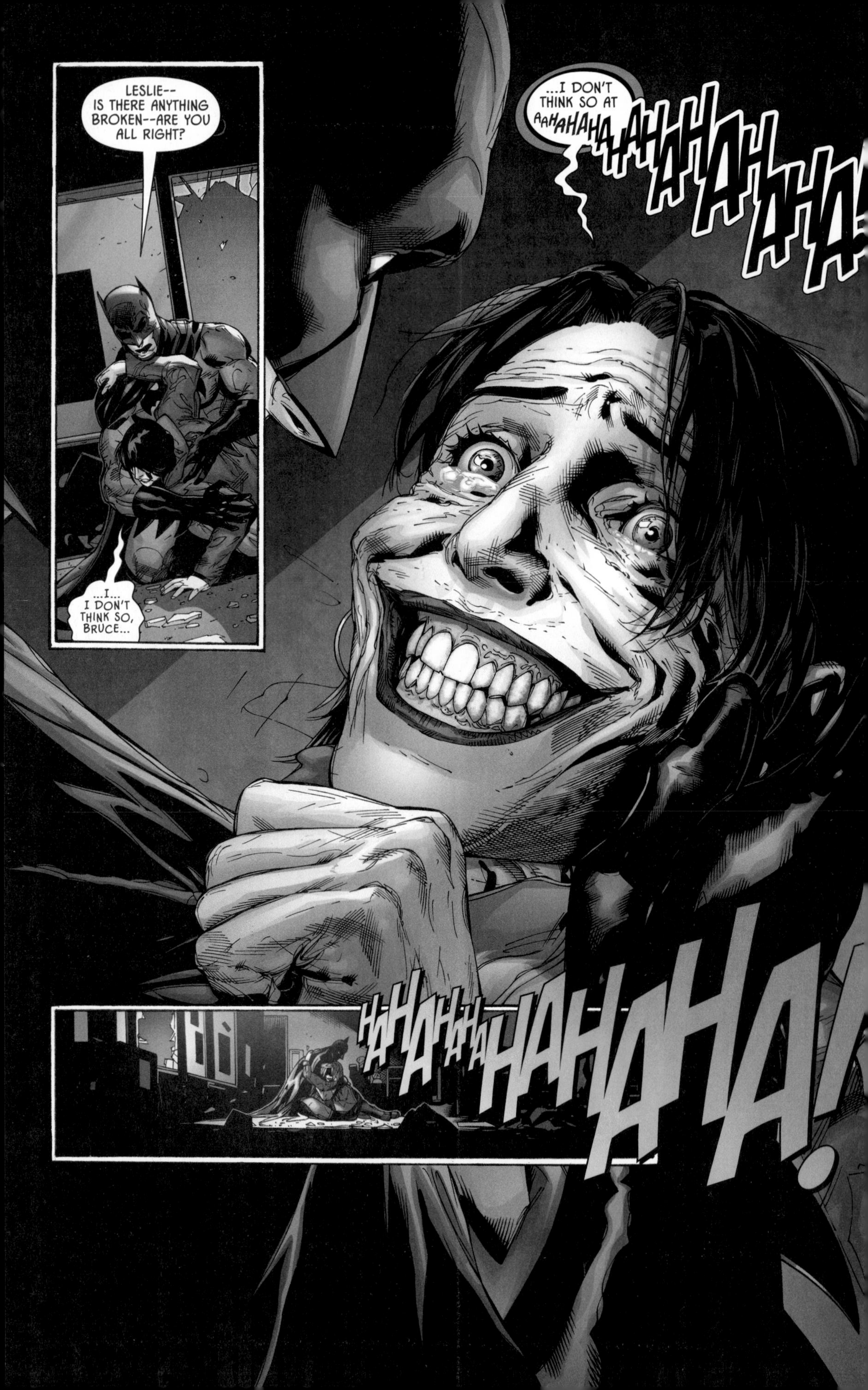
LESLIE-- IS THERE ANYTHING BROKEN--ARE YOU ALL RIGHT?
...I... I DON'T THINK SO, BRUCE...
...I DON'T THINK SO AT AAHAHAHAHAHAHAHAHAHA
HAHAHAHAHAHAHAHA!

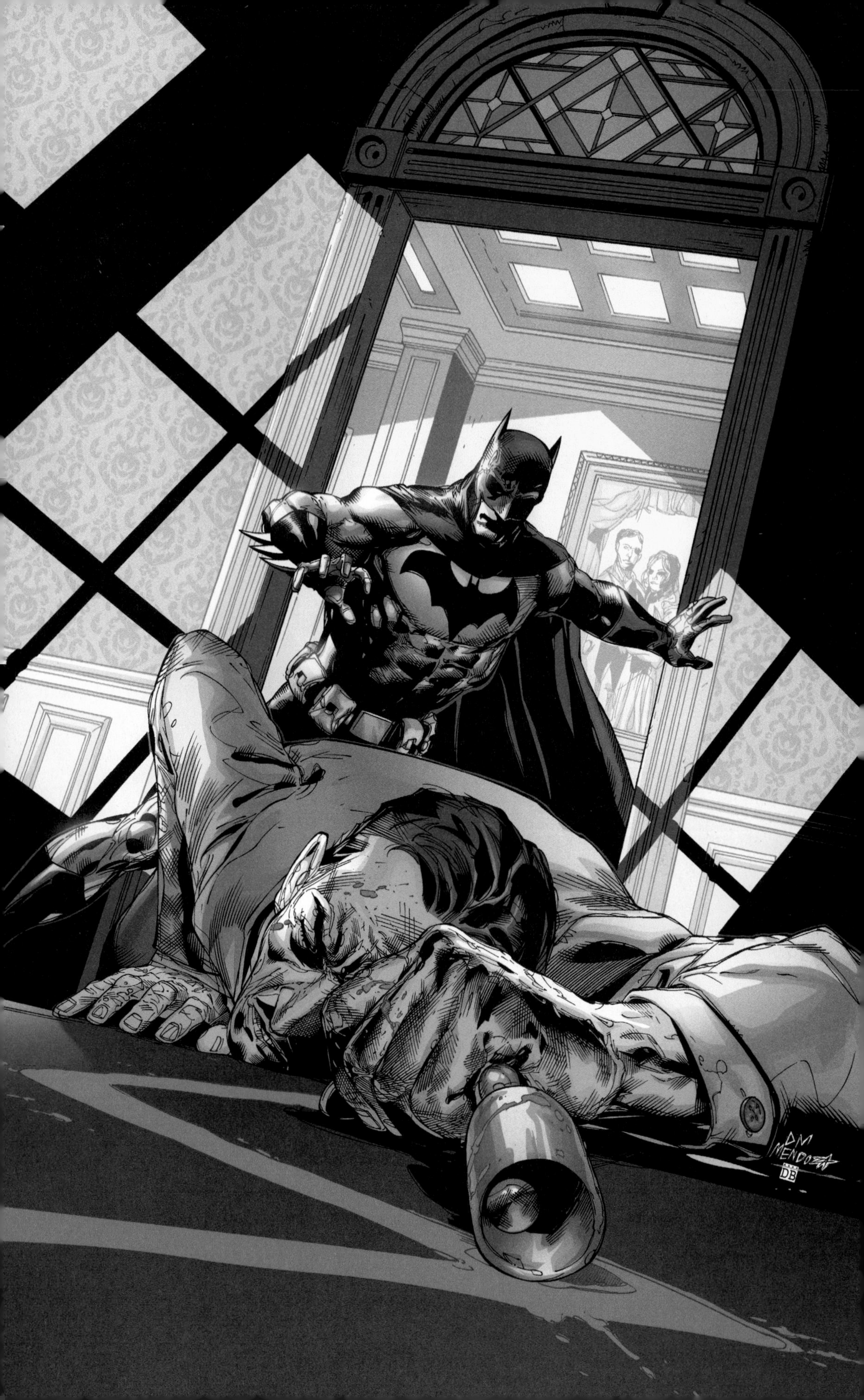

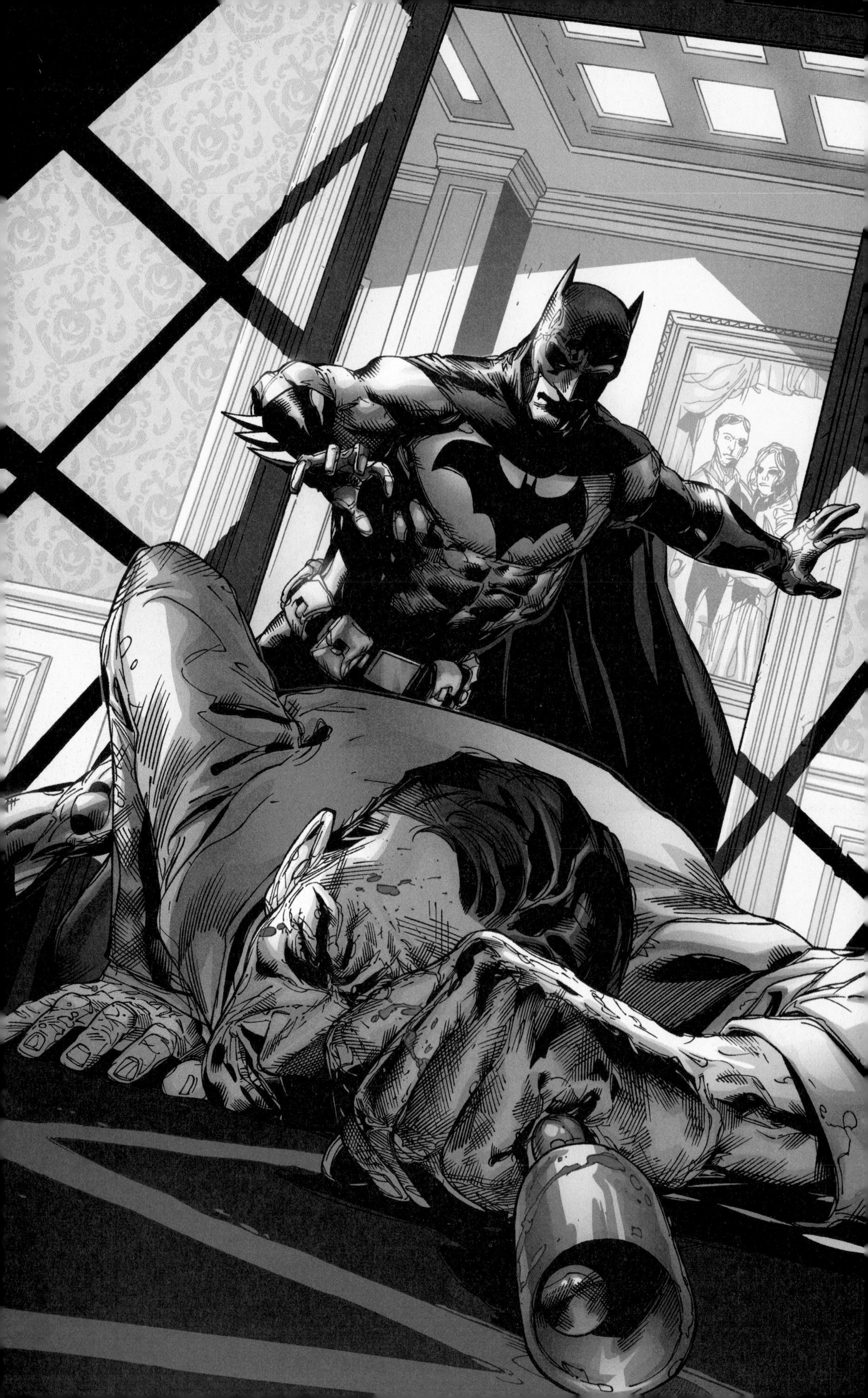

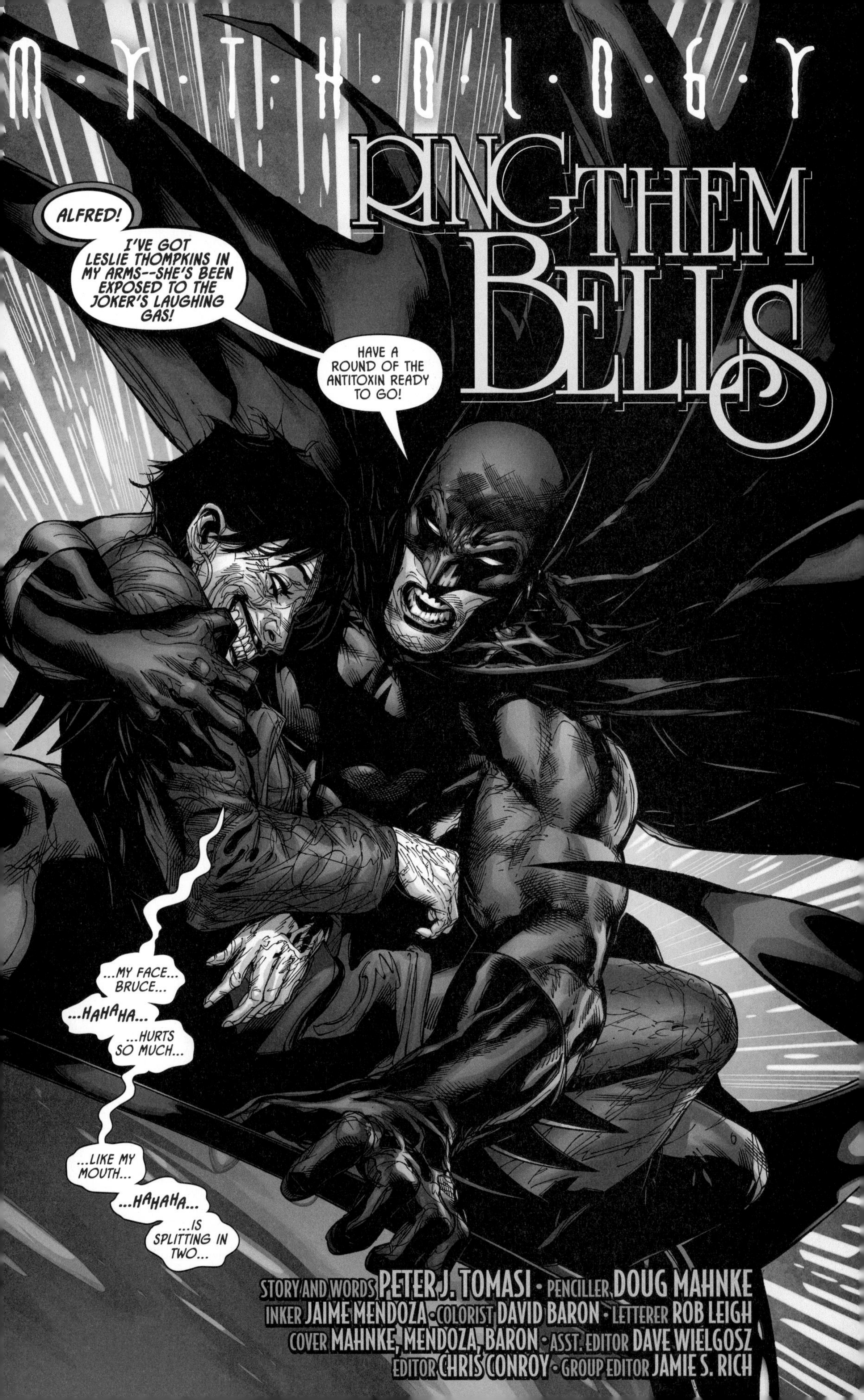

MYTHOLOGY
RING THEM BELLS
ALFRED!
I'VE GOT LESLIE THOMPKINS IN MY ARMS--SHE'S BEEN EXPOSED TO THE JOKER'S LAUGHING GAS!
HAVE A ROUND OF THE ANTITOXIN READY TO GO!
...MY FACE... BRUCE...
...HAHAHA...
...HURTS SO MUCH...
...LIKE MY MOUTH...
...HAHAHA...
...IS SPLITTING IN TWO...
STORY AND WORDS PETER J. TOMASI · PENCILLER DOUG MAHNKE
INKER JAIME MENDOZA · COLORIST DAVID BARON · LETTERER ROB LEIGH
COVER MAHNKE, MENDOZA, BARON · ASST. EDITOR DAVE WIELGOSZ
EDITOR CHRIS CONROY · GROUP EDITOR JAMIE S. RICH

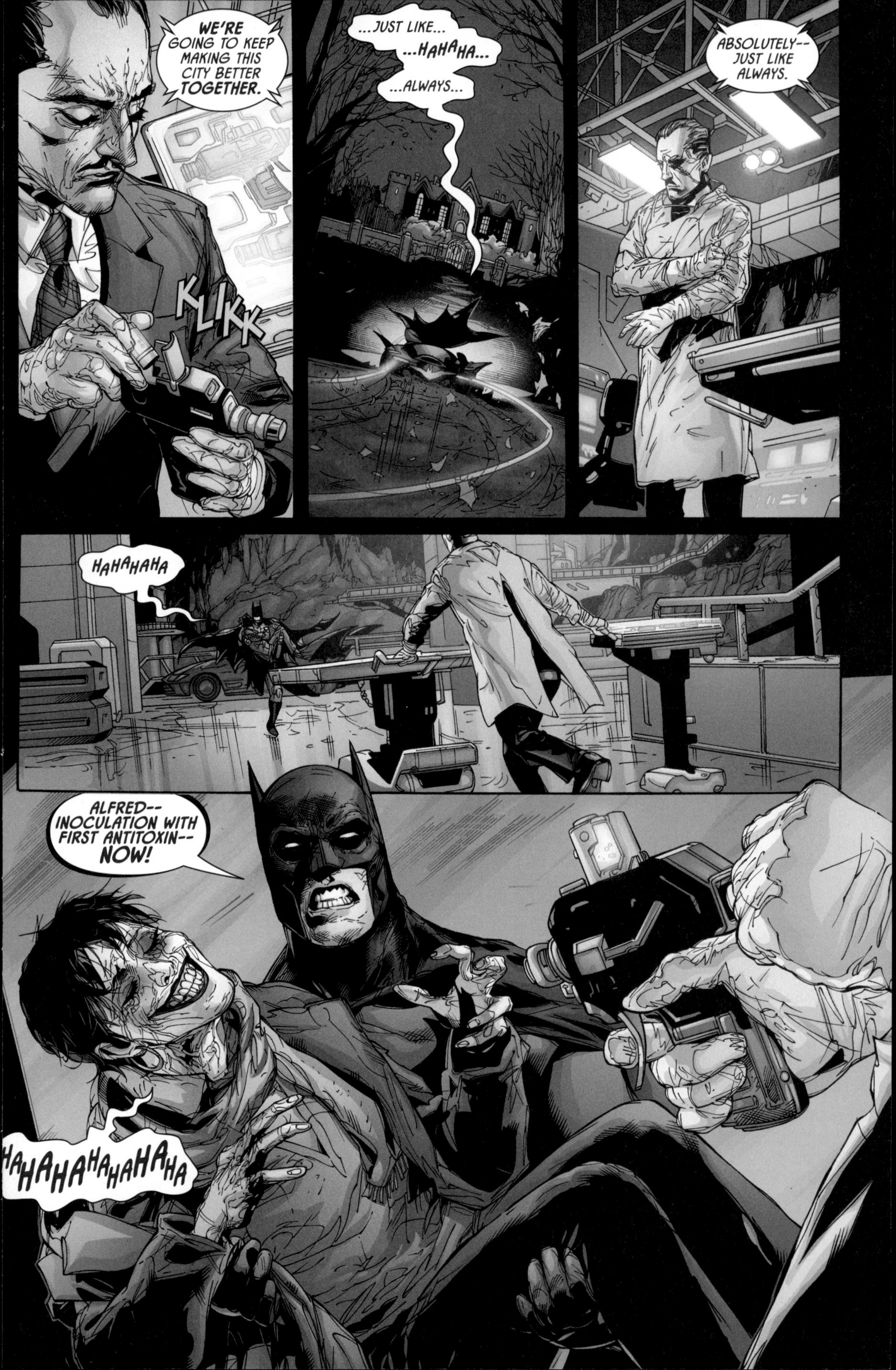
WE'RE GOING TO KEEP MAKING THIS CITY BETTER TOGETHER.
KLIKK
...JUST LIKE...
...HAHAHA...
...ALWAYS...
ABSOLUTELY-- JUST LIKE ALWAYS.
HAHAHAHA
ALFRED-- INOCULATION WITH FIRST ANTITOXIN-- NOW!
HAHAHAHAHAHAHAHA

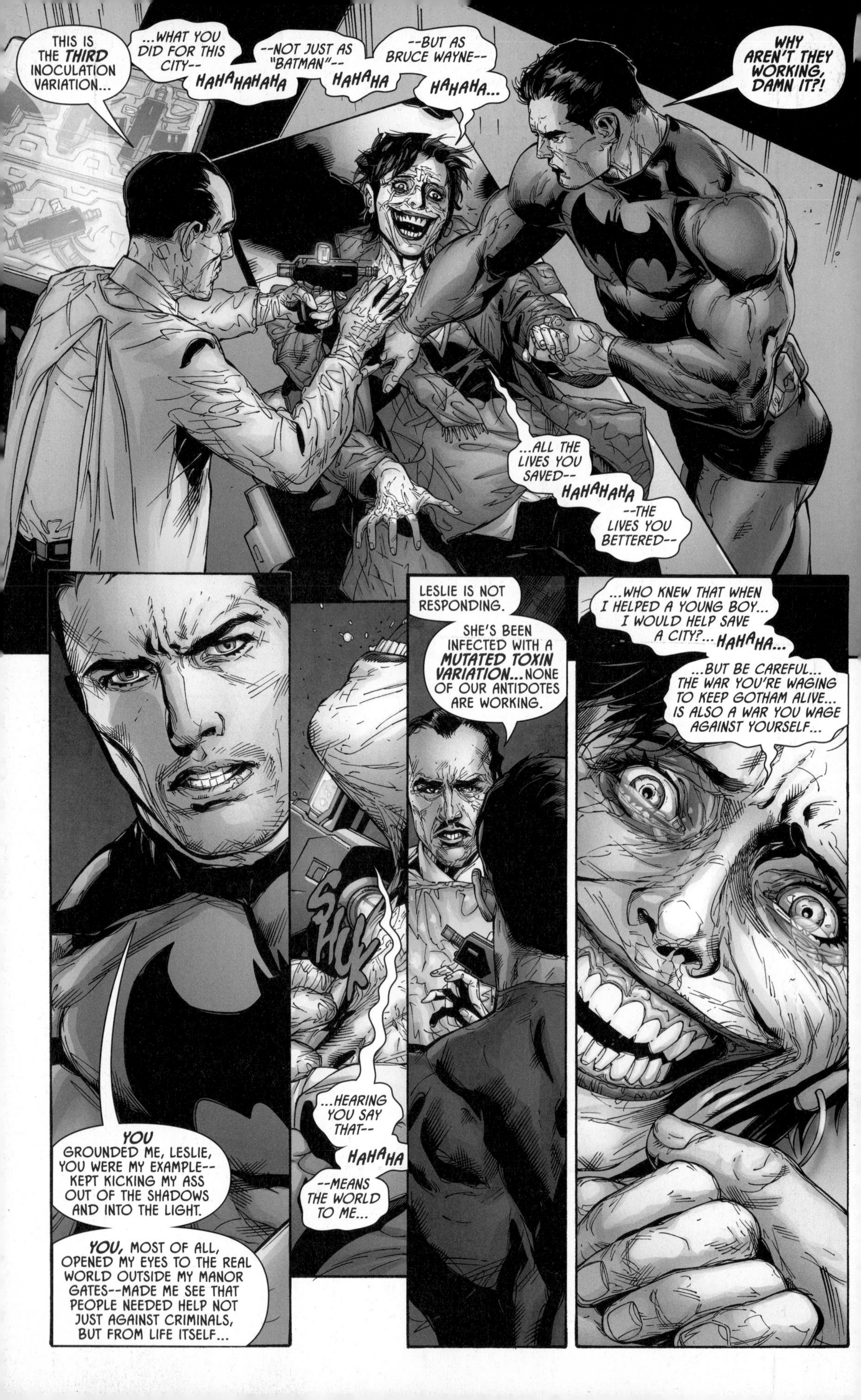

THIS IS THE THIRD INOCULATION VARIATION...
...WHAT YOU DID FOR THIS CITY--
HAHAHAHAHA
--NOT JUST AS "BATMAN"--
HAHAHA
--BUT AS BRUCE WAYNE--
HAHAHA...
WHY AREN'T THEY WORKING, DAMN IT?!
...ALL THE LIVES YOU SAVED--
HAHAHAHA
--THE LIVES YOU BETTERED--
YOU GROUNDED ME, LESLIE, YOU WERE MY EXAMPLE--KEPT KICKING MY ASS OUT OF THE SHADOWS AND INTO THE LIGHT.
YOU, MOST OF ALL, OPENED MY EYES TO THE REAL WORLD OUTSIDE MY MANOR GATES--MADE ME SEE THAT PEOPLE NEEDED HELP NOT JUST AGAINST CRIMINALS, BUT FROM LIFE ITSELF...
SHK
...HEARING YOU SAY THAT--
HAHAHA
--MEANS THE WORLD TO ME...
LESLIE IS NOT RESPONDING.
SHE'S BEEN INFECTED WITH A MUTATED TOXIN VARIATION... NONE OF OUR ANTIDOTES ARE WORKING.
...WHO KNEW THAT WHEN I HELPED A YOUNG BOY... I WOULD HELP SAVE A CITY?... HAHAHA...
...BUT BE CAREFUL... THE WAR YOU'RE WAGING TO KEEP GOTHAM ALIVE... IS ALSO A WAR YOU WAGE AGAINST YOURSELF...

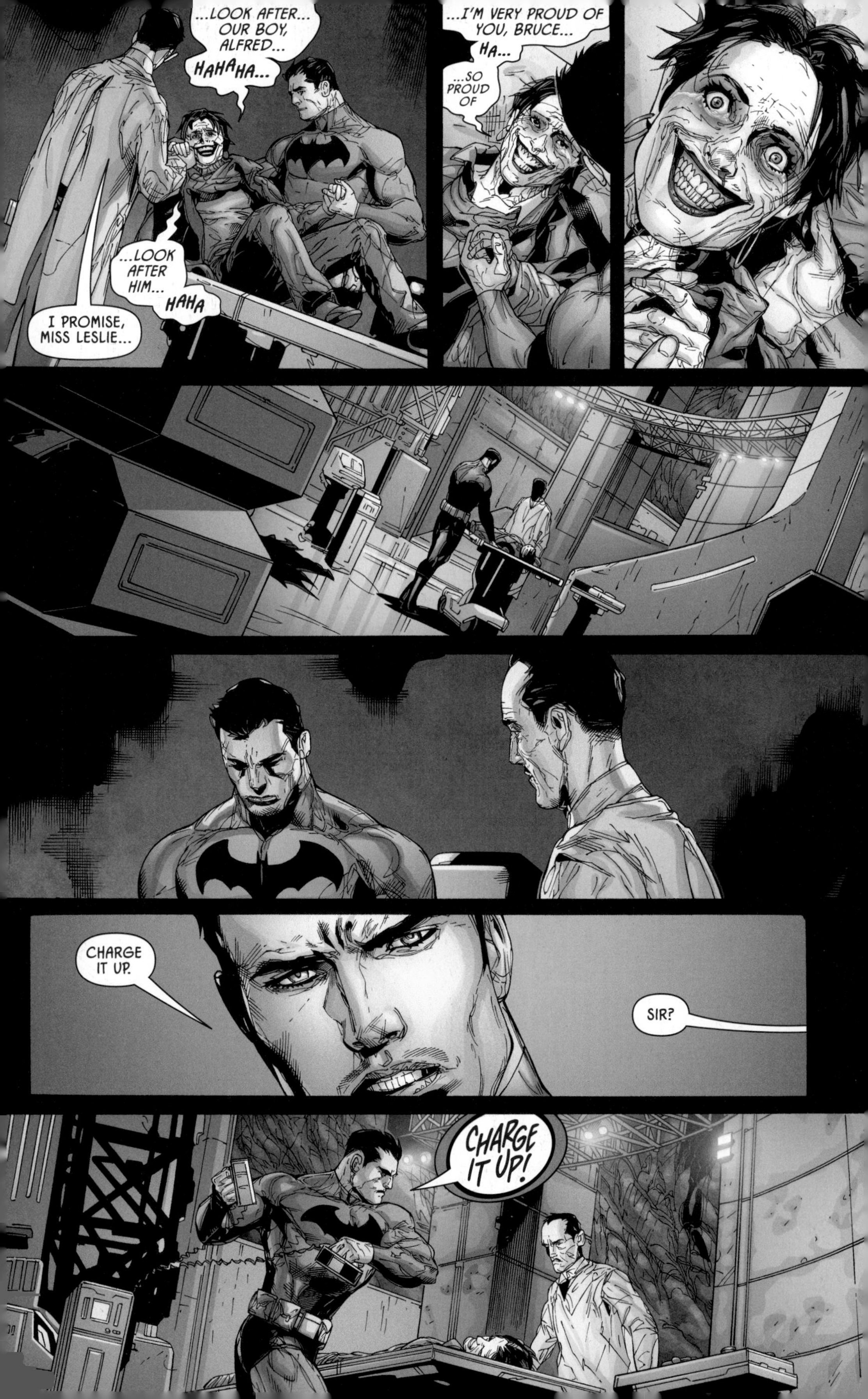
...LOOK AFTER... OUR BOY, ALFRED...
HAHAHA...
...LOOK AFTER HIM...
HAHA
I PROMISE, MISS LESLIE...
...I'M VERY PROUD OF YOU, BRUCE...
HA...
...SO PROUD OF
CHARGE IT UP.
SIR?
CHARGE IT UP!

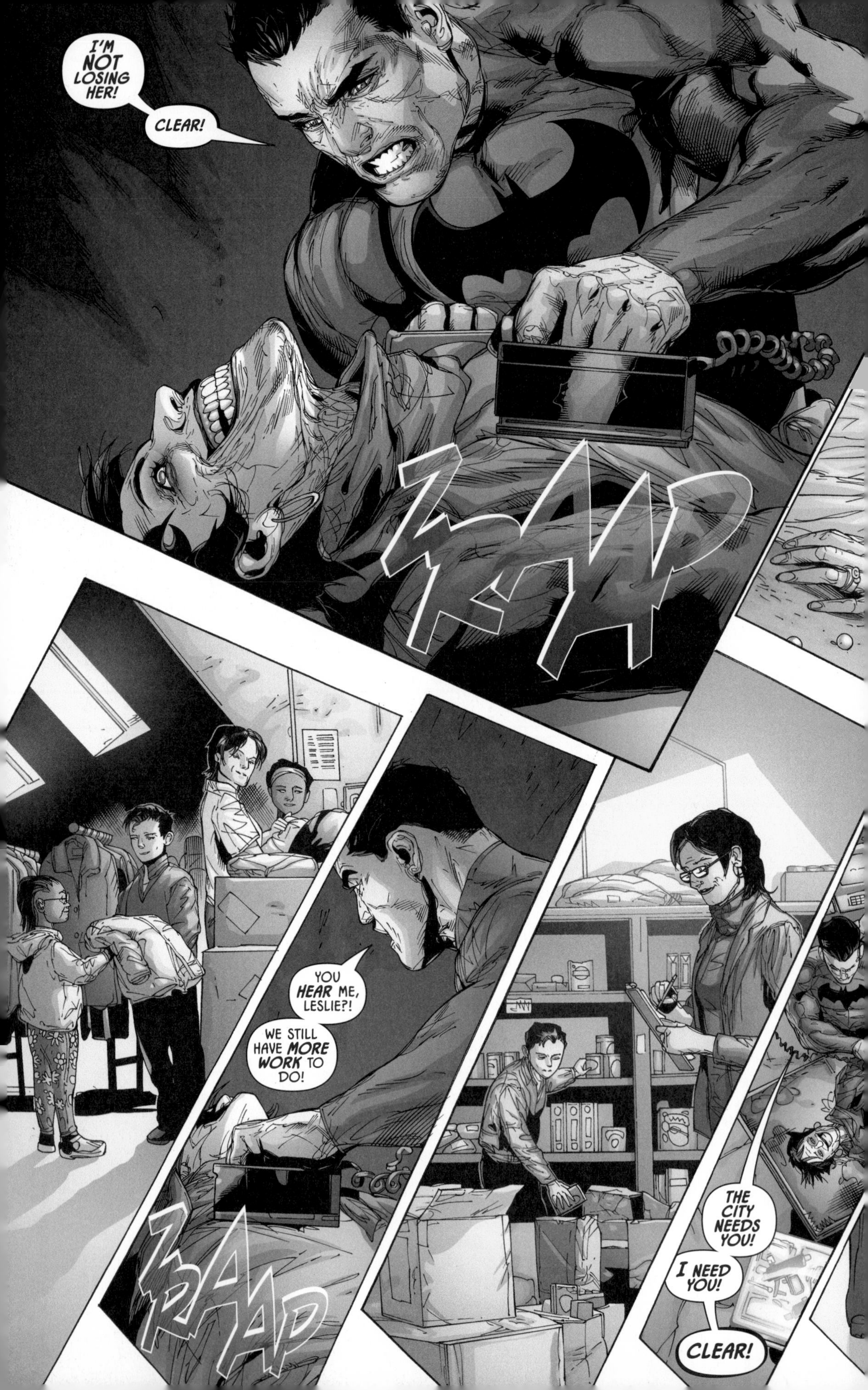
I'M NOT LOSING HER!
CLEAR!
ZAAP
YOU HEAR ME, LESLIE?!
WE STILL HAVE MORE WORK TO DO!
ZAAP
THE CITY NEEDS YOU!
I NEED YOU!
CLEAR!

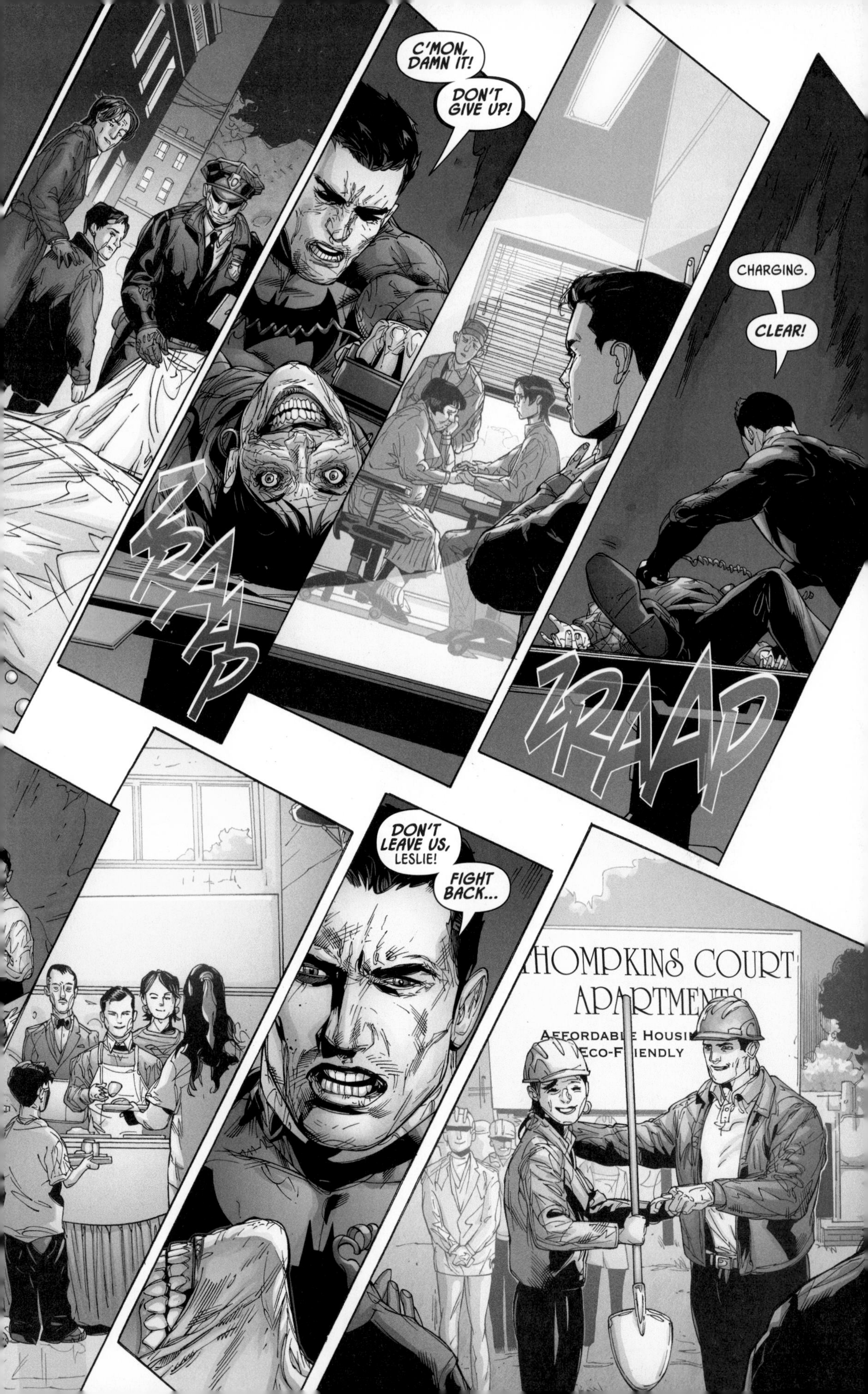
C'MON, DAMN IT!
DON'T GIVE UP!
ZZRAAP
CHARGING.
CLEAR!
ZZRAAP
DON'T LEAVE US, LESLIE!
FIGHT BACK...
THOMPKINS COURT APARTMENTS

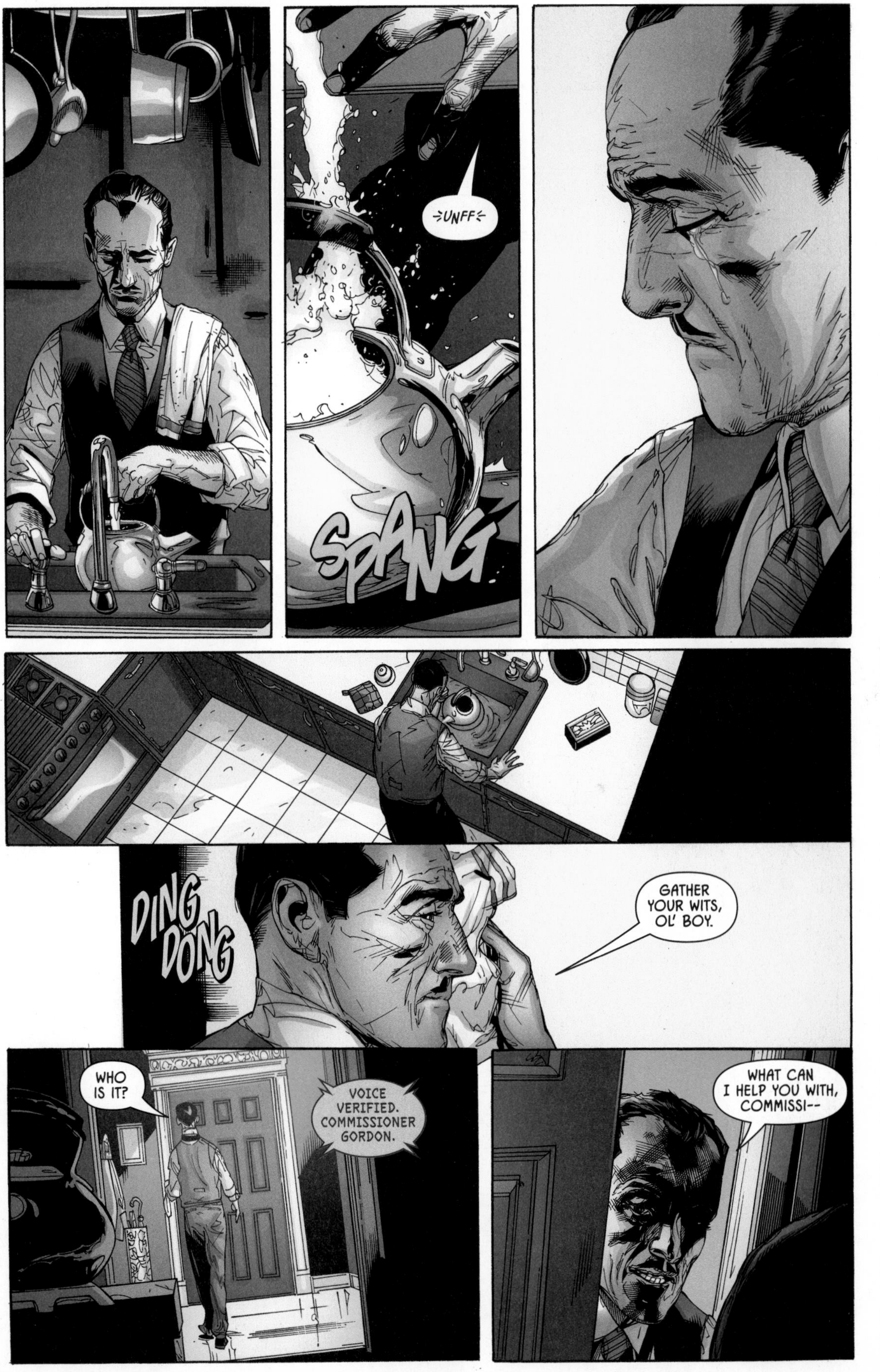
UNFF
SPANG
DING DONG
GATHER YOUR WITS, OL' BOY.
WHO IS IT?
VOICE VERIFIED. COMMISSIONER GORDON.
WHAT CAN I HELP YOU WITH, COMMISSI--

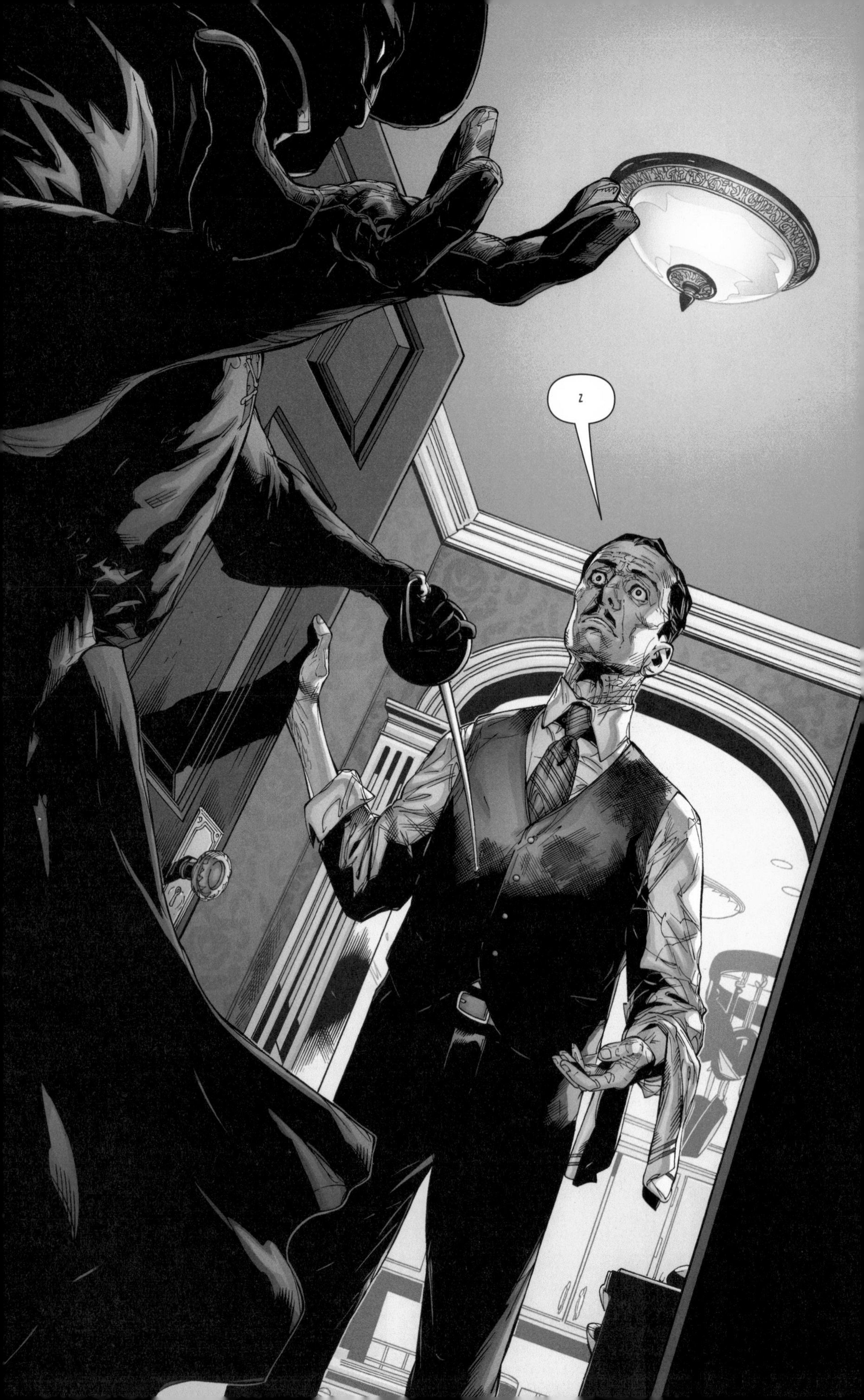
Z

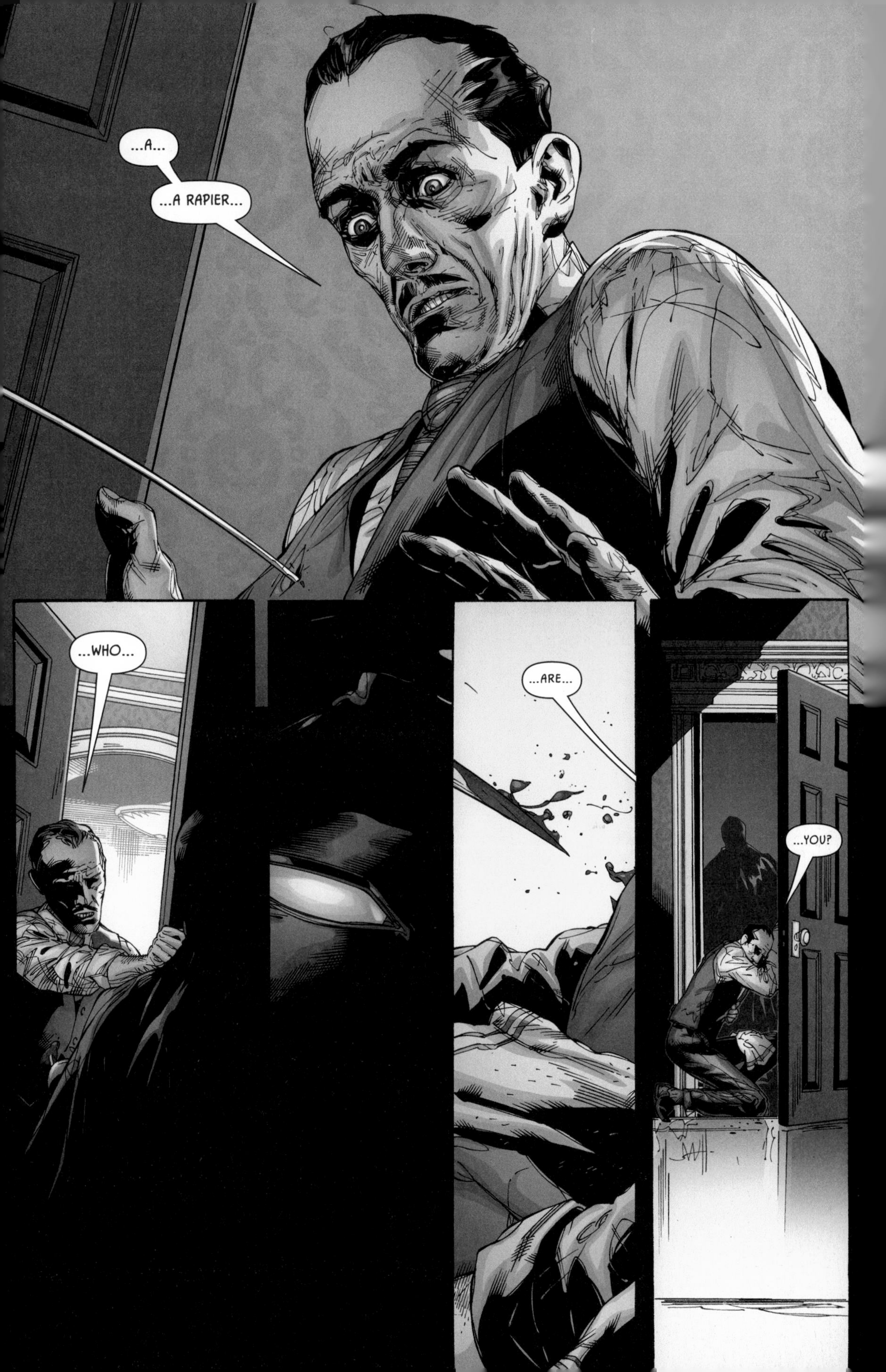

...A...
...A RAPIER...
...WHO...
...ARE...
...YOU?

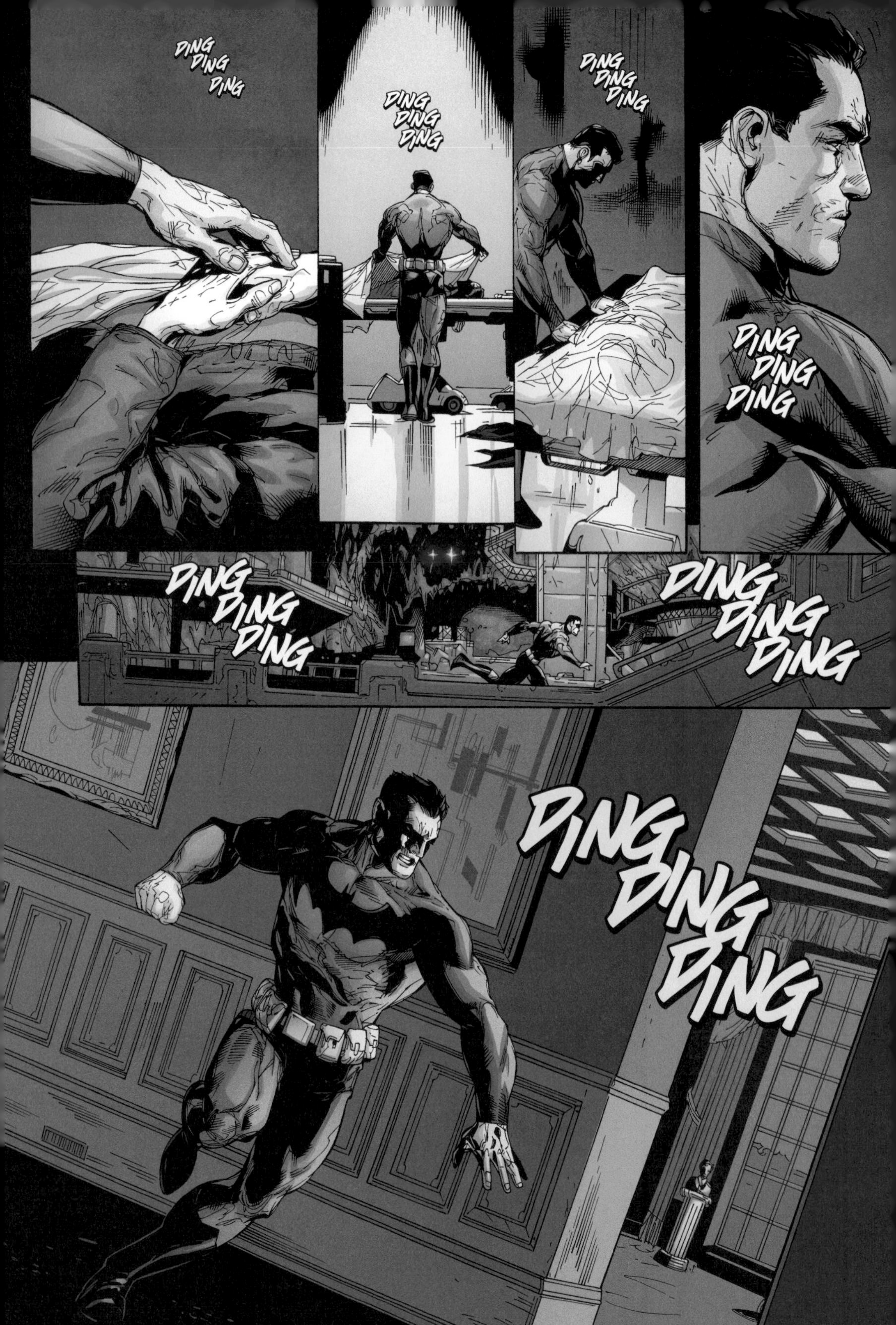
DING DING DING
DING DING DING
DING DING DING
DING DING DING
DING DING DING
DING DING DING
DING DING DING

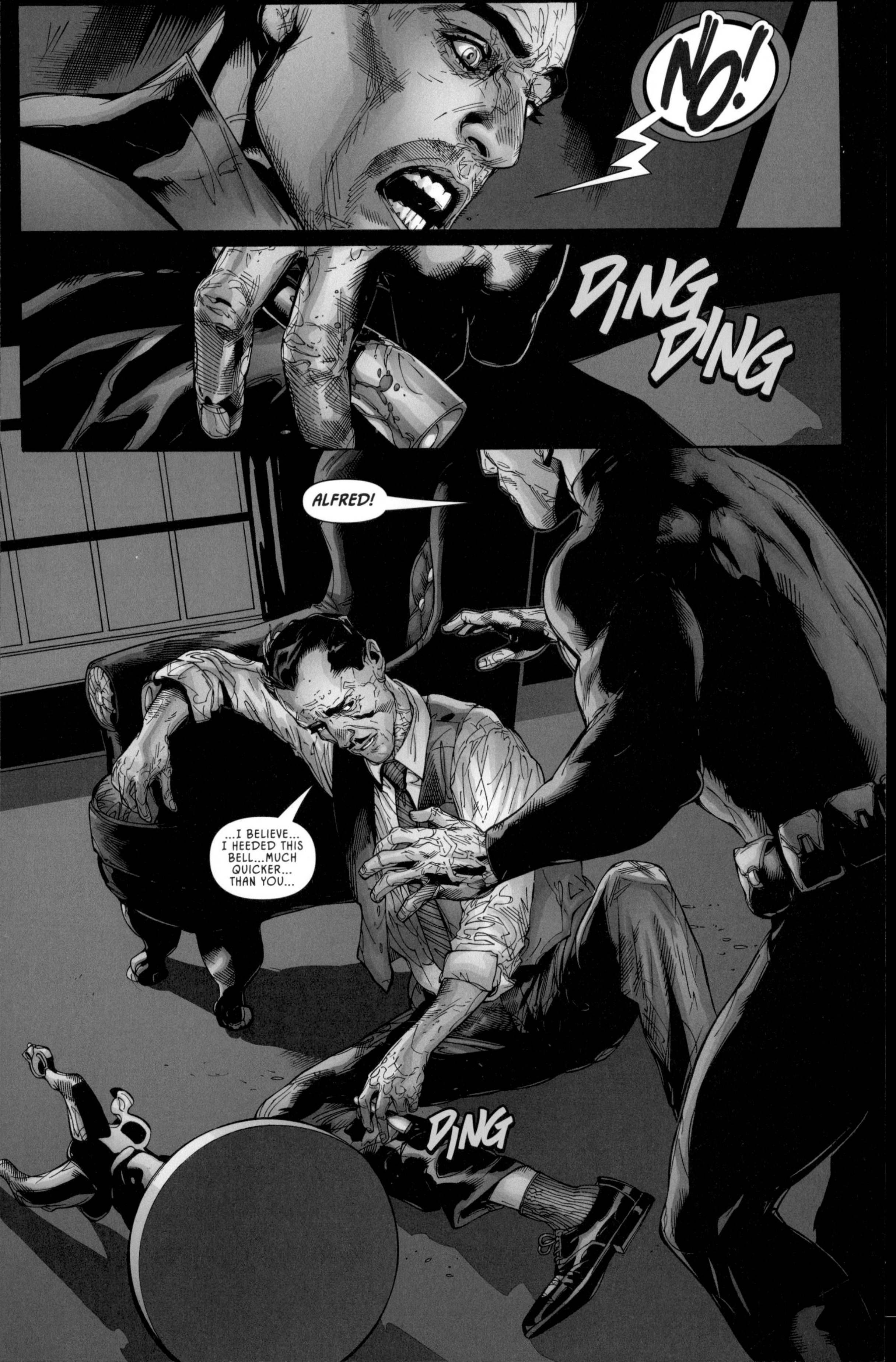
NO!
DING DING
ALFRED!
...I BELIEVE... I HEEDED THIS BELL...MUCH QUICKER... THAN YOU...
DING

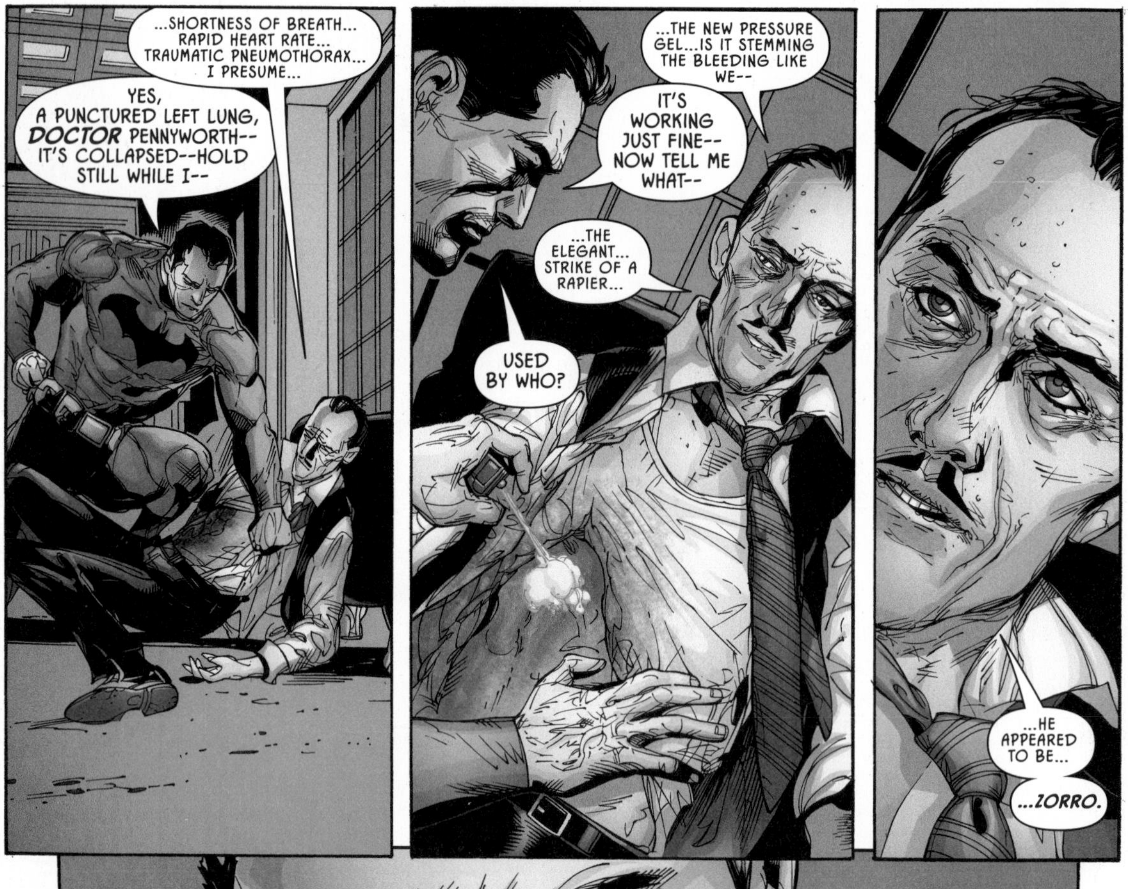

...SHORTNESS OF BREATH... RAPID HEART RATE... TRAUMATIC PNEUMOTHORAX... I PRESUME...
YES, A PUNCTURED LEFT LUNG, DOCTOR PENNYWORTH--IT'S COLLAPSED--HOLD STILL WHILE I--
...THE NEW PRESSURE GEL...IS IT STEMMING THE BLEEDING LIKE WE--
IT'S WORKING JUST FINE--NOW TELL ME WHAT--
...THE ELEGANT... STRIKE OF A RAPIER...
USED BY WHO?
...HE APPEARED TO BE...
...ZORRO.
YOU NEED IMMEDIATE SURGERY--TO REPAIR THE LUNG TISSUE AND SUCTION OUT--
...CALL DAMIAN TO PERFORM IT... HE'S AT MERCY HALL...
WHAT MAKES YOU THINK DAMIAN CAN--
...HE OPERATED... AND FIXED YOUR PUNCTURED LUNG...AFTER THE OWLS...
ONCE DAMIAN'S HERE AND YOU'RE OUT OF DANGER, I'M PUTTING THE HOUSE ON LOCKDOWN...
...AND GOING OUT.

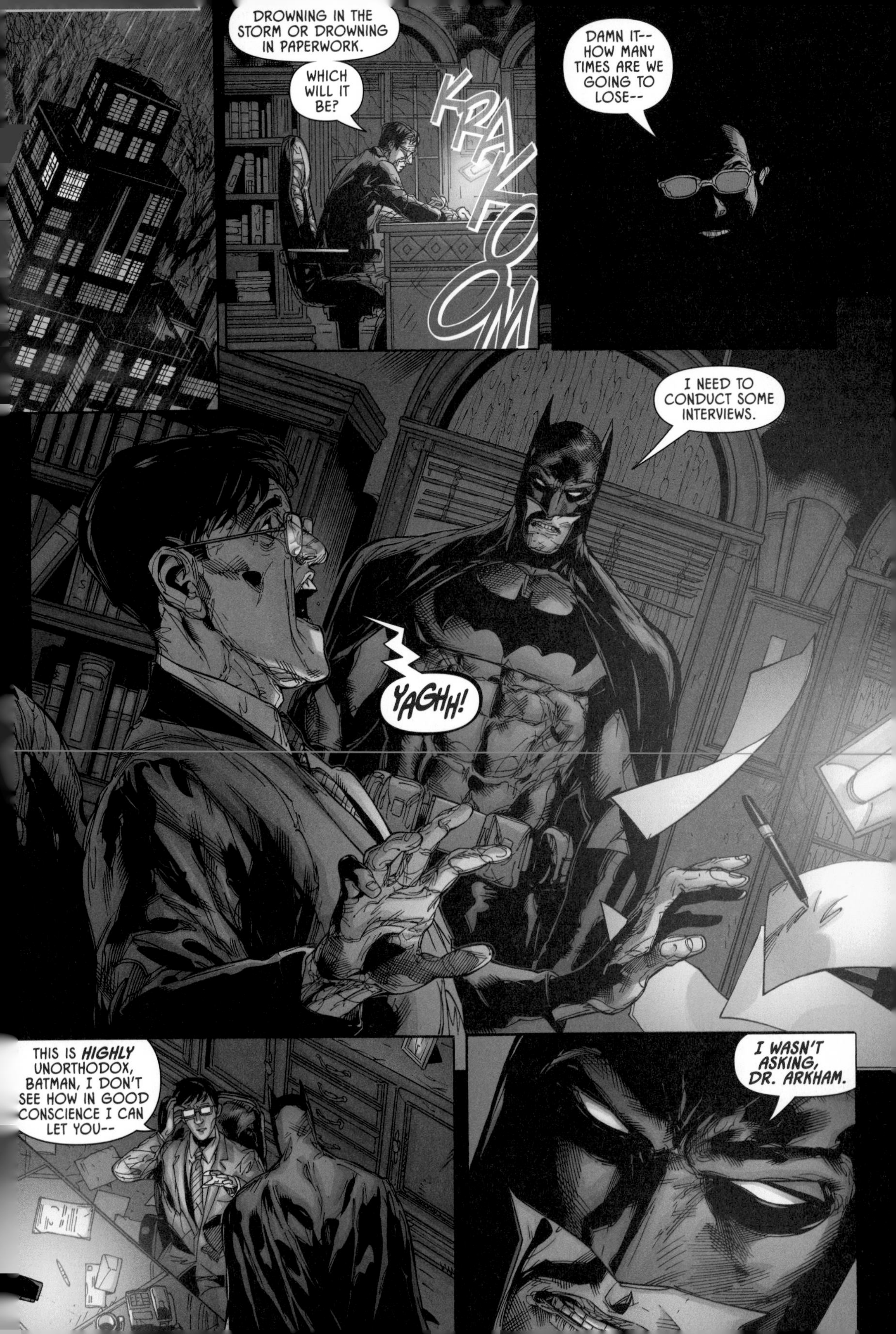
DROWNING IN THE STORM OR DROWNING IN PAPERWORK.
WHICH WILL IT BE?
KRAKOOM
DAMN IT-- HOW MANY TIMES ARE WE GOING TO LOSE--
I NEED TO CONDUCT SOME INTERVIEWS.
YAGHH!
THIS IS HIGHLY UNORTHODOX, BATMAN, I DON'T SEE HOW IN GOOD CONSCIENCE I CAN LET YOU--
I WASN'T ASKING, DR. ARKHAM.

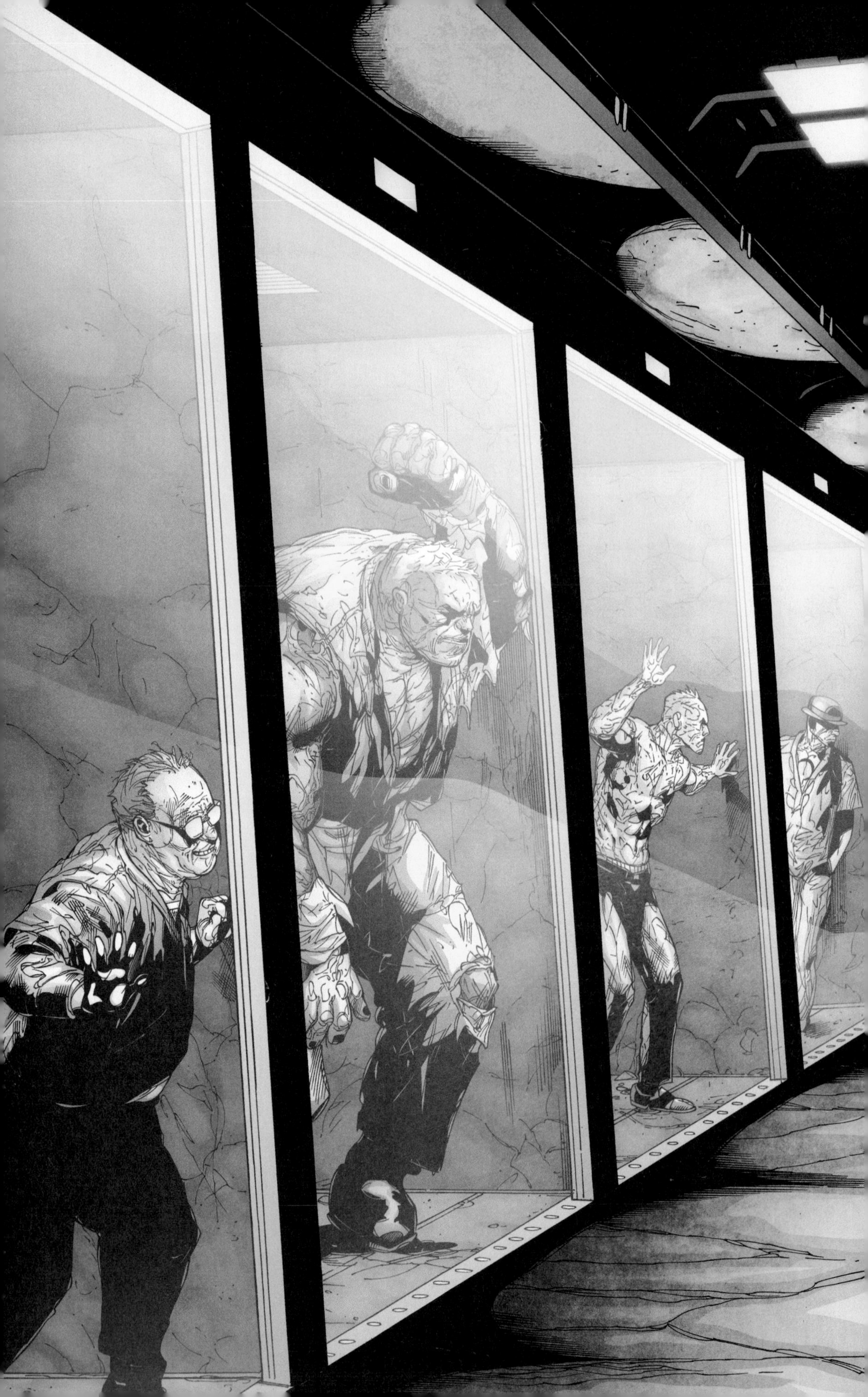

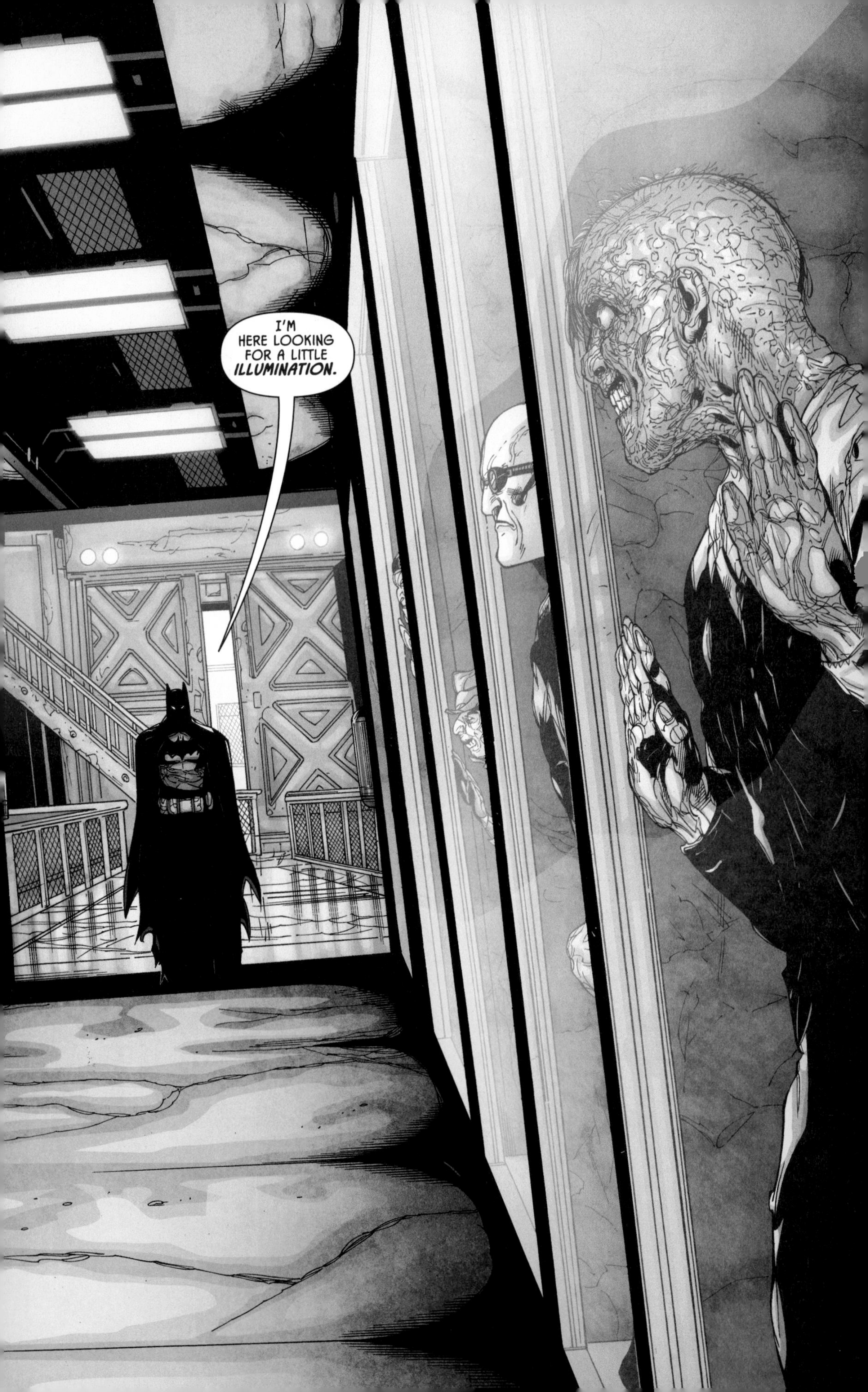
I'M HERE LOOKING FOR A LITTLE ILLUMINATION.

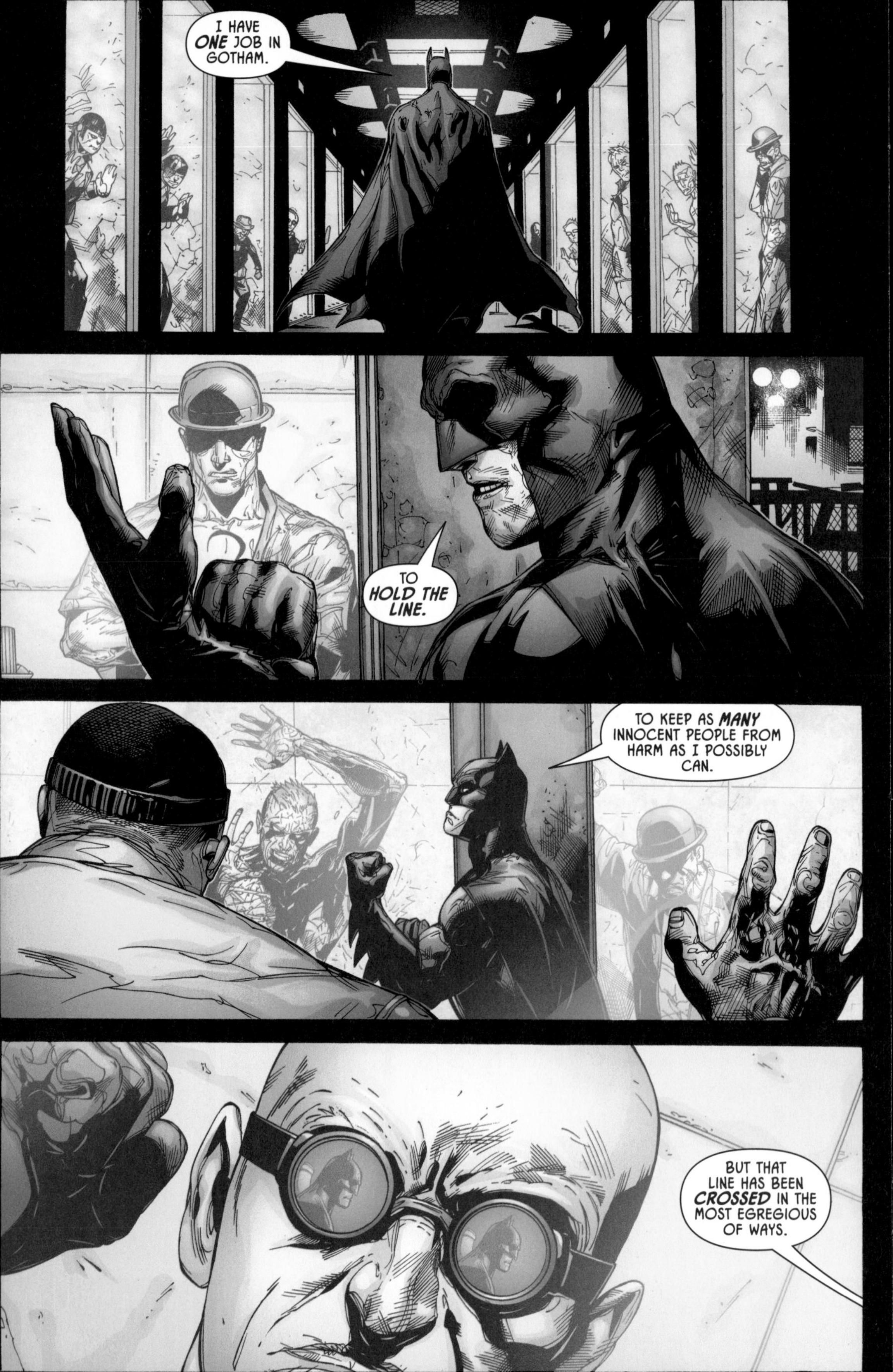
I HAVE ONE JOB IN GOTHAM.
TO HOLD THE LINE.
TO KEEP AS MANY INNOCENT PEOPLE FROM HARM AS I POSSIBLY CAN.
BUT THAT LINE HAS BEEN CROSSED IN THE MOST EGREGIOUS OF WAYS.

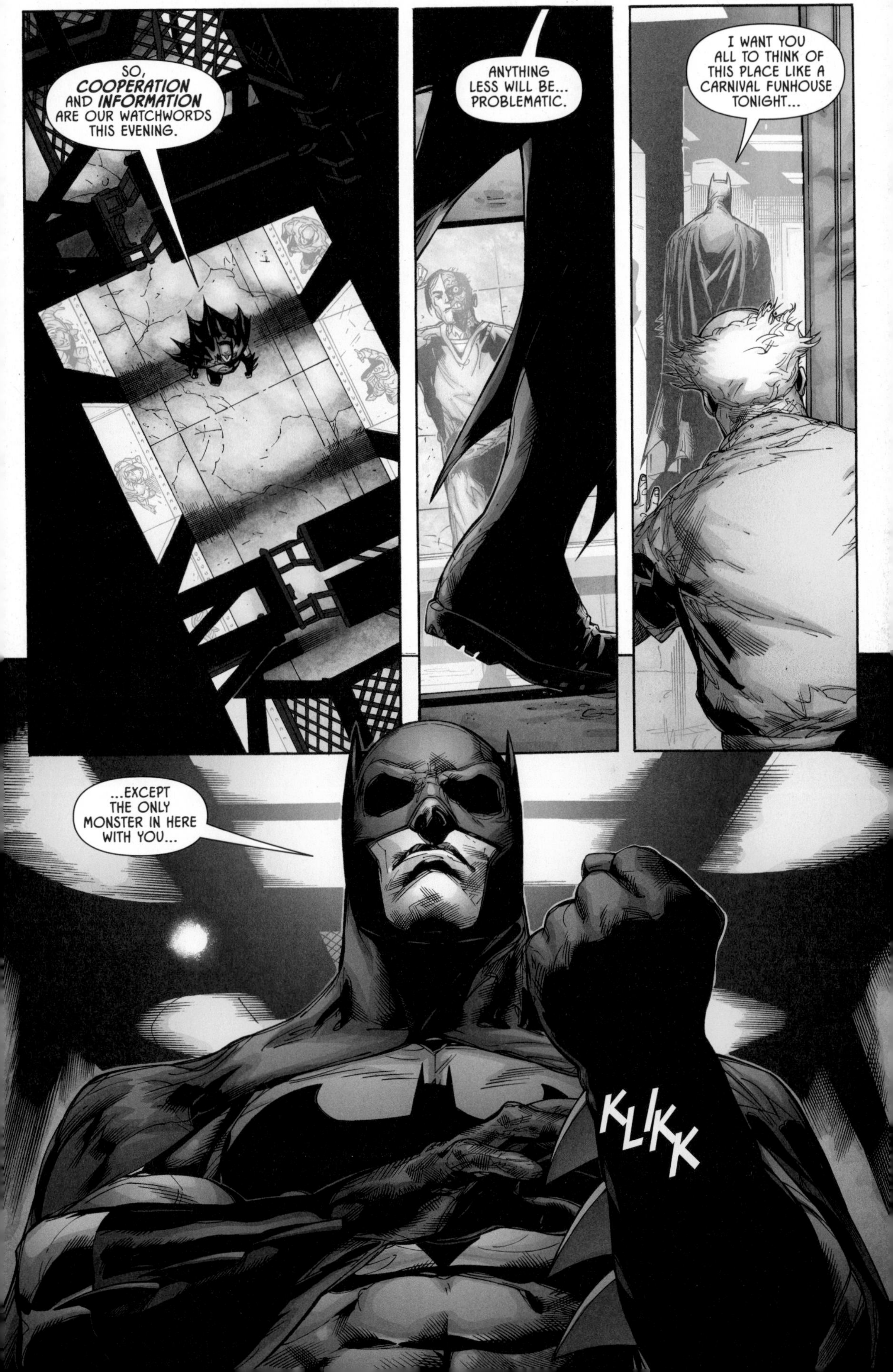
SO, COOPERATION AND INFORMATION ARE OUR WATCHWORDS THIS EVENING.
ANYTHING LESS WILL BE... PROBLEMATIC.
I WANT YOU ALL TO THINK OF THIS PLACE LIKE A CARNIVAL FUNHOUSE TONIGHT...
...EXCEPT THE ONLY MONSTER IN HERE WITH YOU...
KLIKK

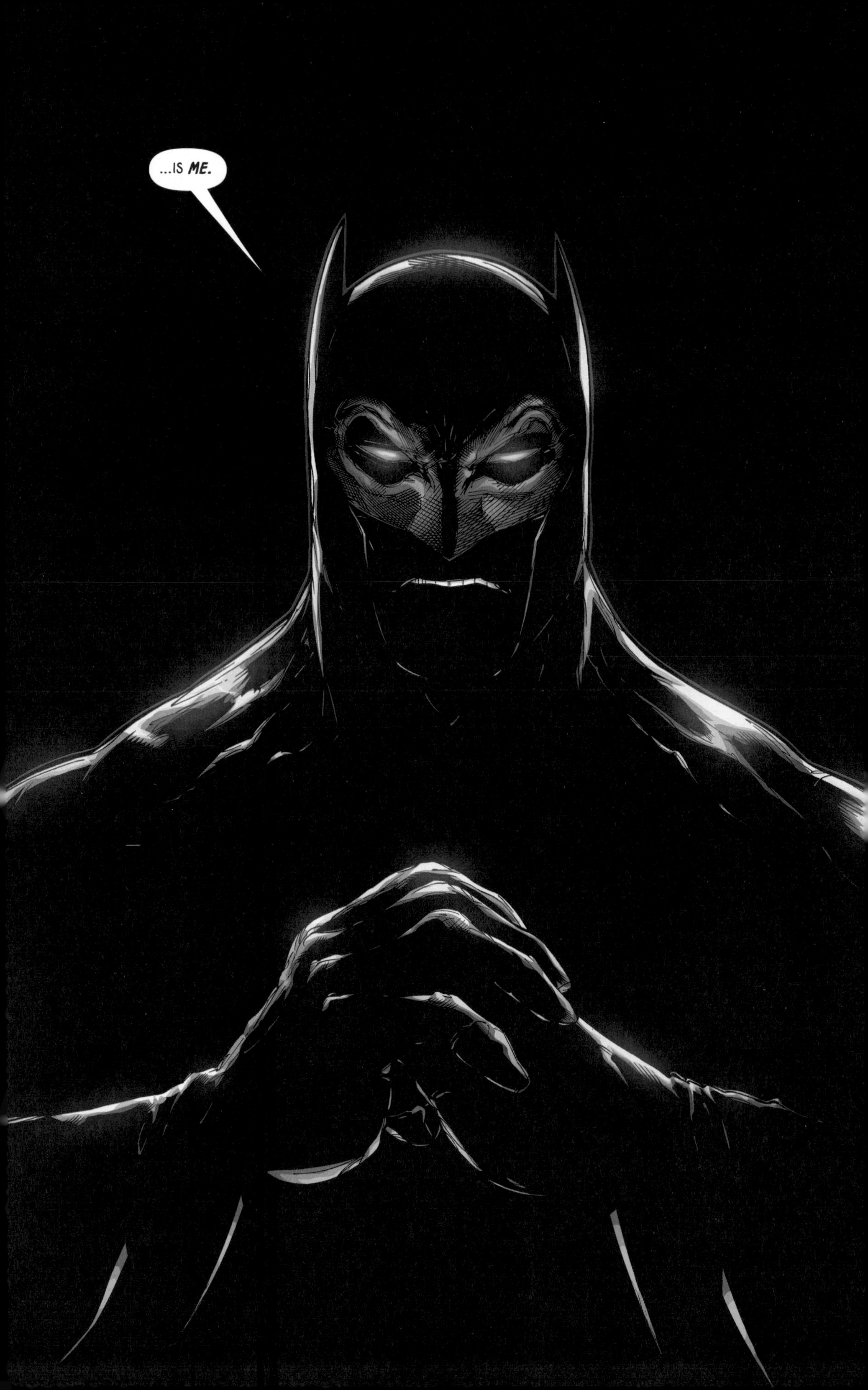
...IS ME.

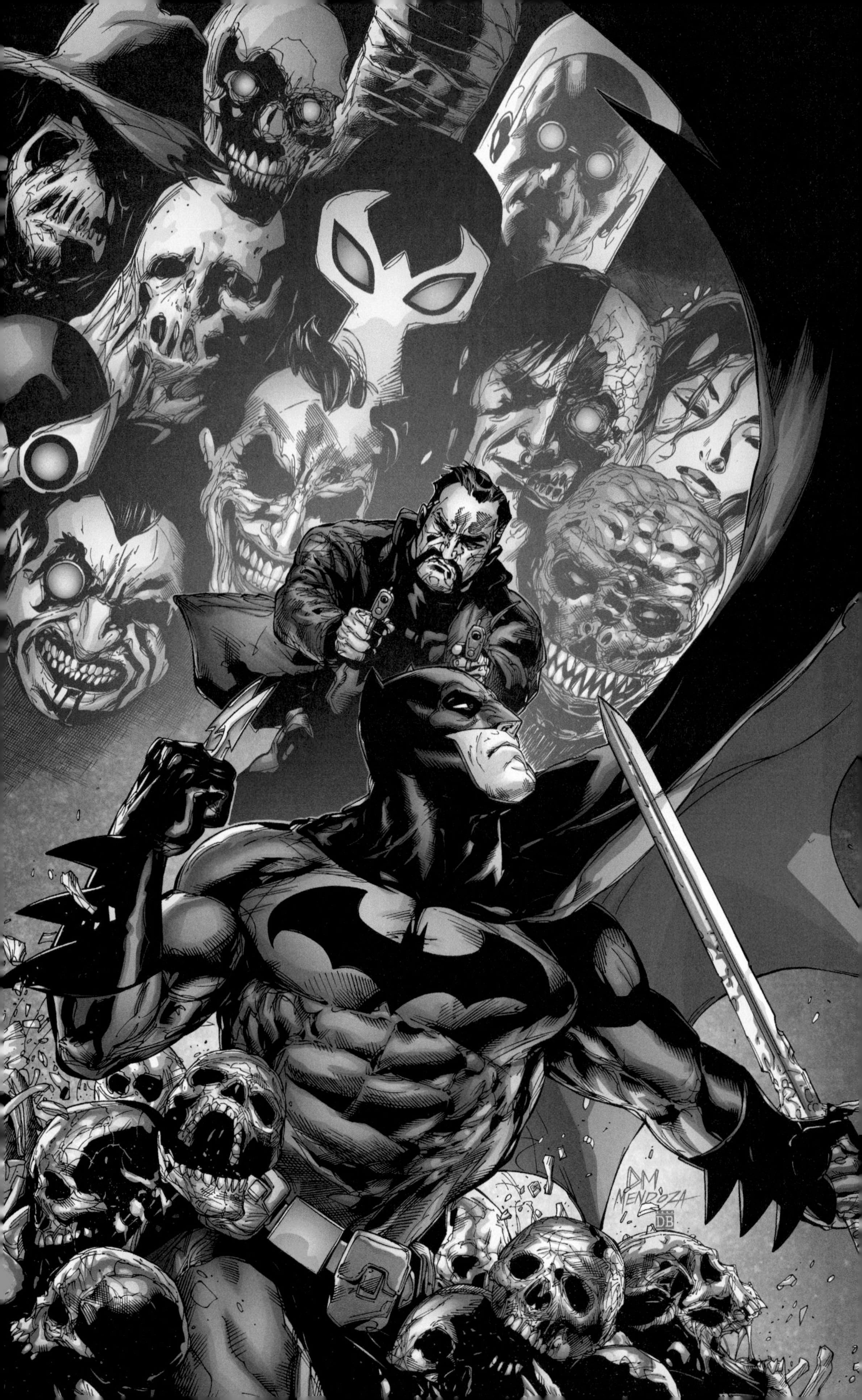
DM
MENDOZA
DB

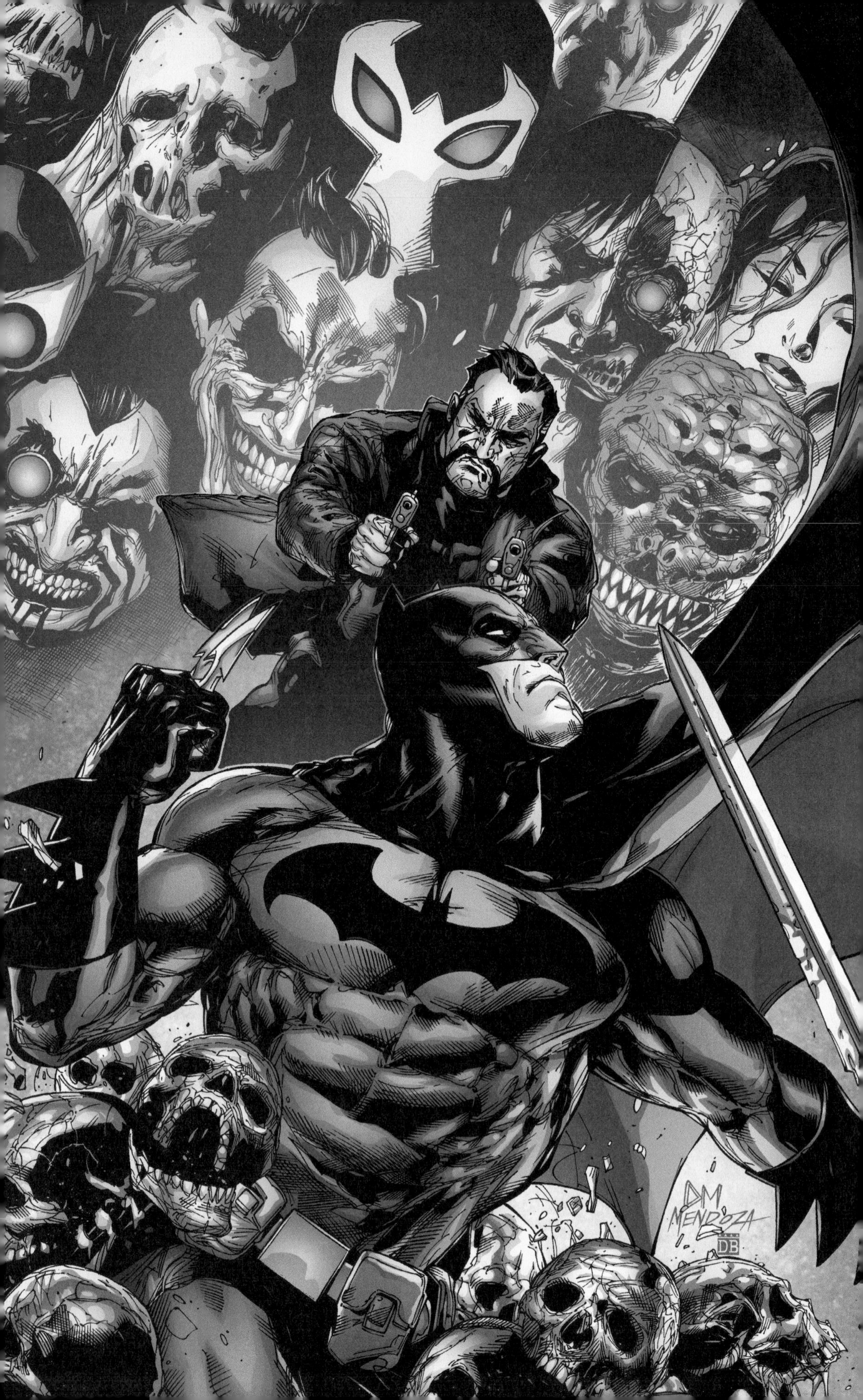
DM
MENDOZA
DB

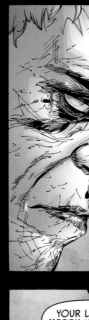

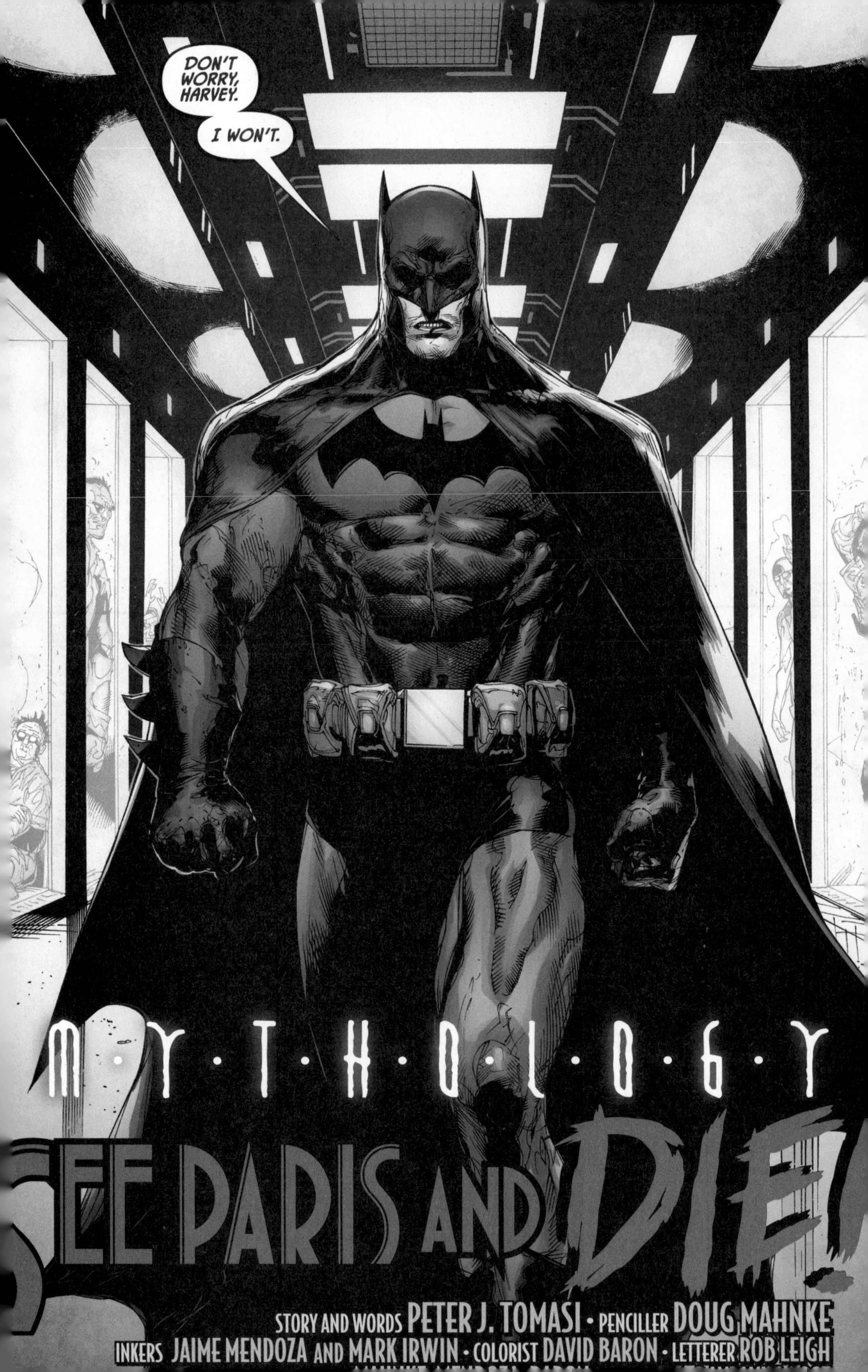
DON'T WORRY, HARVEY.
I WON'T.
M·Y·T·H·O·L·O·G·Y
SEE PARIS AND DIE!
STORY AND WORDS PETER J. TOMASI • PENCILLER DOUG MAHNKE
INKERS JAIME MENDOZA AND MARK IRWIN • COLORIST DAVID BARON • LETTERER ROB LEIGH

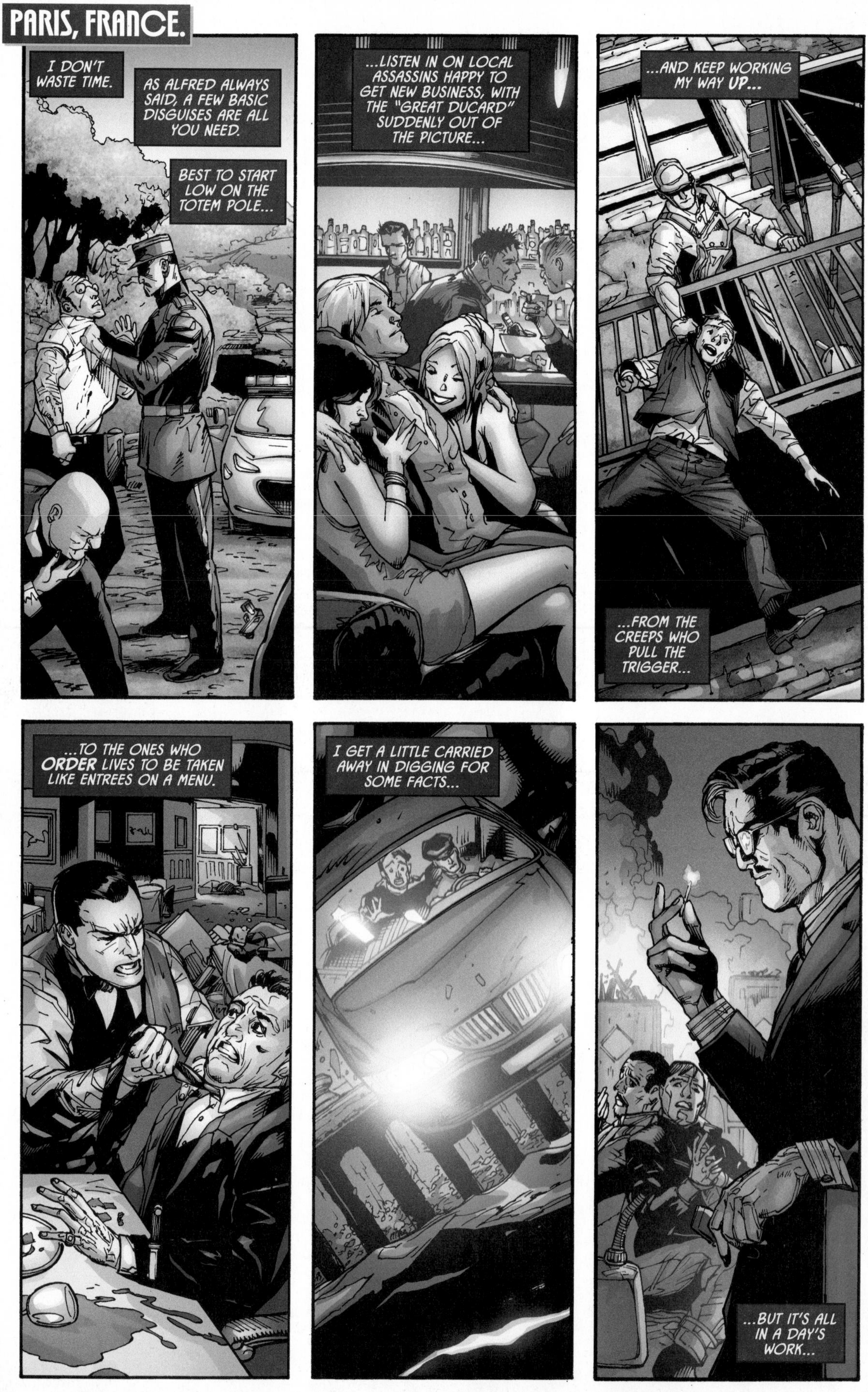
PARIS, FRANCE.
I DON'T WASTE TIME.
AS ALFRED ALWAYS SAID, A FEW BASIC DISGUISES ARE ALL YOU NEED.
BEST TO START LOW ON THE TOTEM POLE...
...LISTEN IN ON LOCAL ASSASSINS HAPPY TO GET NEW BUSINESS, WITH THE "GREAT DUCARD" SUDDENLY OUT OF THE PICTURE...
...AND KEEP WORKING MY WAY UP...
...FROM THE CREEPS WHO PULL THE TRIGGER...
...TO THE ONES WHO ORDER LIVES TO BE TAKEN LIKE ENTREES ON A MENU.
I GET A LITTLE CARRIED AWAY IN DIGGING FOR SOME FACTS...
...BUT IT'S ALL IN A DAY'S WORK...

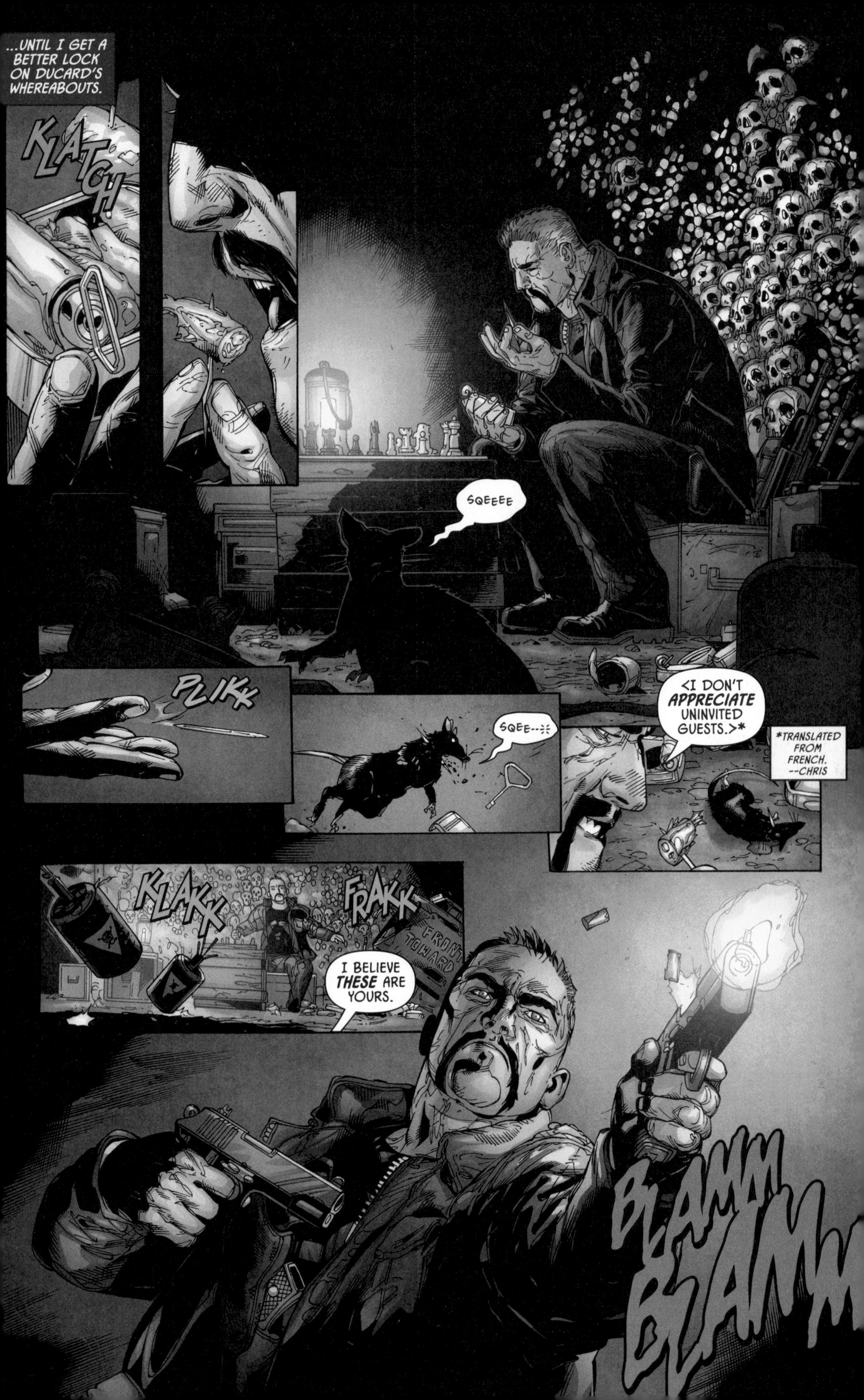
...UNTIL I GET A BETTER LOCK ON DUCARD'S WHEREABOUTS.
KLATCH
SQEEEE
PLIKK
SQEE--
<I DON'T APPRECIATE UNINVITED GUESTS.>*
*TRANSLATED FROM FRENCH. --CHRIS
KLAKK
FRAKK
FRONT TOWARD
I BELIEVE THESE ARE YOURS.
BLAMM
BLAMM

YOUR DISTASTE FOR FIREARMS AGAINST YOUR PREY IS STILL A...*THING*, HMM?

MY *PREY'S* LEARNED I DON'T *NEED* A GUN TO HURT OR STOP THEM.

KLAK

YES, MY SON, *MORGAN*, WAS QUITE AWARE OF THAT.

LET'S GET THIS STRAIGHT, DUCARD-- YOU SENT YOUR SON TO KILL ME--HE *FAILED*--I THREW HIM BACK IN YOUR FACE, ALIVE-- AND THEN PROBABLY TO PROVE TO YOU WHAT A MEAN BASTARD HE WAS, HE DECIDED TO TRY AGAIN *AND* TAKE *MY* SON.

UNFORTUNATELY, AGAINST MY WISHES, DAMIAN TOOK HIS LIFE.*

*AS SEEN IN THE *BATMAN & ROBIN: BAD BLOOD* TPB, ON SALE NOW! --CHRIS.

YES, DAMIAN HAS *QUITE* THE REPUTATION.

A BOY OF IRON PREPARED TO DO WHAT IS NECESSARY.

I HAVE NO DOUBT I'D LIKE HIM.

BUT YOU KNEW THAT ALREADY BECAUSE MORGAN-- AS *NOBODY*-- RECORDED EVERYTHING AND ASSUMED HE'D BE SHOWING YOU HIS FINAL VICTORY INSTEAD OF HIS DEFEAT, DIDN'T HE?

YES, I SAT AND WATCHED THOUSANDS OF MILES AWAY, HELPLESS, AS YOUR BOY KILLED MY ONLY SON ON A LIVE FEED.

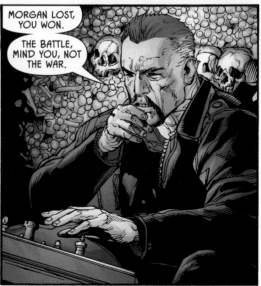

MORGAN LOST, YOU WON.

THE BATTLE, MIND YOU, NOT THE WAR.

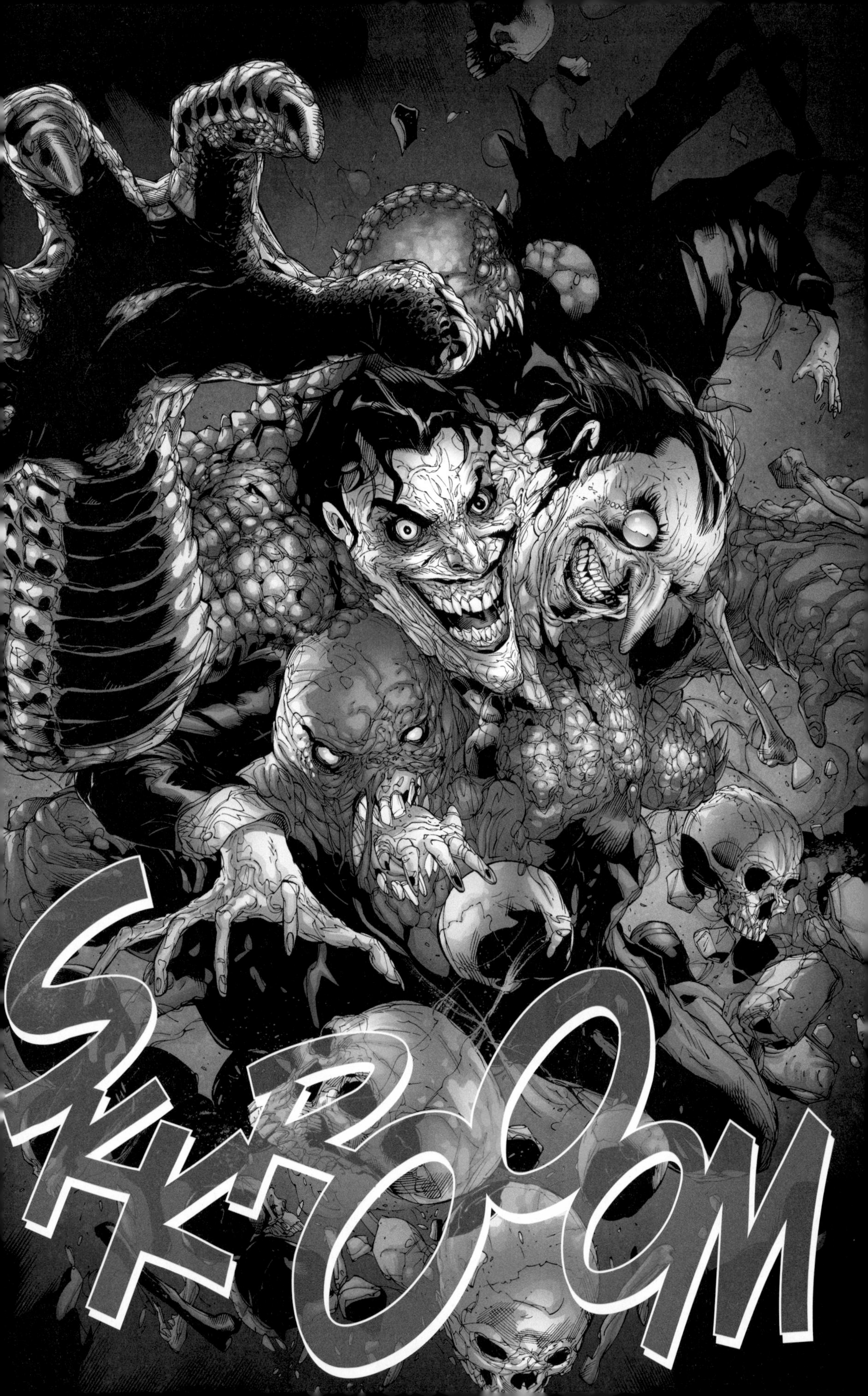
SKROOOM

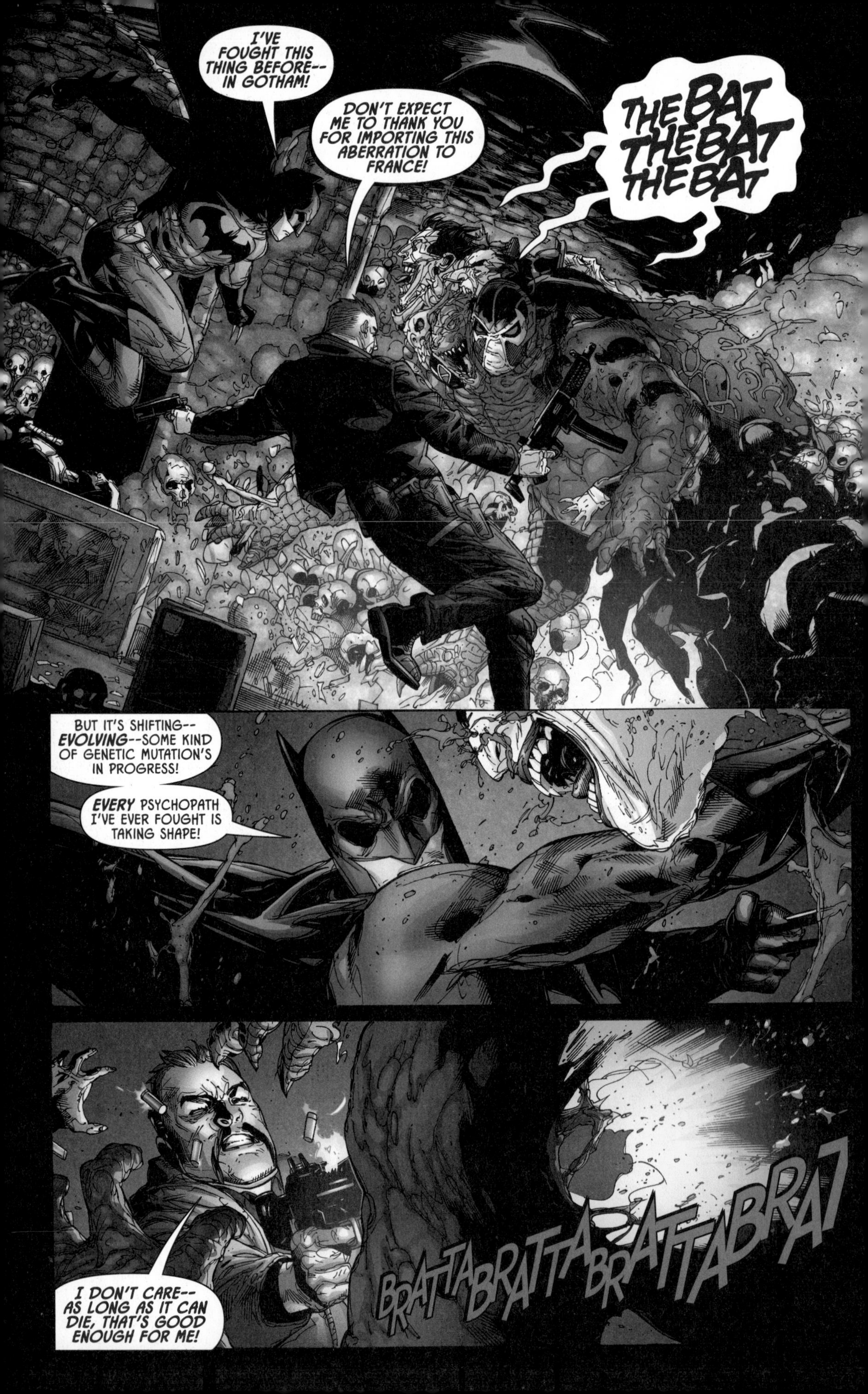
I'VE FOUGHT THIS THING BEFORE-- IN GOTHAM!
DON'T EXPECT ME TO THANK YOU FOR IMPORTING THIS ABERRATION TO FRANCE!
THE BAT THE BAT THE BAT
BUT IT'S SHIFTING-- EVOLVING--SOME KIND OF GENETIC MUTATION'S IN PROGRESS!
EVERY PSYCHOPATH I'VE EVER FOUGHT IS TAKING SHAPE!
I DON'T CARE-- AS LONG AS IT CAN DIE, THAT'S GOOD ENOUGH FOR ME!
BRATTABRATTABRATTABRAT

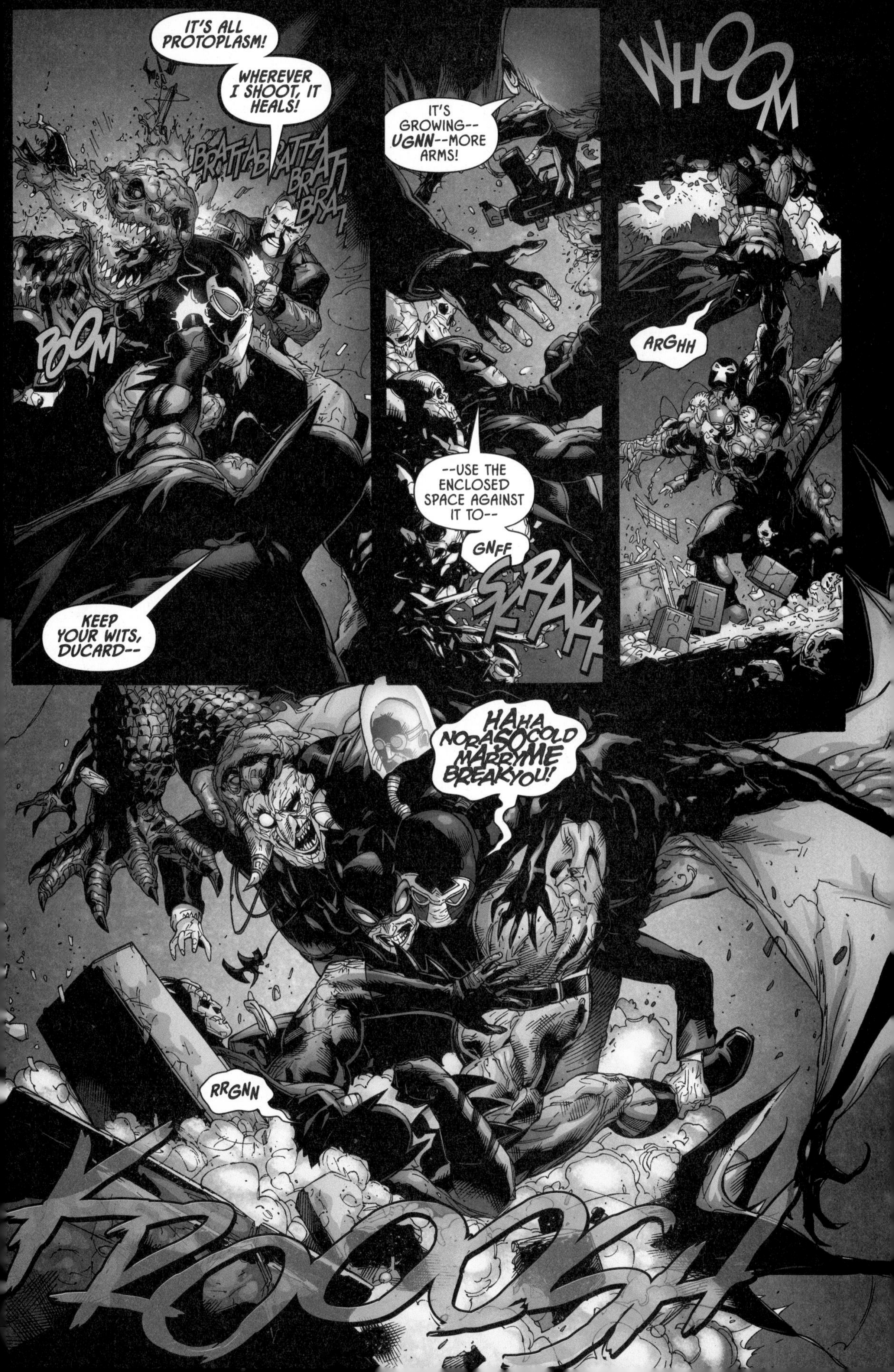

IT'S ALL PROTOPLASM!
WHEREVER I SHOOT, IT HEALS!
BRATTABRATTA BRATTABRATTA BRAT BRAT
POOM
KEEP YOUR WITS, DUCARD--
IT'S GROWING-- UGNN--MORE ARMS!
--USE THE ENCLOSED SPACE AGAINST IT TO--
GNFF
SKRAKK
WHOOM
ARGHH
HAHA NORASOCOLD MARRYME BREAKYOU!
RRGNN
KROOSH

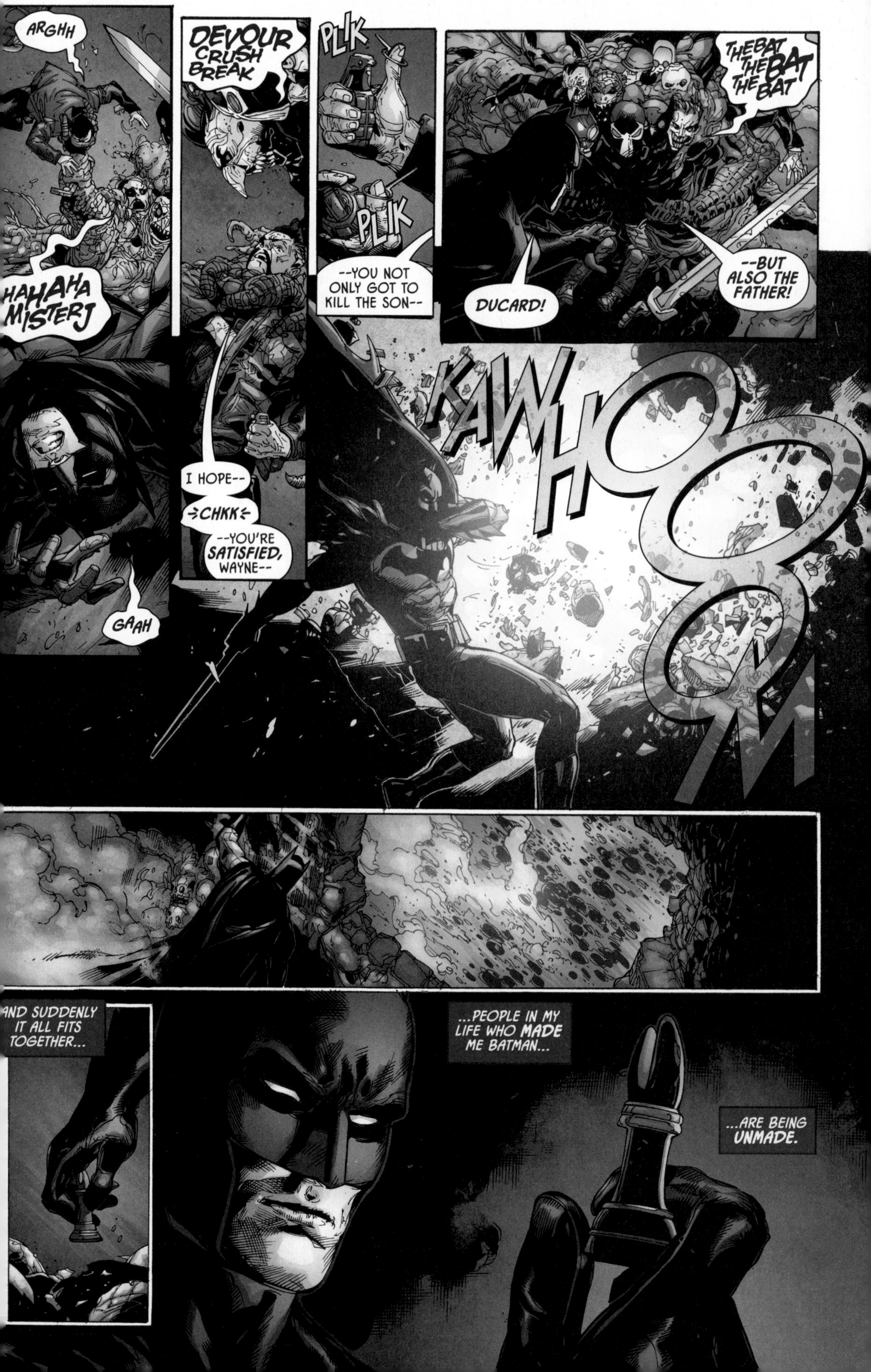
ARGHH
HAHAHA MISTER J
GAAH
DEVOUR CRUSH BREAK
I HOPE--
CHKK
--YOU'RE SATISFIED, WAYNE--
PLIK
PLIK
--YOU NOT ONLY GOT TO KILL THE SON--
THE BAT THE BAT THE BAT
DUCARD!
--BUT ALSO THE FATHER!
KAWHOOOM
AND SUDDENLY IT ALL FITS TOGETHER...
...PEOPLE IN MY LIFE WHO MADE ME BATMAN...
...ARE BEING UNMADE.

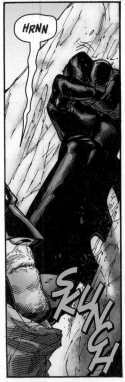

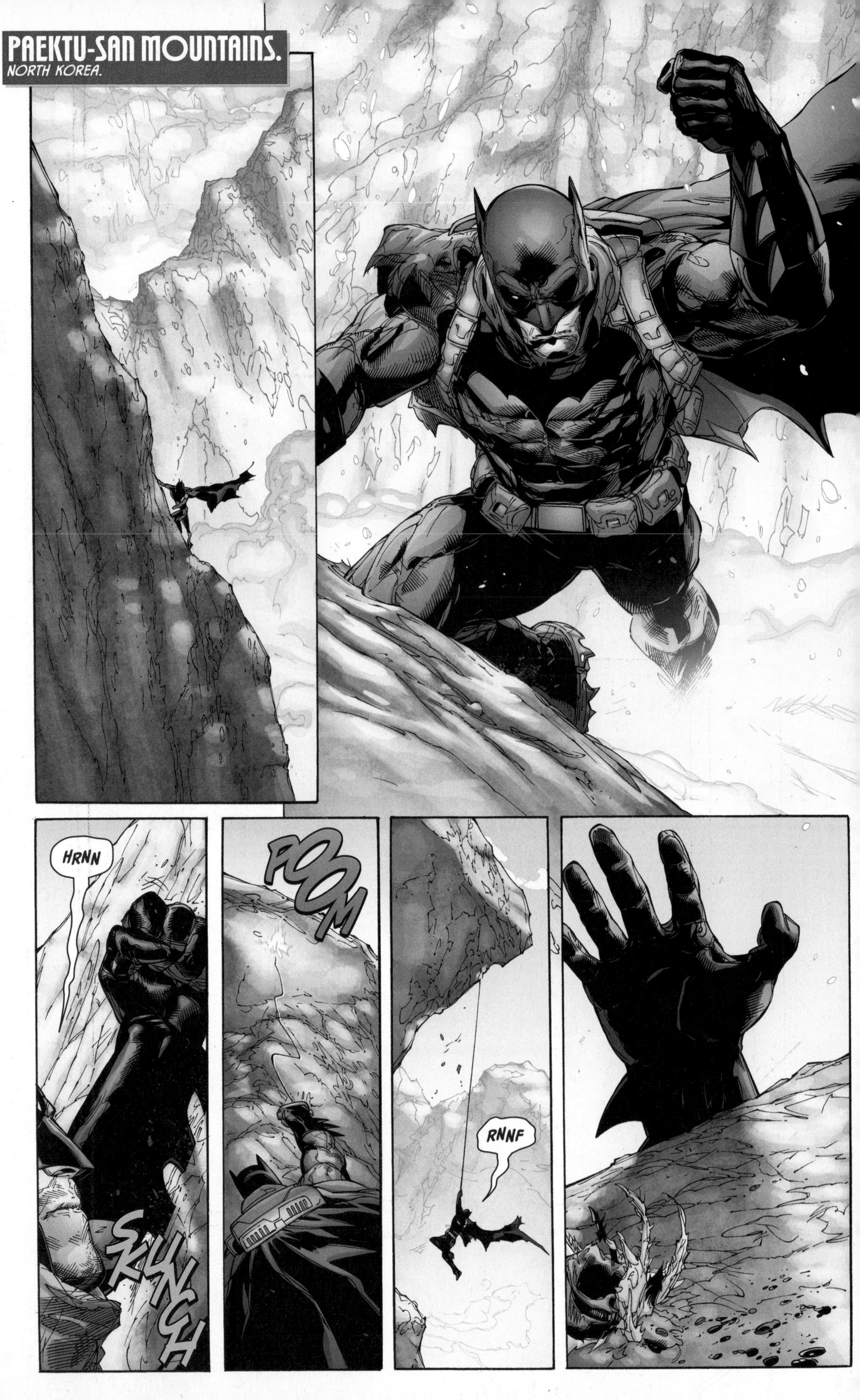
PAEKTU-SAN MOUNTAINS.
NORTH KOREA.
HRNN
SKLUNCH
POOM
RNNF

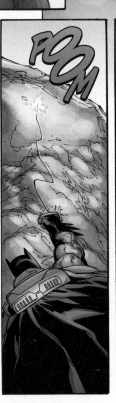

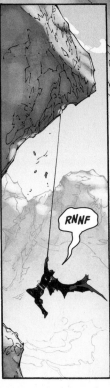

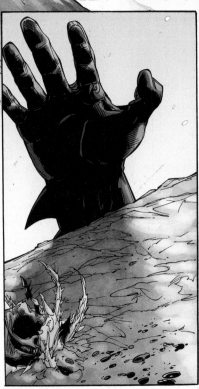

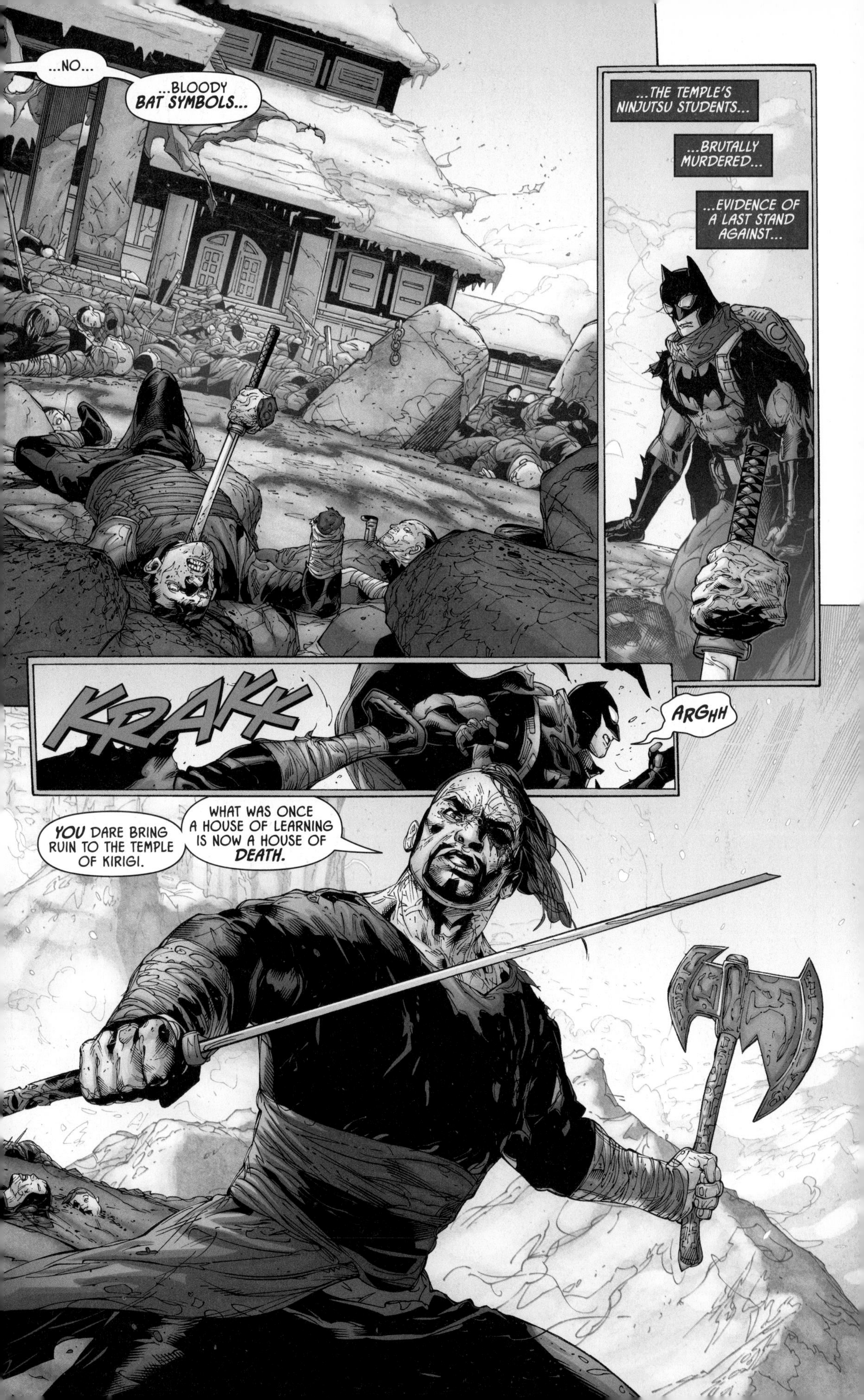
...NO...
...BLOODY BAT SYMBOLS...
...THE TEMPLE'S NINJUTSU STUDENTS...
...BRUTALLY MURDERED...
...EVIDENCE OF A LAST STAND AGAINST...
KRAKK
ARGHH
YOU DARE BRING RUIN TO THE TEMPLE OF KIRIGI.
WHAT WAS ONCE A HOUSE OF LEARNING IS NOW A HOUSE OF DEATH.

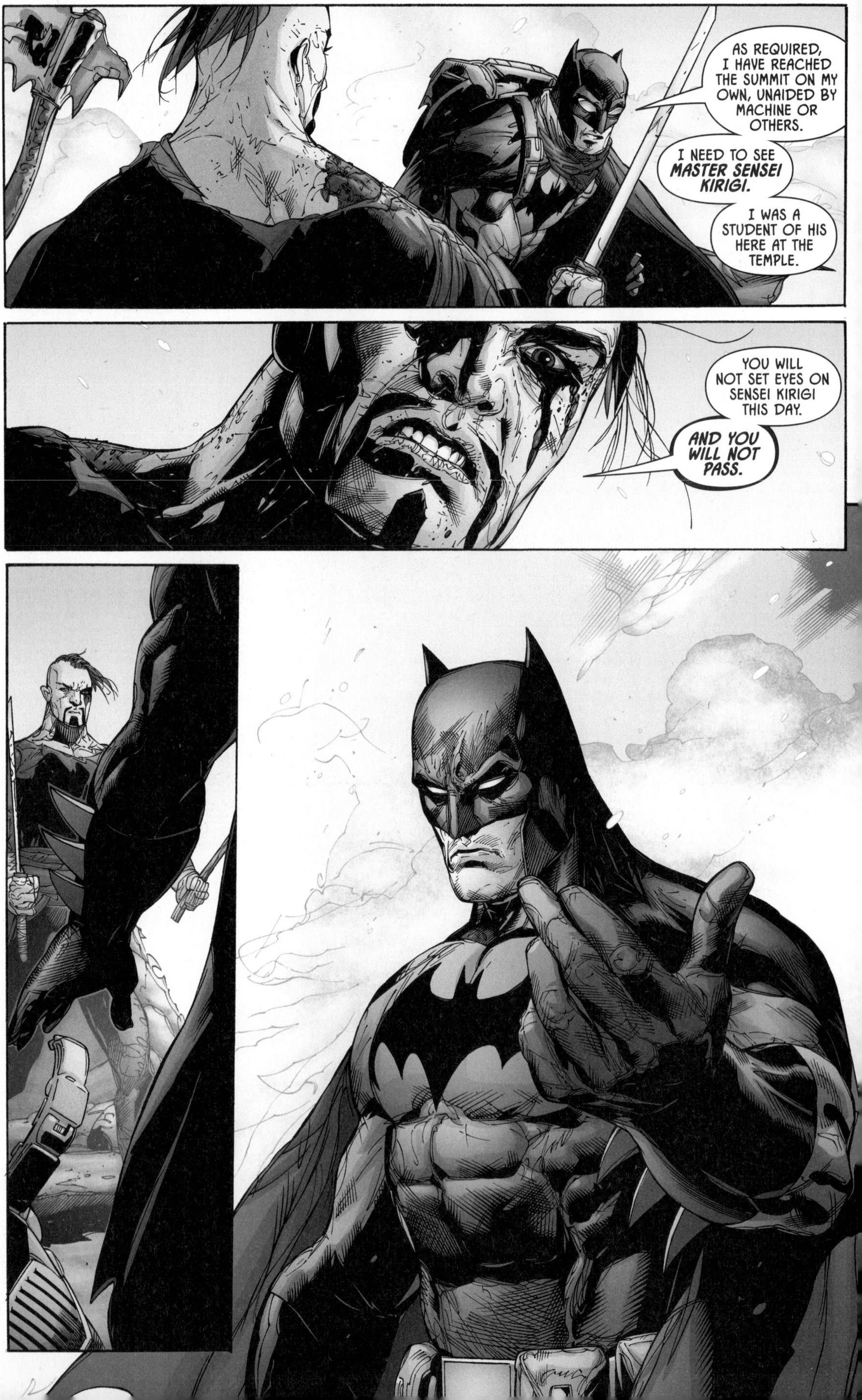
AS REQUIRED, I HAVE REACHED THE SUMMIT ON MY OWN, UNAIDED BY MACHINE OR OTHERS.
I NEED TO SEE MASTER SENSEI KIRIGI.
I WAS A STUDENT OF HIS HERE AT THE TEMPLE.
YOU WILL NOT SET EYES ON SENSEI KIRIGI THIS DAY.
AND YOU WILL NOT PASS.

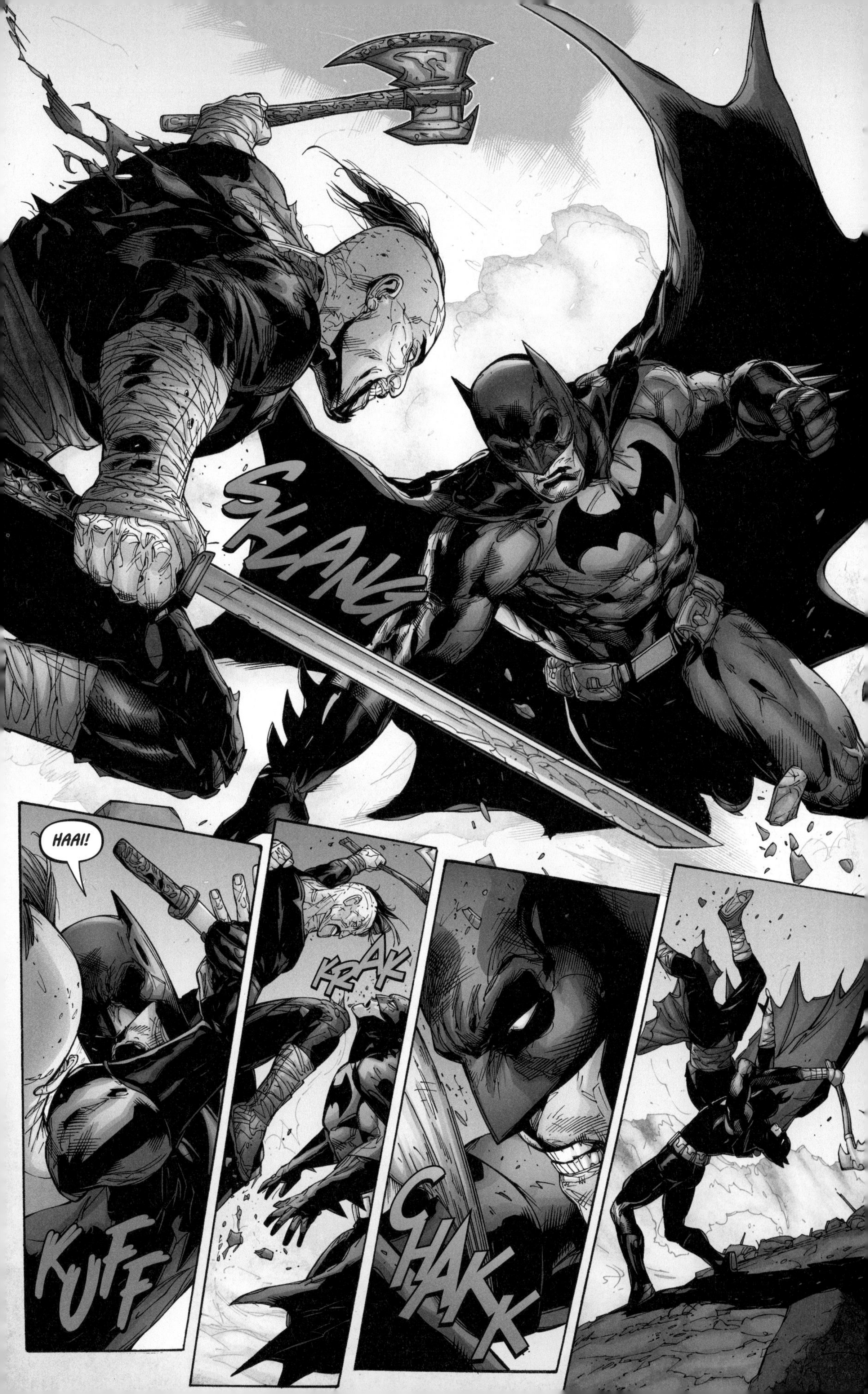
SKLANG
HAAI!
KUFF
KRAK
CHAKK

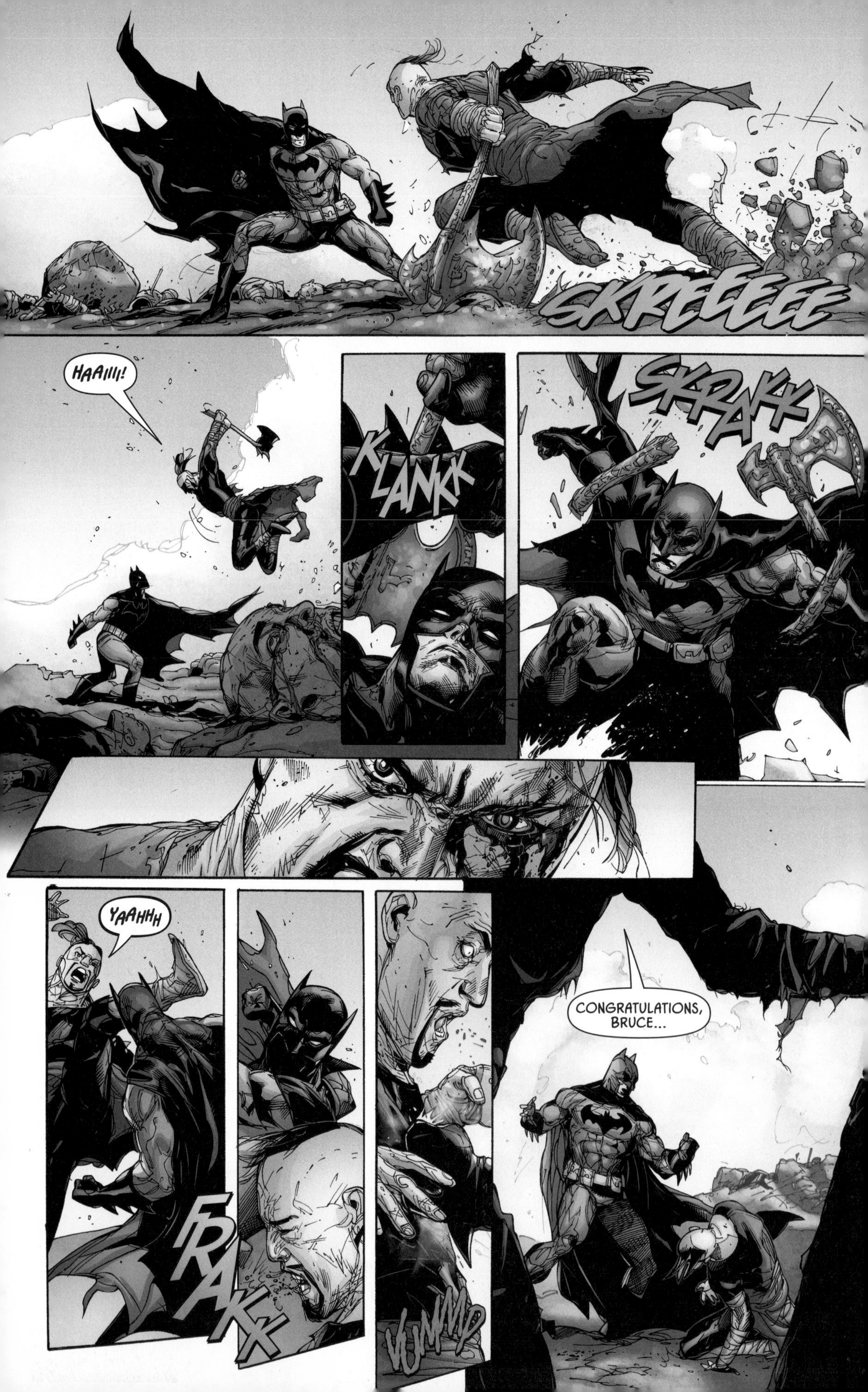
SKREEEEEE
HAAIIII!
KLANKK
SKRAKK
YAAHHH
FRAKK
VUMMP
CONGRATULATIONS, BRUCE...

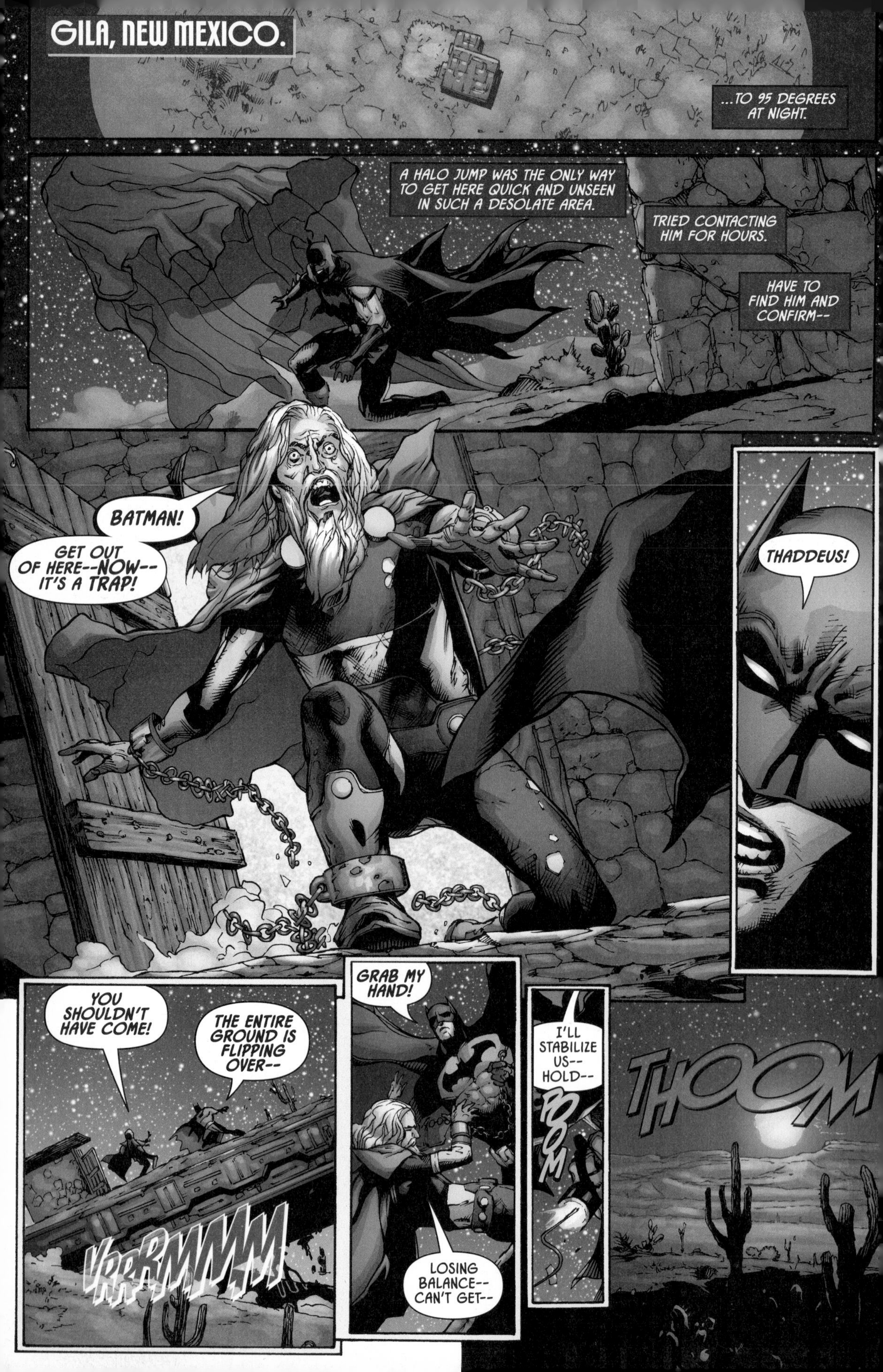
GILA, NEW MEXICO.
...TO 95 DEGREES AT NIGHT.
A HALO JUMP WAS THE ONLY WAY TO GET HERE QUICK AND UNSEEN IN SUCH A DESOLATE AREA.
TRIED CONTACTING HIM FOR HOURS.
HAVE TO FIND HIM AND CONFIRM--
BATMAN!
GET OUT OF HERE--NOW--IT'S A TRAP!
THADDEUS!
YOU SHOULDN'T HAVE COME!
THE ENTIRE GROUND IS FLIPPING OVER--
VRRRMMMM
GRAB MY HAND!
LOSING BALANCE--CAN'T GET--
I'LL STABILIZE US--HOLD--
BOOM
THOOM

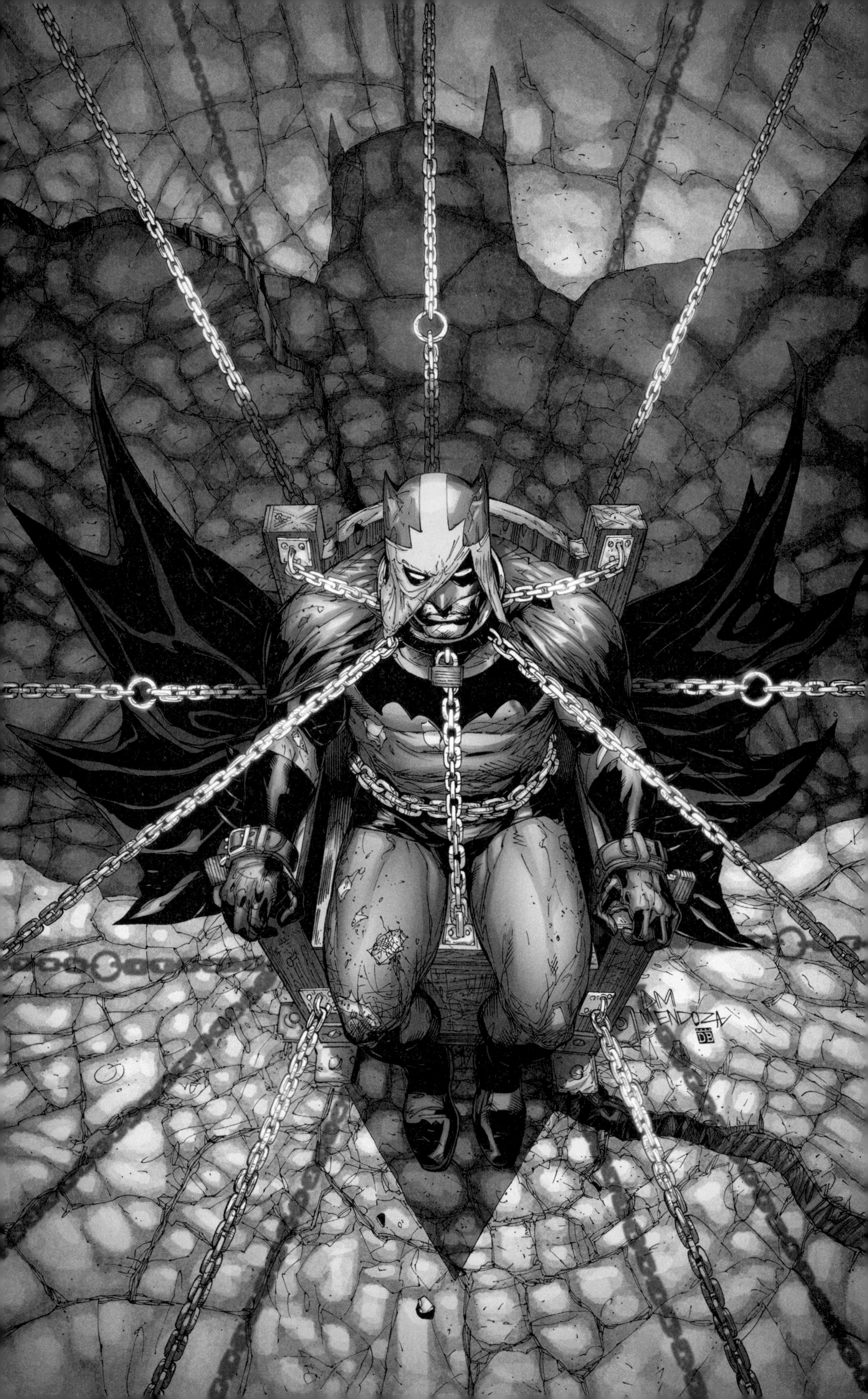
DM MENDOZA
DB

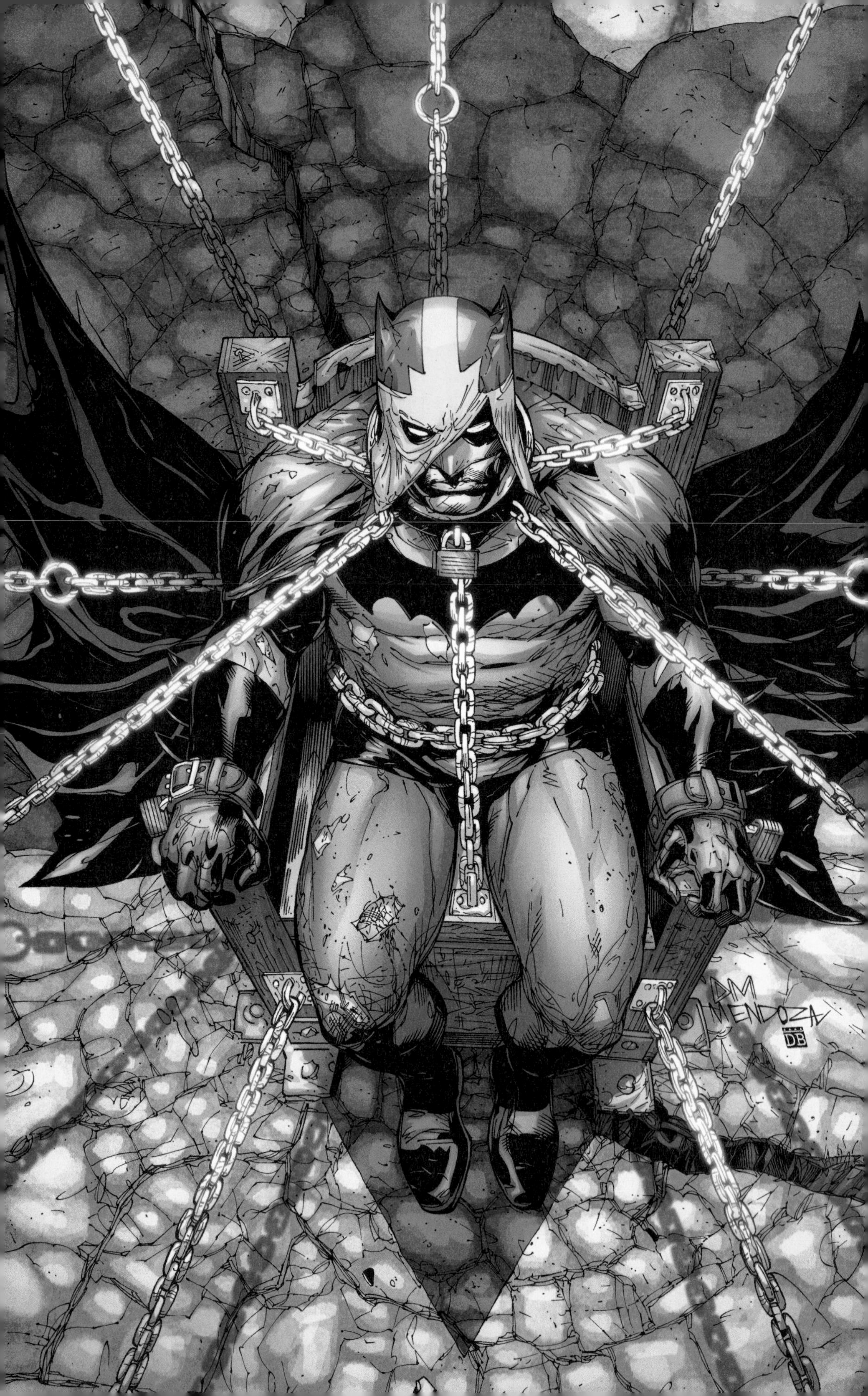
DM MENDOZA
DB

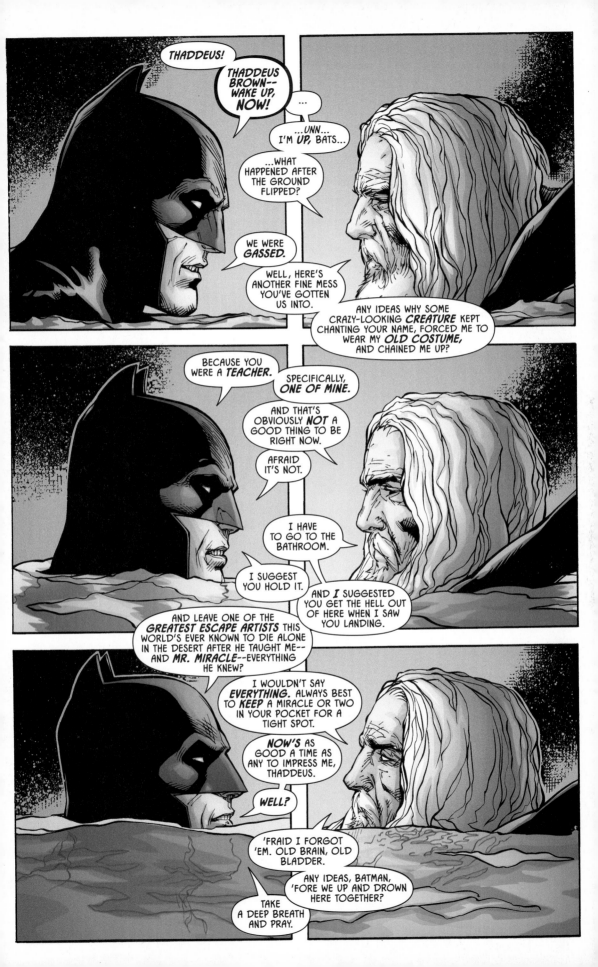

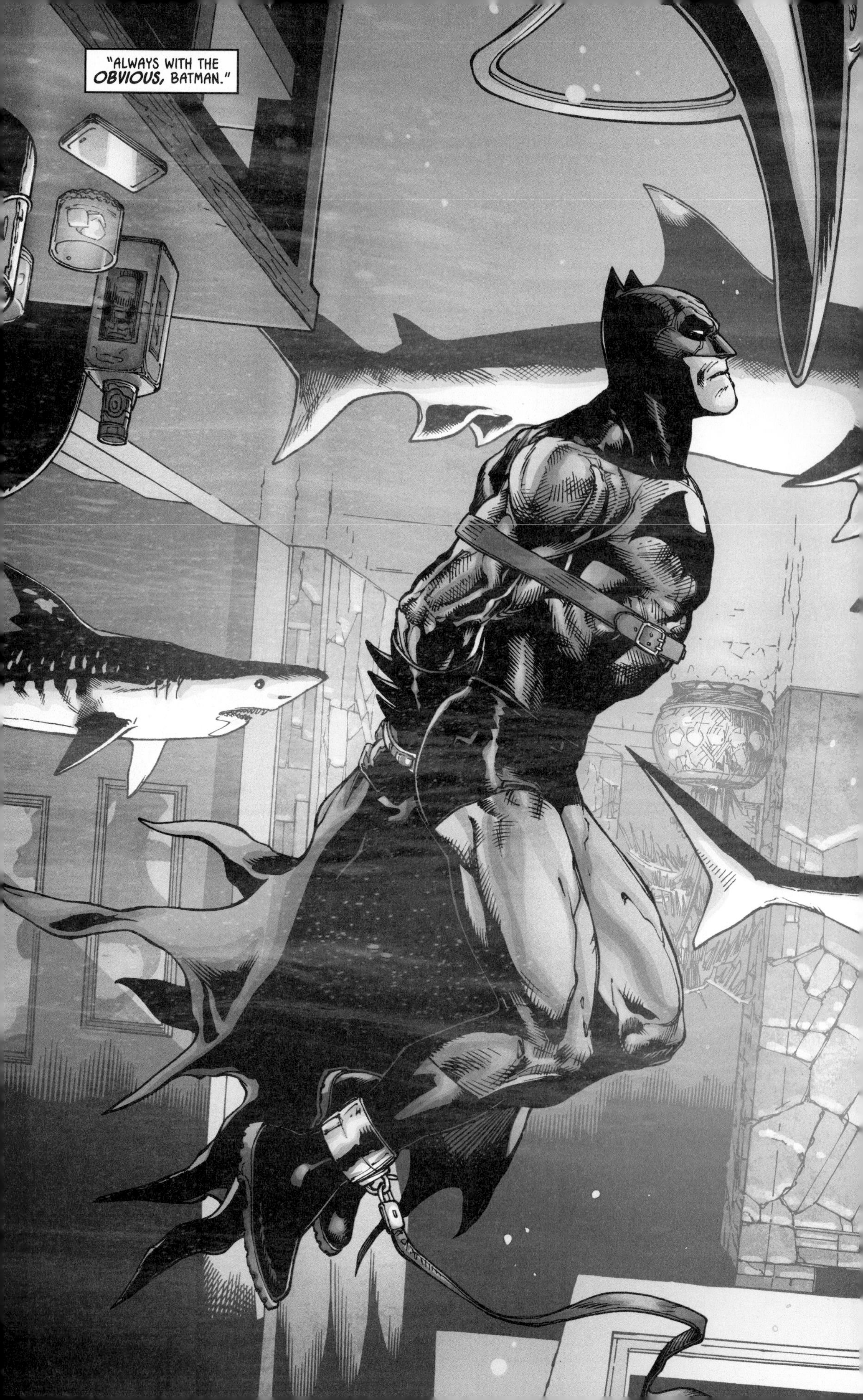
"ALWAYS WITH THE
OBVIOUS, BATMAN."

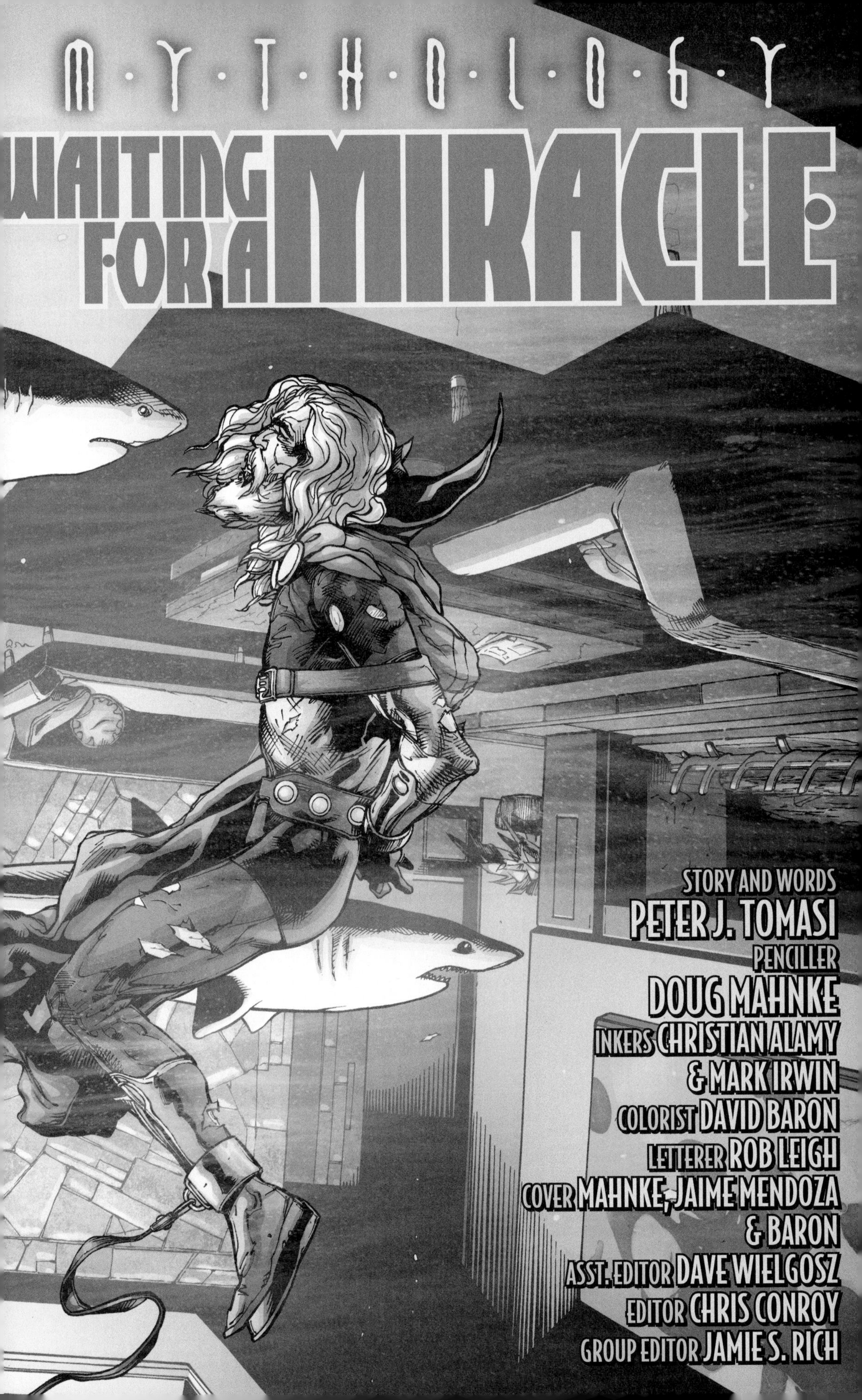
MYTHOLOGY
WAITING FOR A MIRACLE.
STORY AND WORDS PETER J. TOMASI
PENCILLER DOUG MAHNKE
INKERS CHRISTIAN ALAMY & MARK IRWIN
COLORIST DAVID BARON
LETTERER ROB LEIGH
COVER MAHNKE, JAIME MENDOZA & BARON
ASST. EDITOR DAVE WIELGOSZ
EDITOR CHRIS CONROY
GROUP EDITOR JAMIE S. RICH

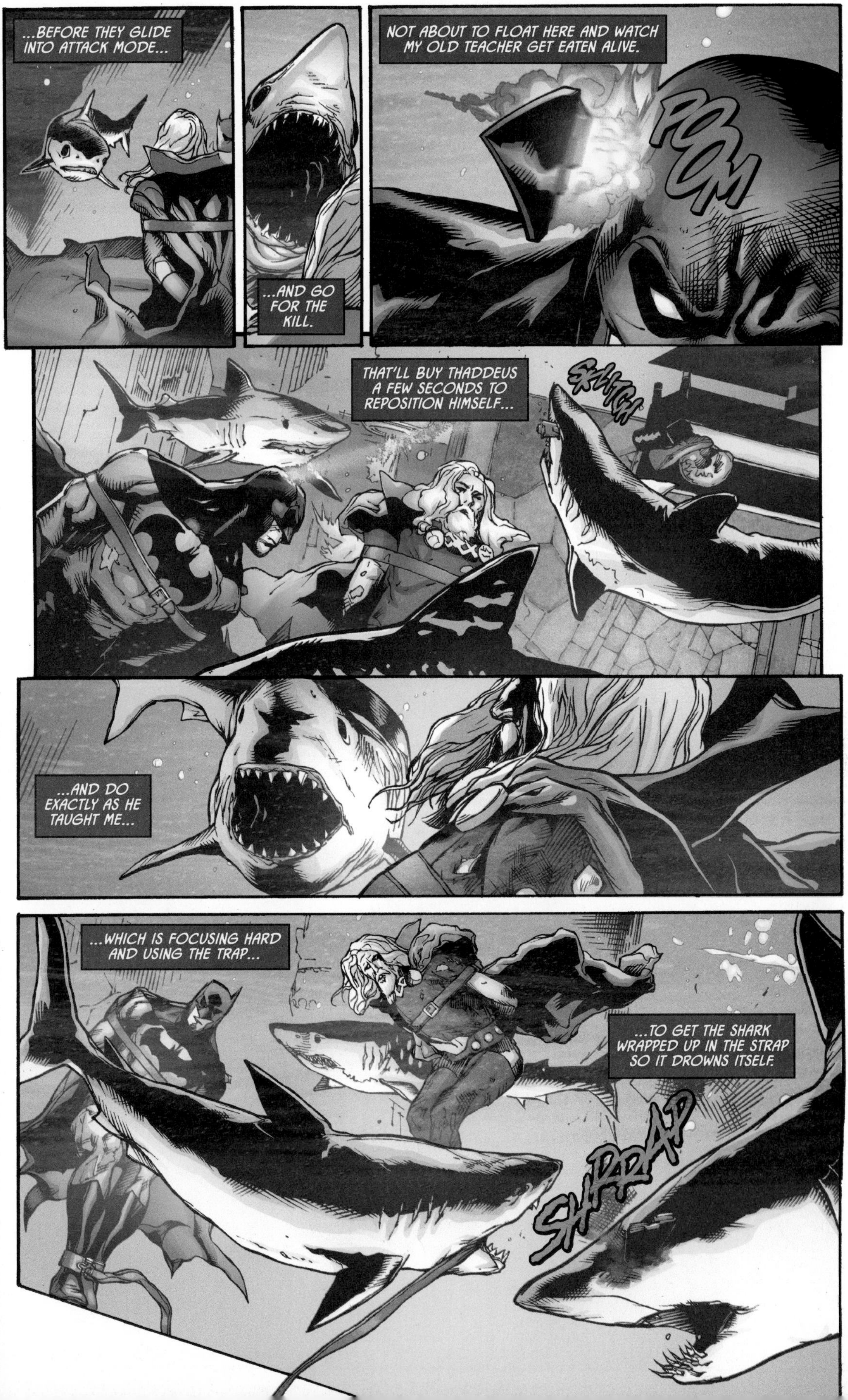
...BEFORE THEY GLIDE INTO ATTACK MODE...
...AND GO FOR THE KILL.
NOT ABOUT TO FLOAT HERE AND WATCH MY OLD TEACHER GET EATEN ALIVE.
POOM
THAT'LL BUY THADDEUS A FEW SECONDS TO REPOSITION HIMSELF...
SKLITCH
...AND DO EXACTLY AS HE TAUGHT ME...
...WHICH IS FOCUSING HARD AND USING THE TRAP...
...TO GET THE SHARK WRAPPED UP IN THE STRAP SO IT DROWNS ITSELF.
SHRRAP

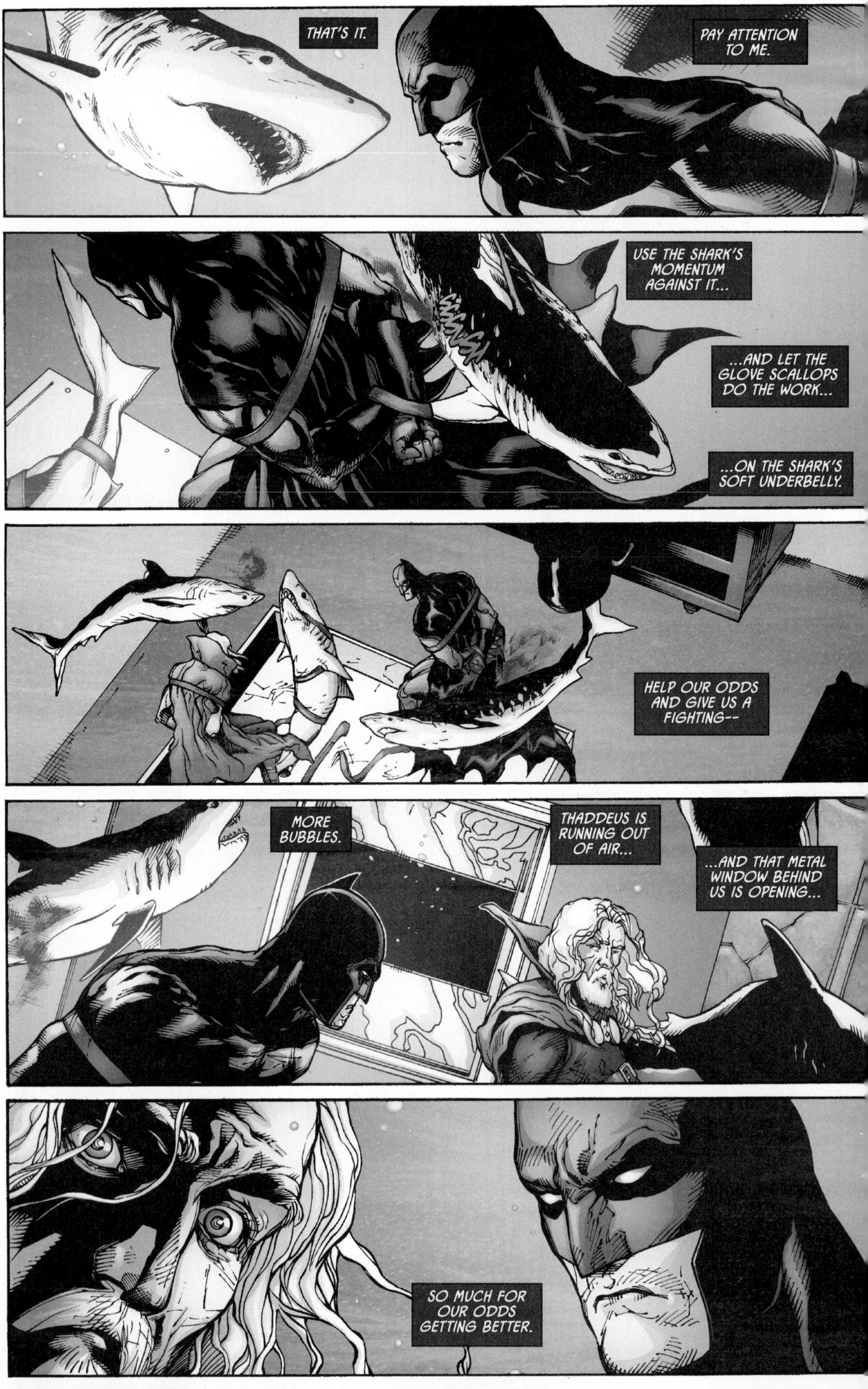
THAT'S IT.
PAY ATTENTION TO ME.
USE THE SHARK'S MOMENTUM AGAINST IT...
SHSHSH
...AND LET THE GLOVE SCALLOPS DO THE WORK...
...ON THE SHARK'S SOFT UNDERBELLY.
HELP OUR ODDS AND GIVE US A FIGHTING--
MORE BUBBLES.
THADDEUS IS RUNNING OUT OF AIR...
...AND THAT METAL WINDOW BEHIND US IS OPENING...
SO MUCH FOR OUR ODDS GETTING BETTER.

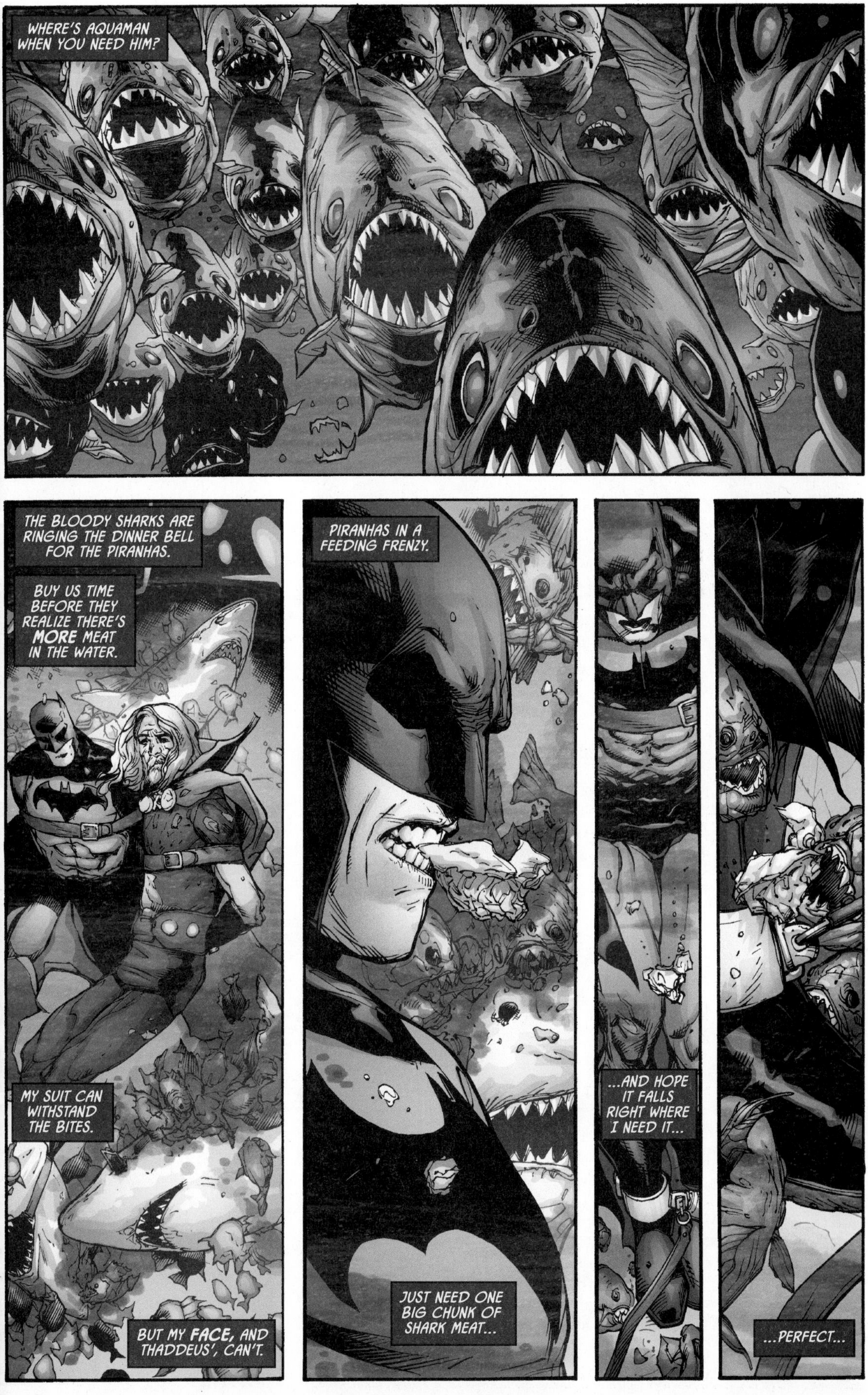
WHERE'S AQUAMAN WHEN YOU NEED HIM?
THE BLOODY SHARKS ARE RINGING THE DINNER BELL FOR THE PIRANHAS.
BUY US TIME BEFORE THEY REALIZE THERE'S MORE MEAT IN THE WATER.
MY SUIT CAN WITHSTAND THE BITES.
BUT MY FACE, AND THADDEUS', CAN'T.
PIRANHAS IN A FEEDING FRENZY.
JUST NEED ONE BIG CHUNK OF SHARK MEAT...
...AND HOPE IT FALLS RIGHT WHERE I NEED IT...
...PERFECT...

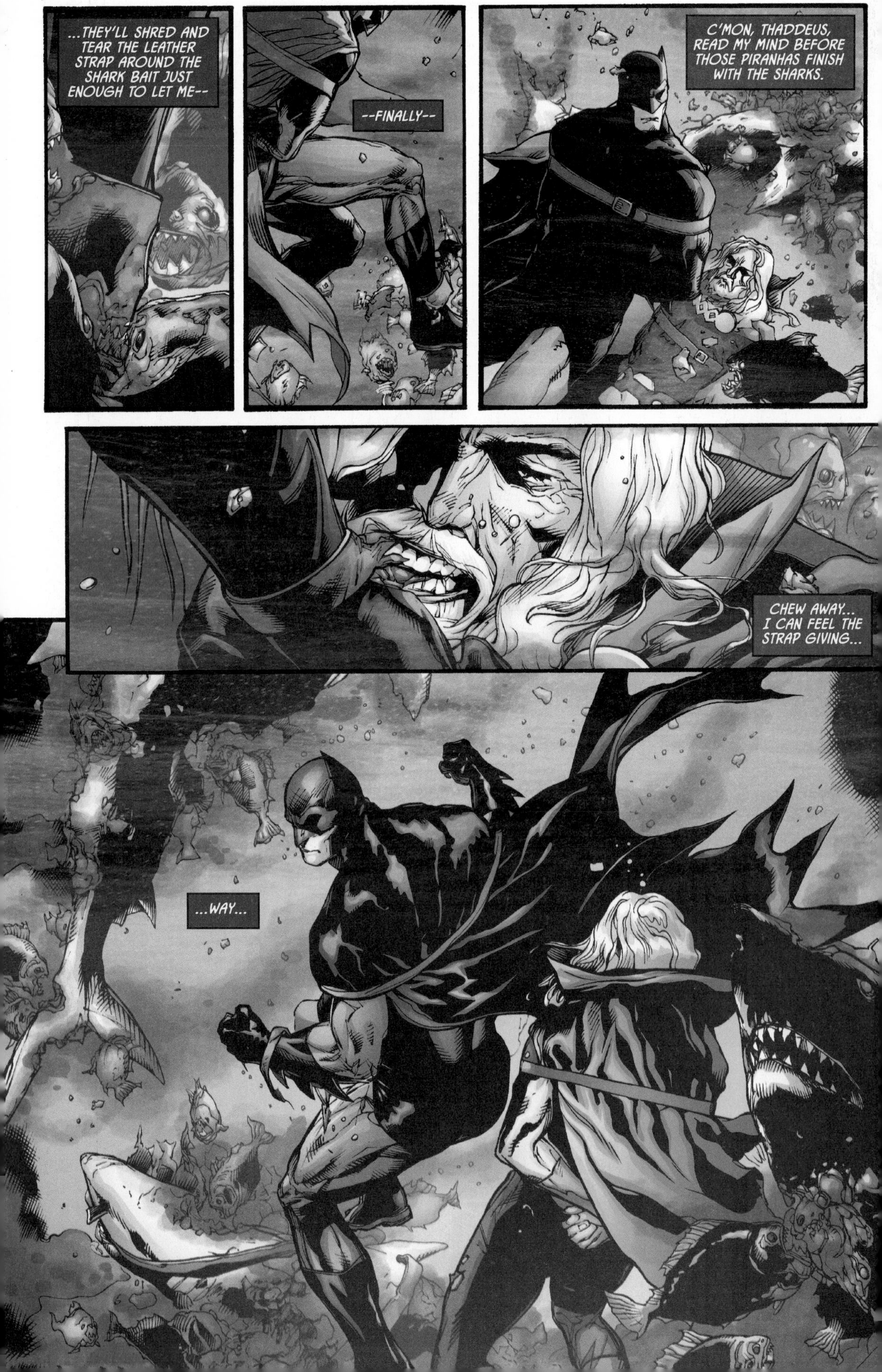
...THEY'LL SHRED AND TEAR THE LEATHER STRAP AROUND THE SHARK BAIT JUST ENOUGH TO LET ME--
--FINALLY--
C'MON, THADDEUS, READ MY MIND BEFORE THOSE PIRANHAS FINISH WITH THE SHARKS.
CHEW AWAY... I CAN FEEL THE STRAP GIVING...
...WAY...

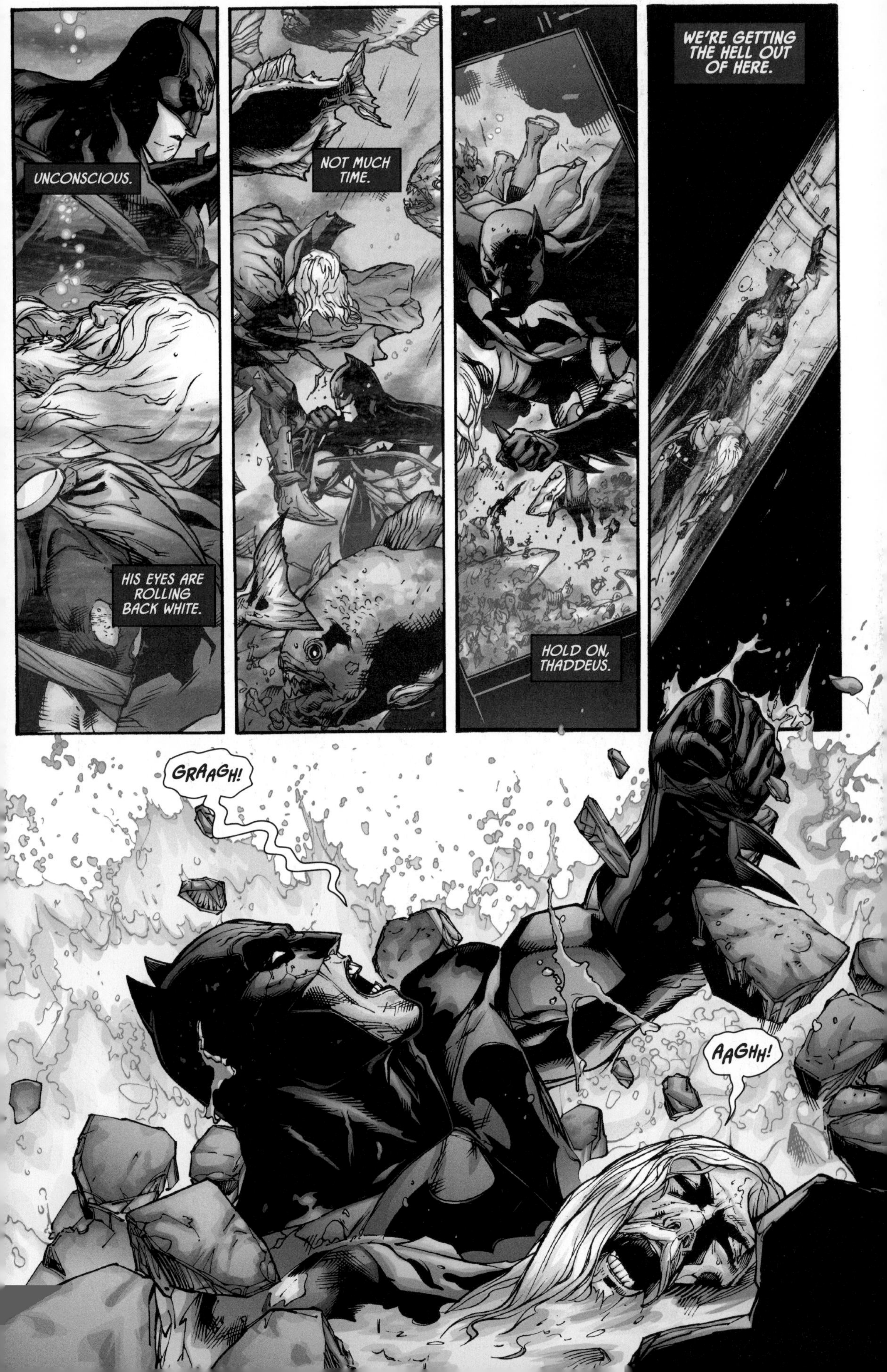
UNCONSCIOUS.
HIS EYES ARE ROLLING BACK WHITE.
NOT MUCH TIME.
HOLD ON, THADDEUS.
WE'RE GETTING THE HELL OUT OF HERE.
GRAAGH!
AAGHH!

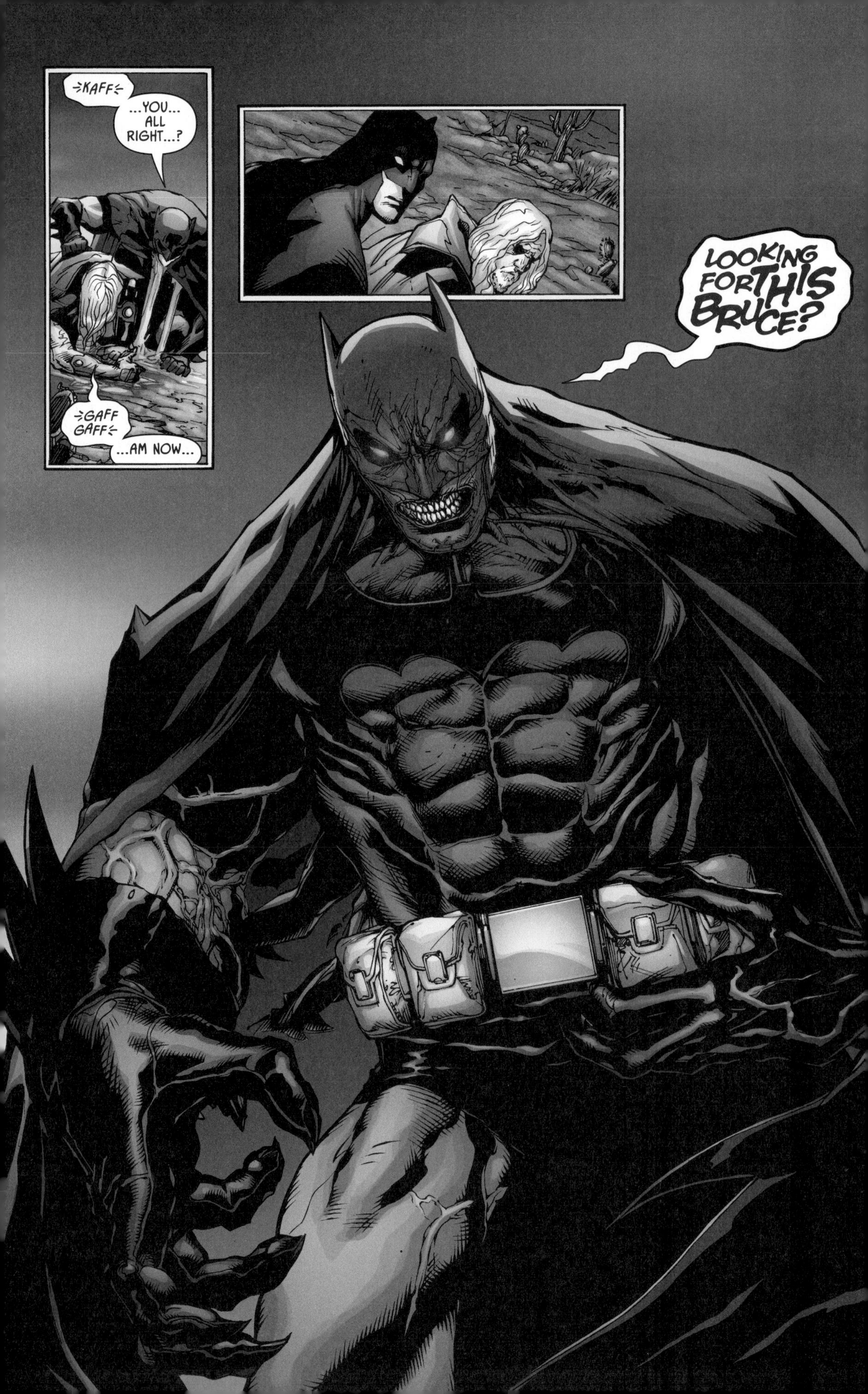

KAFF
...YOU... ALL RIGHT...?
GAFF GAFF
...AM NOW...
LOOKING FOR THIS BRUCE?

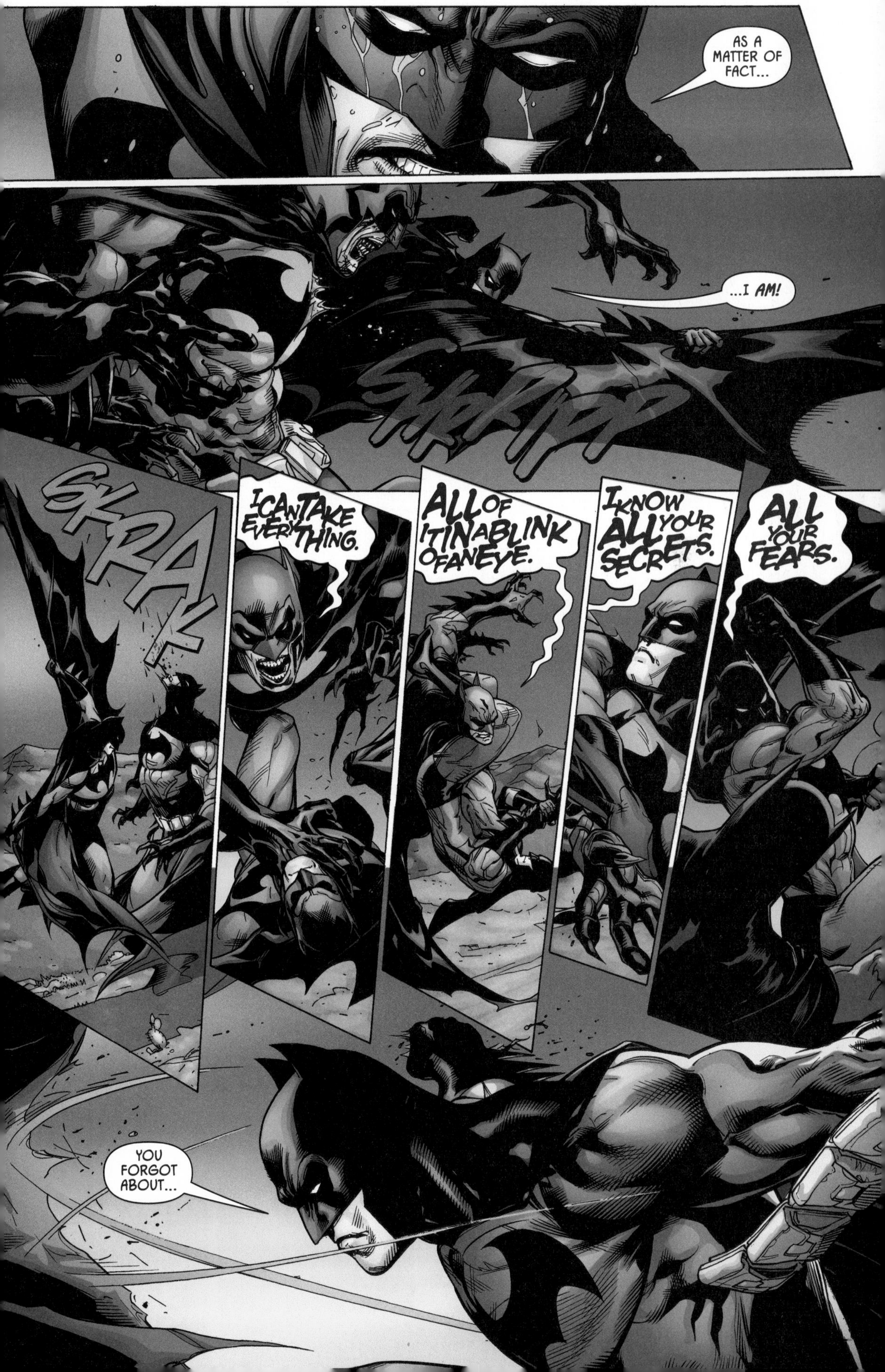
AS A MATTER OF FACT...
...I AM!
SHHHIPP
SKRAK
I CAN TAKE EVERYTHING.
ALL OF IT IN A BLINK OF AN EYE.
I KNOW ALL YOUR SECRETS.
ALL YOUR FEARS.
YOU FORGOT ABOUT...

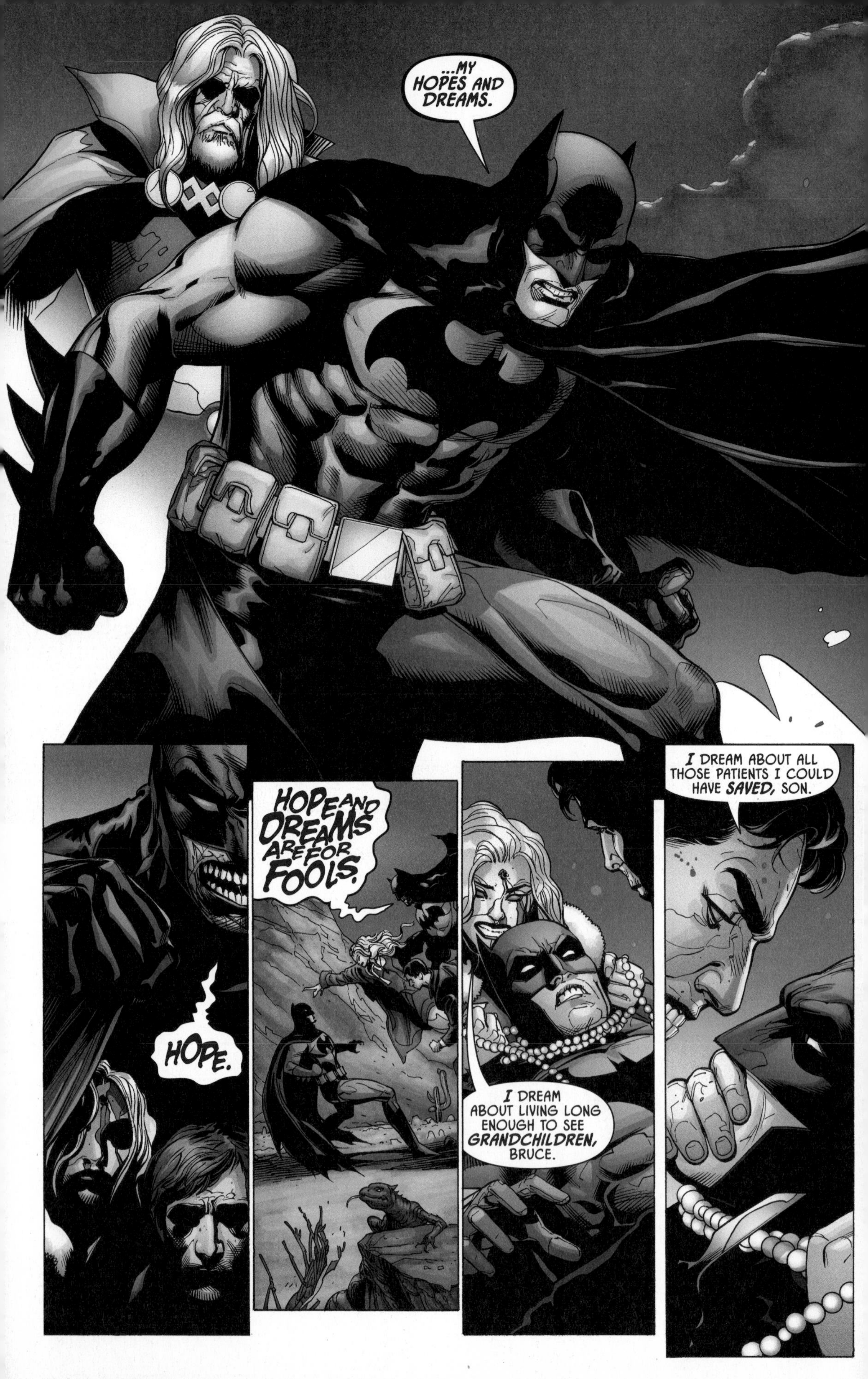
...MY HOPES AND DREAMS.
HOPE.
HOPE AND DREAMS ARE FOR FOOLS.
I DREAM ABOUT LIVING LONG ENOUGH TO SEE GRANDCHILDREN, BRUCE.
I DREAM ABOUT ALL THOSE PATIENTS I COULD HAVE SAVED, SON.

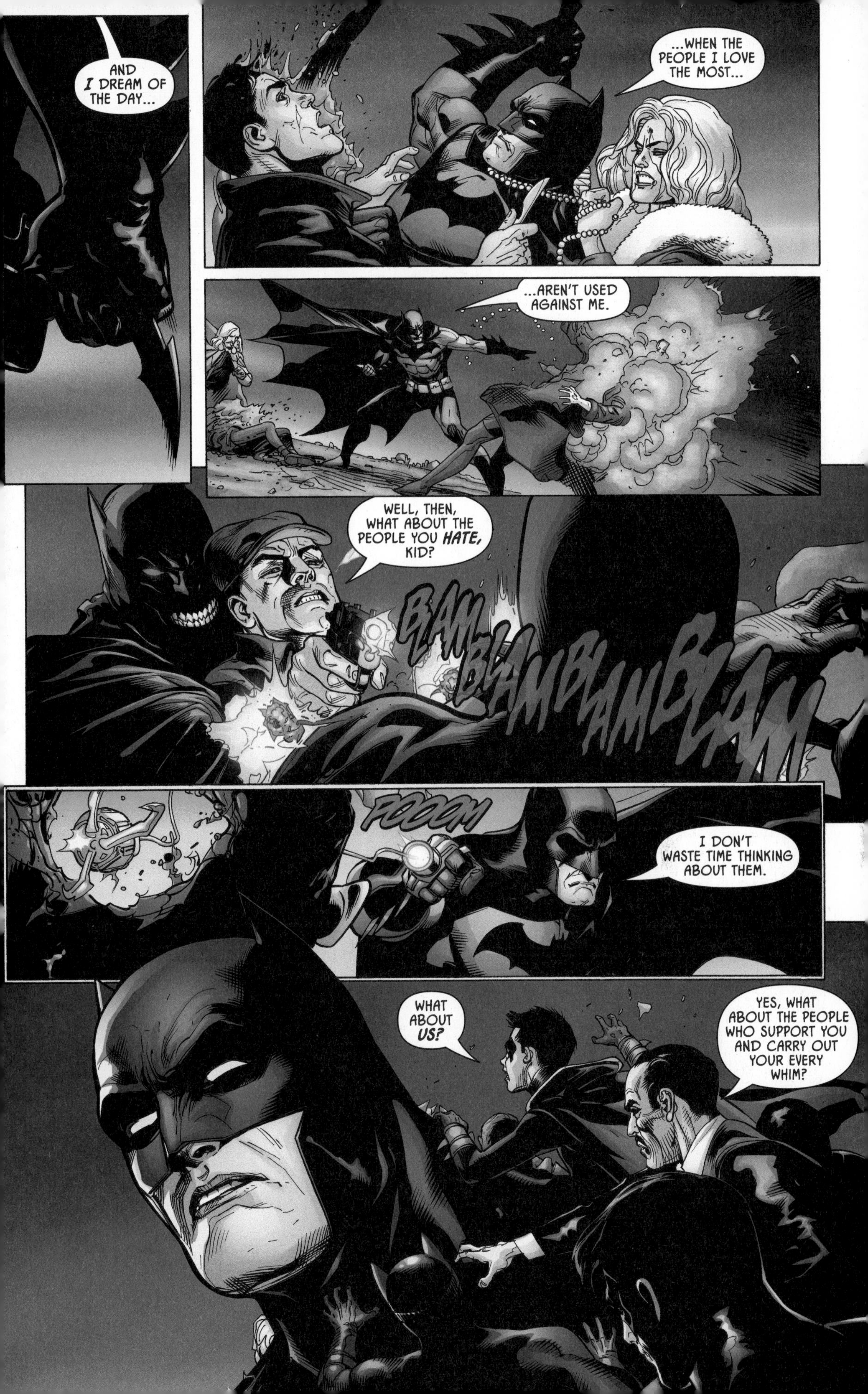
AND I DREAM OF THE DAY...
...WHEN THE PEOPLE I LOVE THE MOST...
...AREN'T USED AGAINST ME.
WELL, THEN, WHAT ABOUT THE PEOPLE YOU HATE, KID?
BLAM BLAM BLAM BLAM BLAM
POOOM
I DON'T WASTE TIME THINKING ABOUT THEM.
WHAT ABOUT US?
YES, WHAT ABOUT THE PEOPLE WHO SUPPORT YOU AND CARRY OUT YOUR EVERY WHIM?

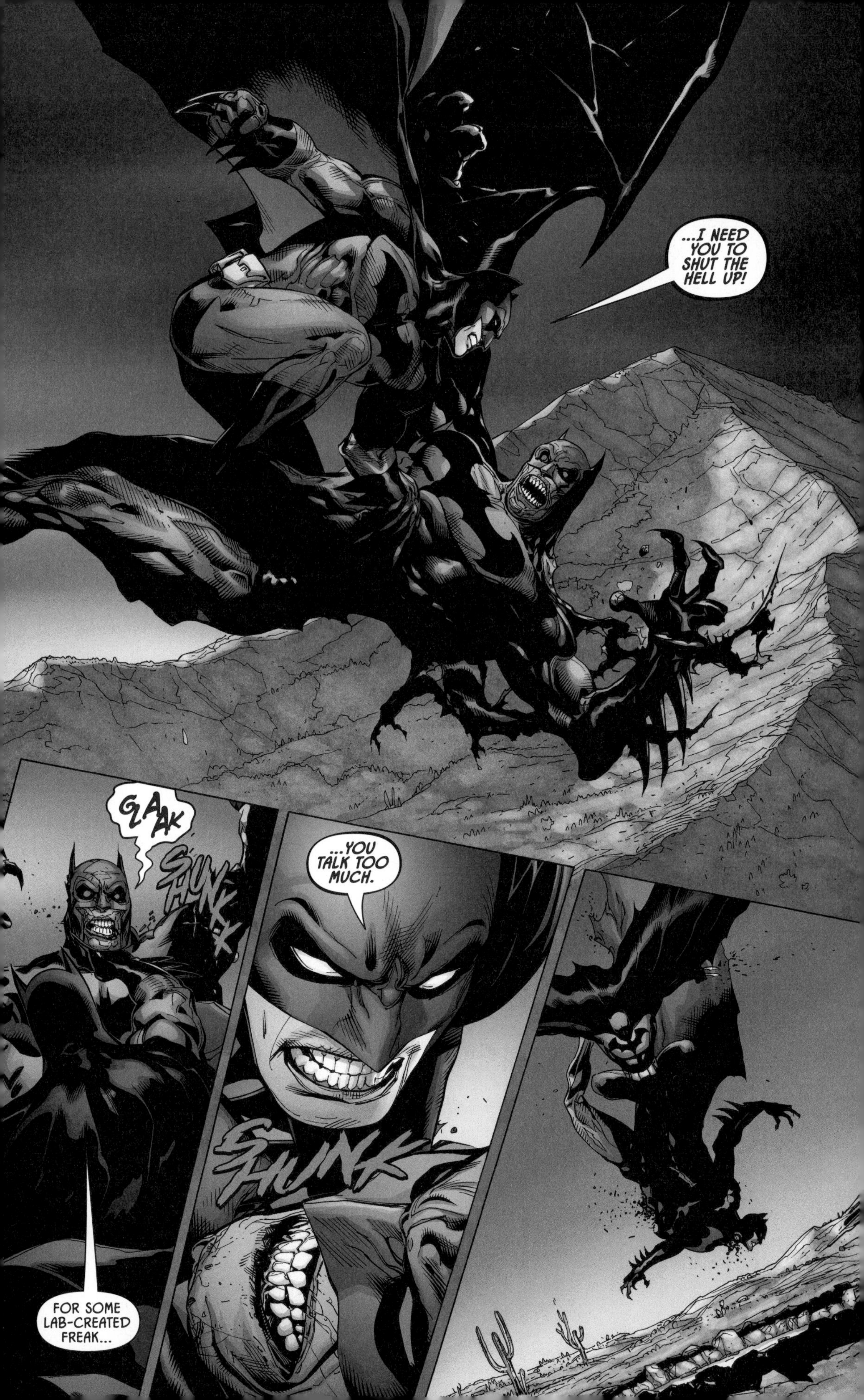
...I NEED YOU TO SHUT THE HELL UP!
GLAAK
SHUNK
...YOU TALK TOO MUCH.
SHUNK
FOR SOME LAB-CREATED FREAK...

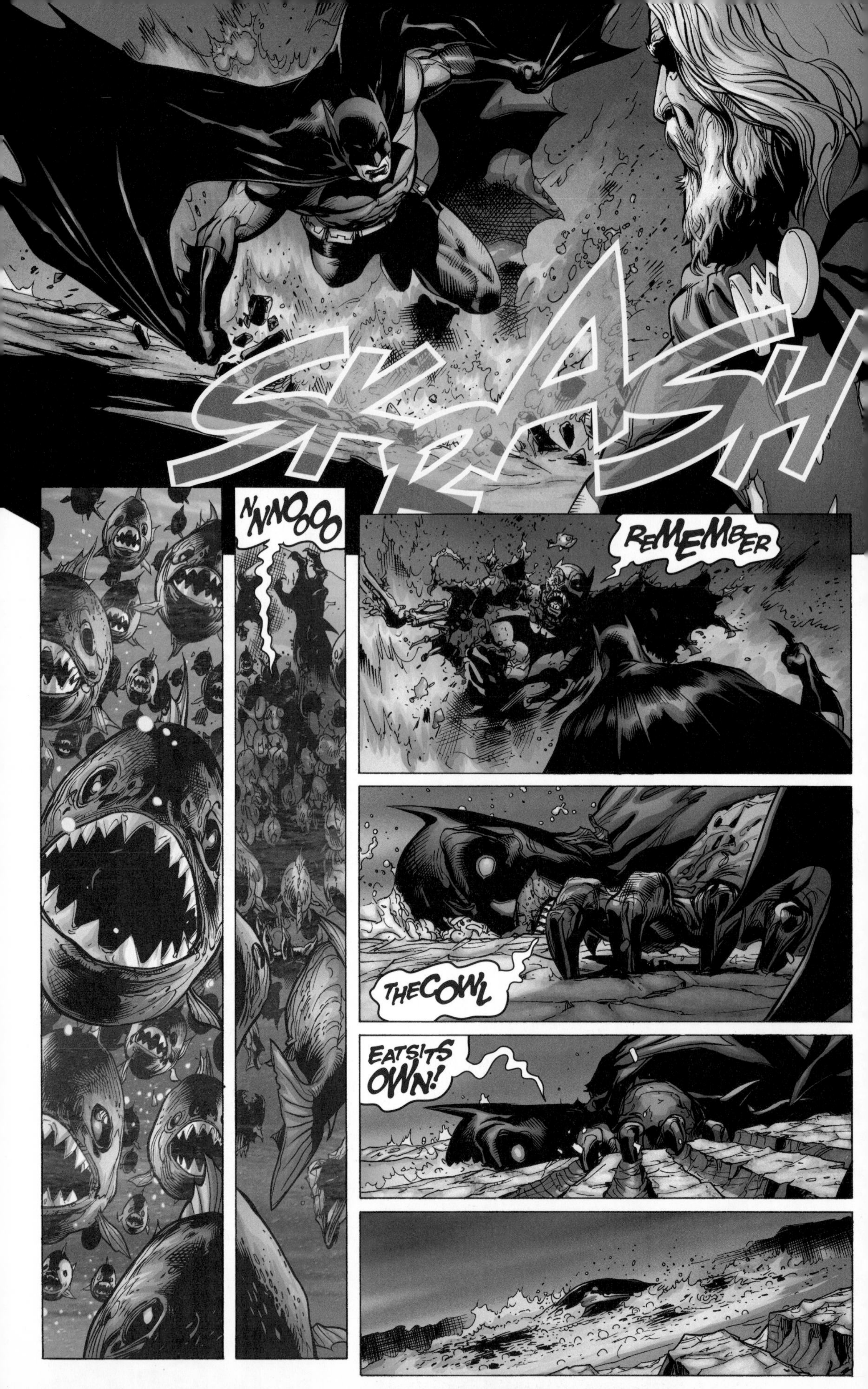
SKRASH
NNNOOOO
REMEMBER
THE COWL
EATS ITS OWN!

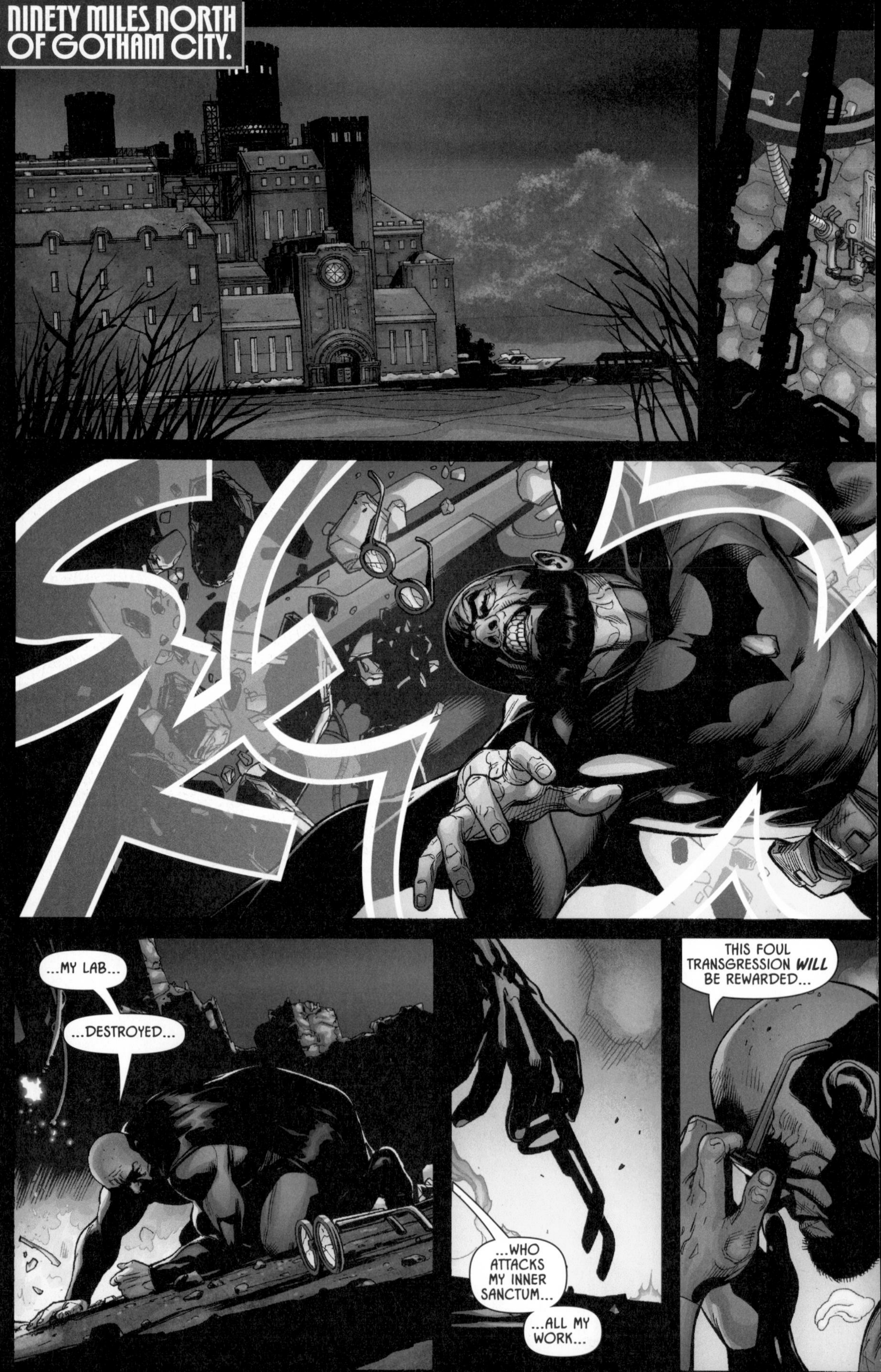
NINETY MILES NORTH OF GOTHAM CITY.
...MY LAB...
...DESTROYED...
...WHO ATTACKS MY INNER SANCTUM...
...ALL MY WORK...
THIS FOUL TRANSGRESSION WILL BE REWARDED...

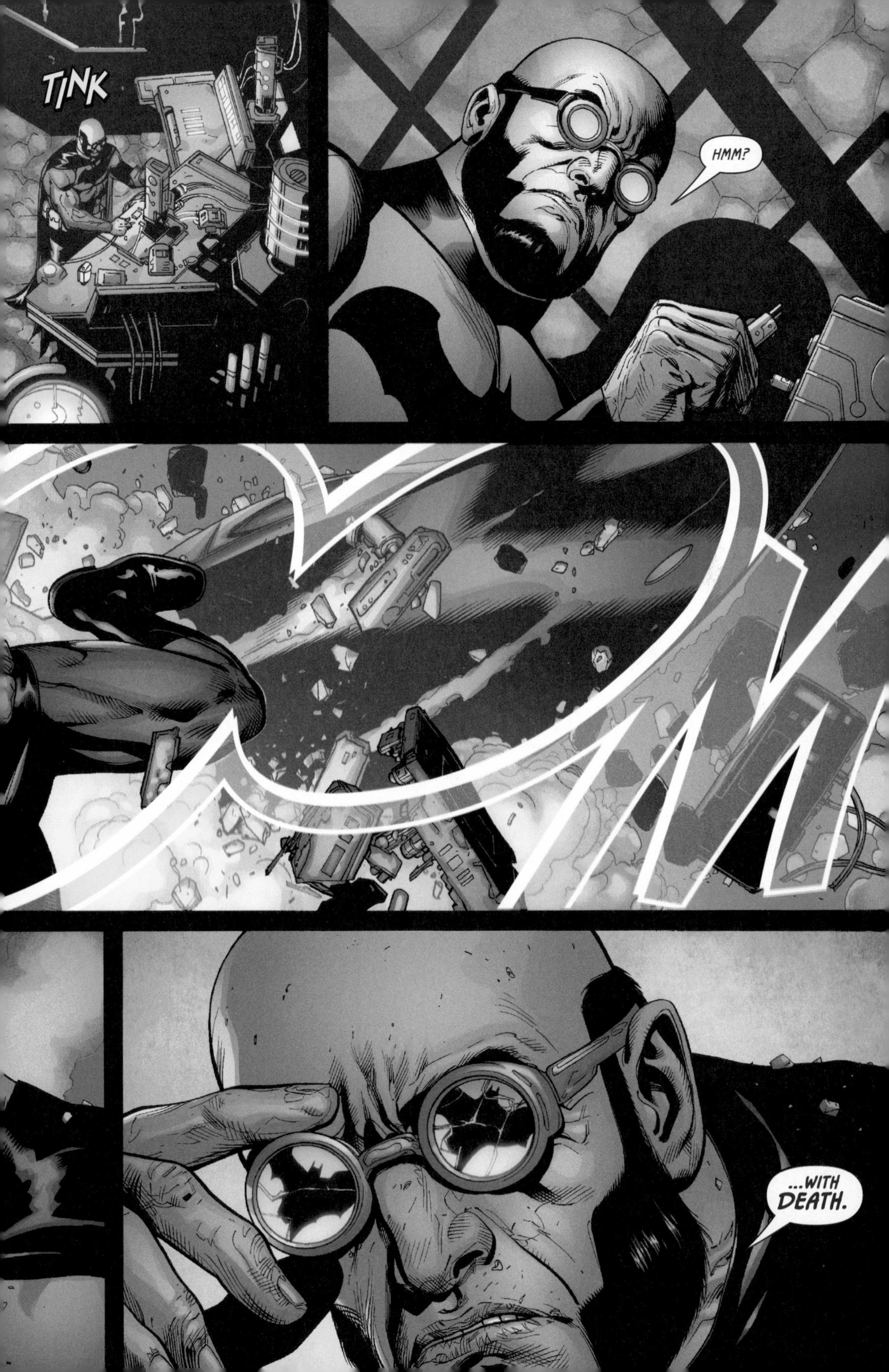
TINK
HMM?
...WITH DEATH.

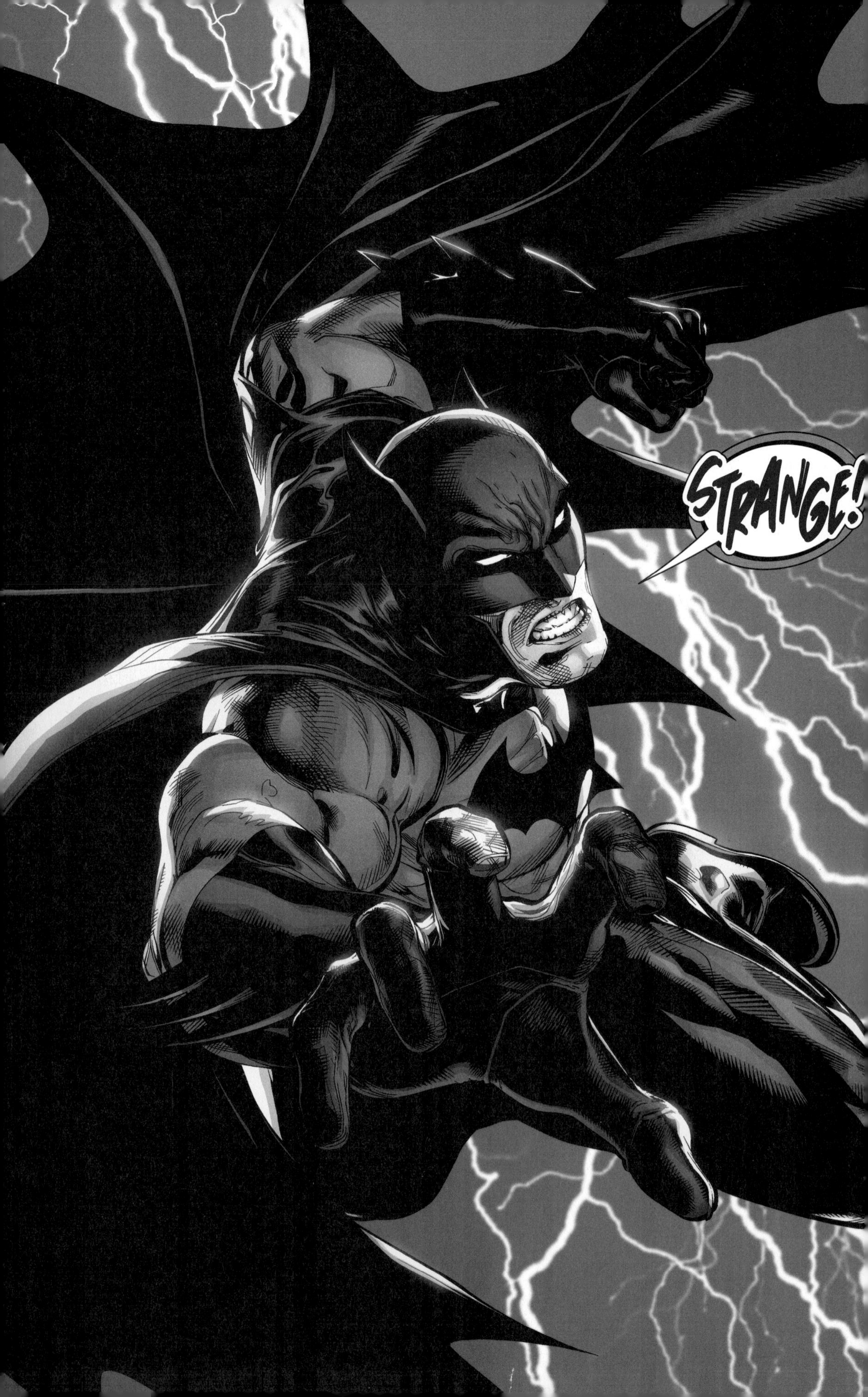
STRANGE!

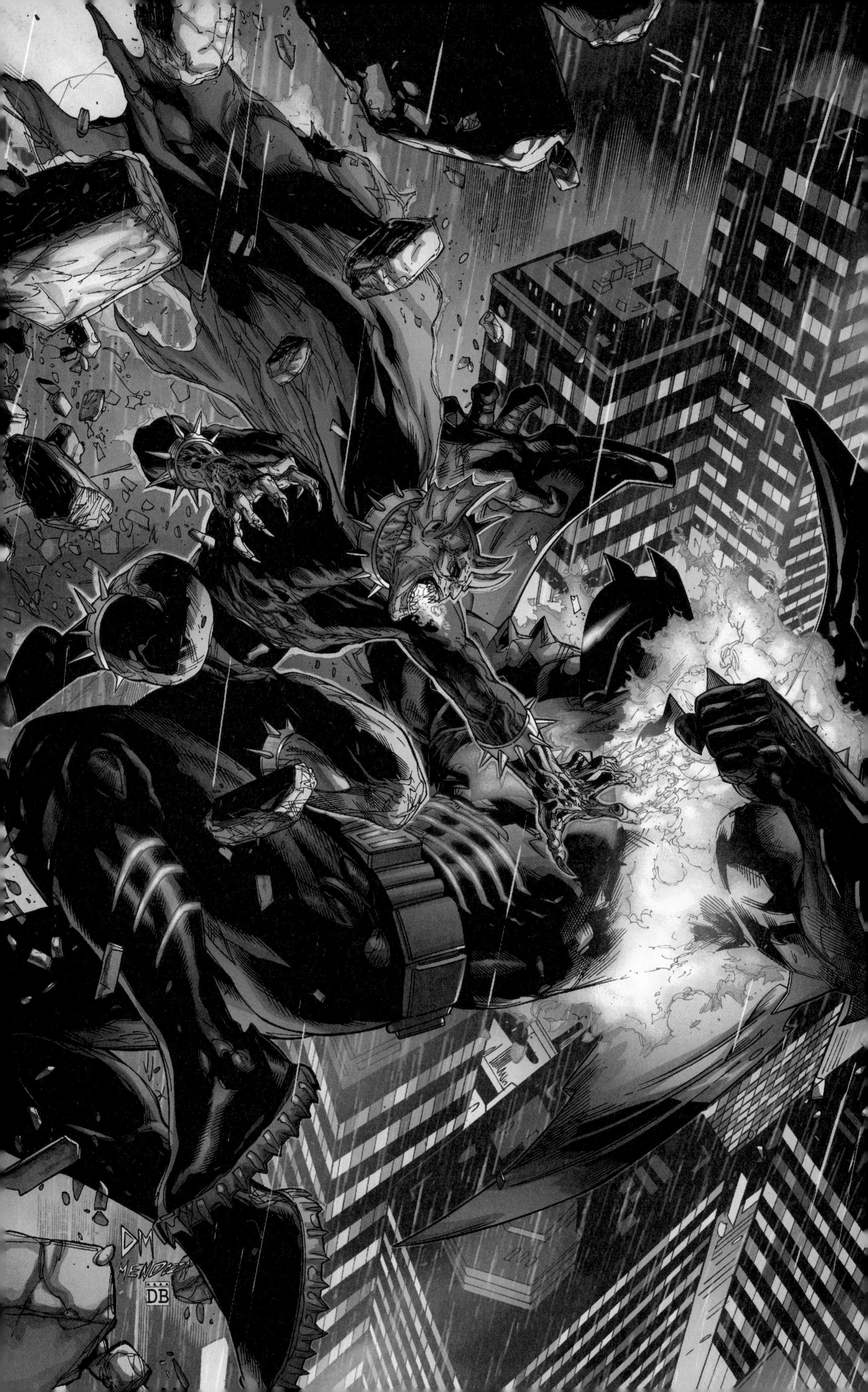
DM
MENDOZA
DB

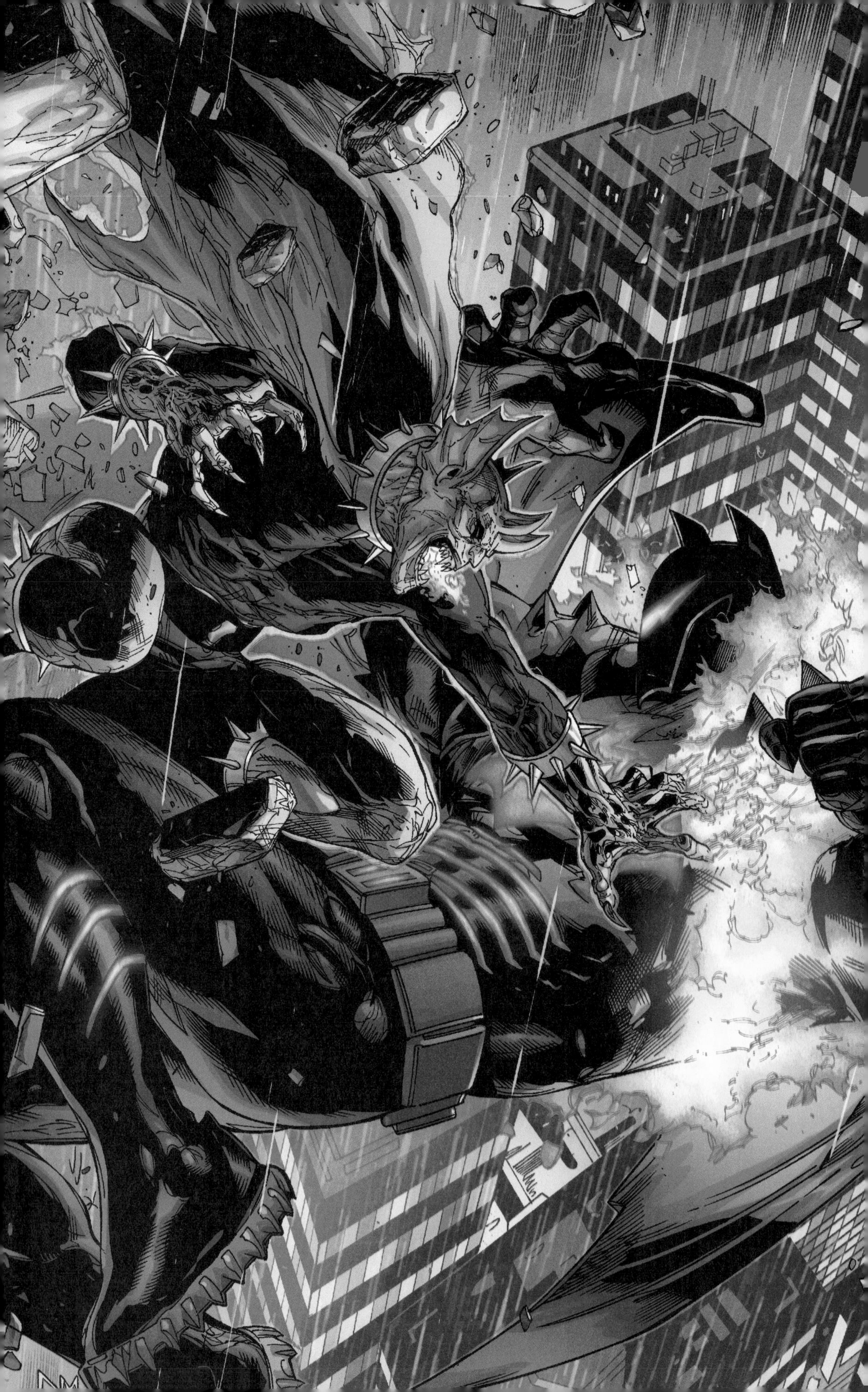

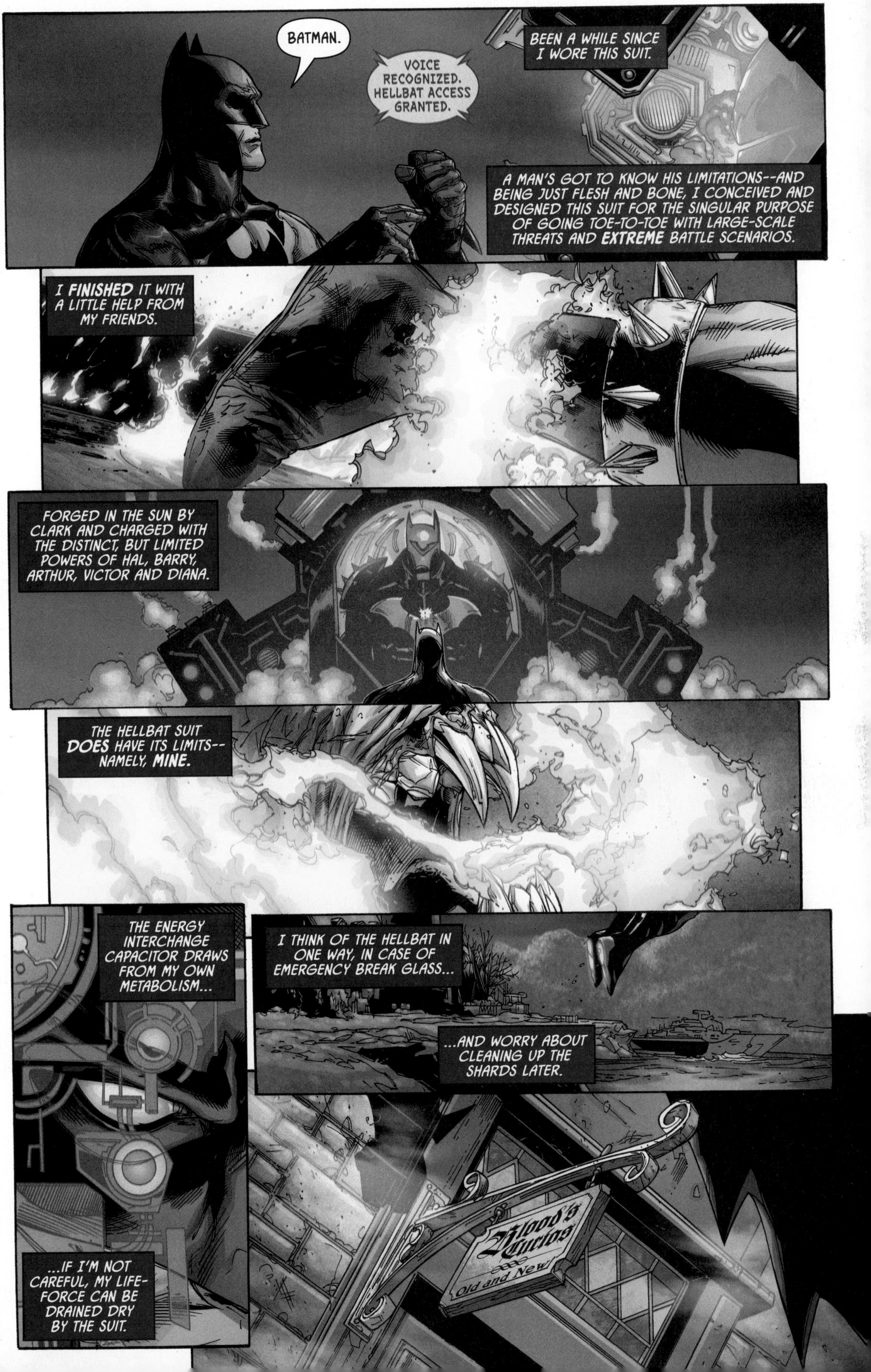
BATMAN.
VOICE RECOGNIZED. HELLBAT ACCESS GRANTED.
BEEN A WHILE SINCE I WORE THIS SUIT.
A MAN'S GOT TO KNOW HIS LIMITATIONS--AND BEING JUST FLESH AND BONE, I CONCEIVED AND DESIGNED THIS SUIT FOR THE SINGULAR PURPOSE OF GOING TOE-TO-TOE WITH LARGE-SCALE THREATS AND EXTREME BATTLE SCENARIOS.
I FINISHED IT WITH A LITTLE HELP FROM MY FRIENDS.
FORGED IN THE SUN BY CLARK AND CHARGED WITH THE DISTINCT, BUT LIMITED POWERS OF HAL, BARRY, ARTHUR, VICTOR AND DIANA.
THE HELLBAT SUIT DOES HAVE ITS LIMITS--NAMELY, MINE.
THE ENERGY INTERCHANGE CAPACITOR DRAWS FROM MY OWN METABOLISM...
I THINK OF THE HELLBAT IN ONE WAY, IN CASE OF EMERGENCY BREAK GLASS...
...AND WORRY ABOUT CLEANING UP THE SHARDS LATER.
...IF I'M NOT CAREFUL, MY LIFE-FORCE CAN BE DRAINED DRY BY THE SUIT.
Old and New

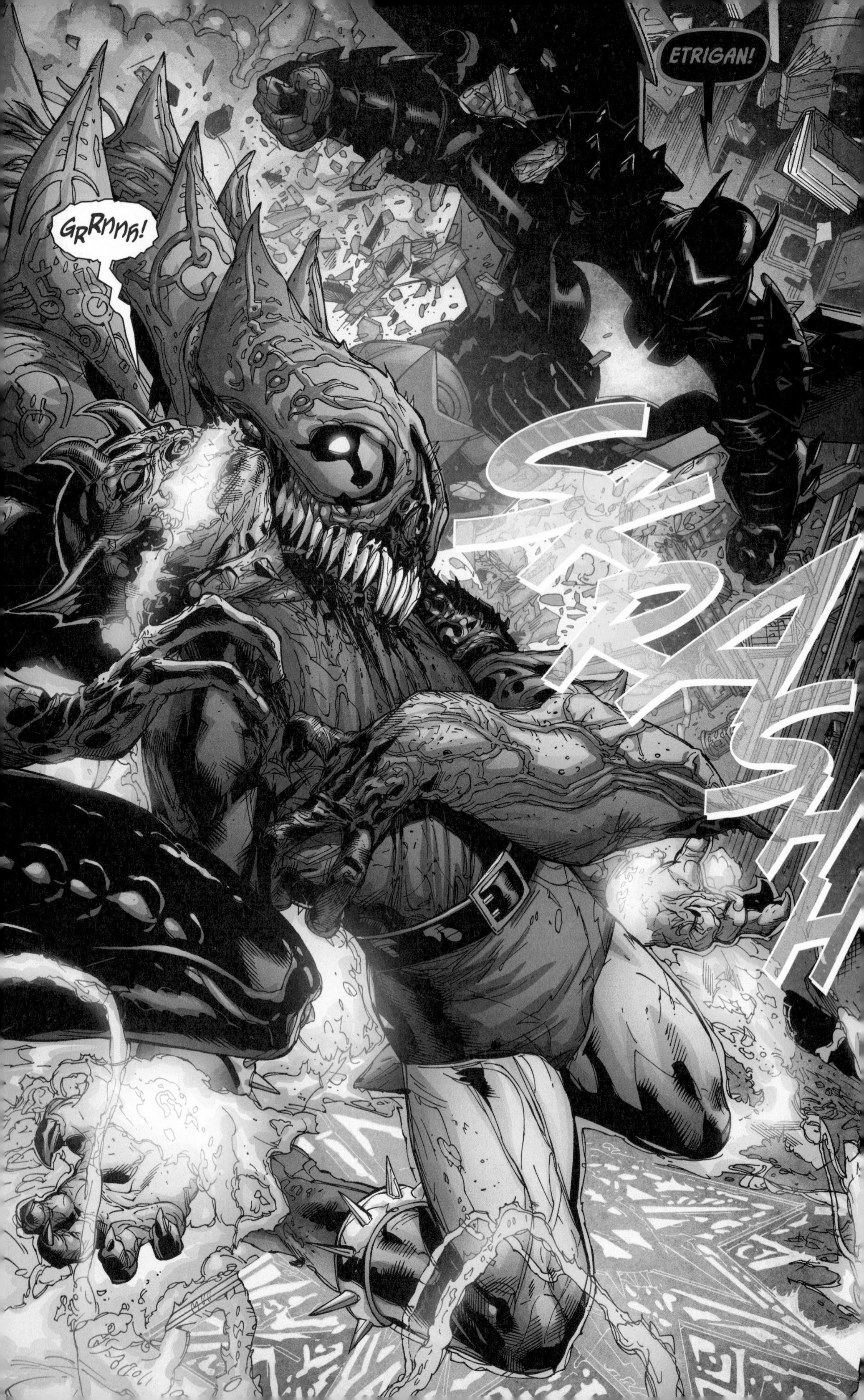
ETRIGAN!
GRRnnn!
SKRASHH

RELEASE ETRIGAN.

I WON'T ASK TWICE.

RRNNFF!

BATS AND DEMONS.

DEMONS AND BATS.

I WILL RELEASE ETRIGAN *ONLY* AFTER I CONSUME *EVERY OUNCE* OF HIS FOUL BLOOD AND EMPOWER--

BLAZZNAK

A MAN OF HIS WORD.

HOW RARE INDEED.

JUST LIKE THE *MEAT* THAT WILL HANG FROM YOUR BONES.

FRROOSH

A MOMENT TO TALK, BUT NOT TO WALK!

THIS CREATURE OF FEAR HAS HOPES TO--

HUSH, HUSH, SWEET ETRIGAN.

THE BAT WILL LEARN WHEN HE BURNS.

GNNF!

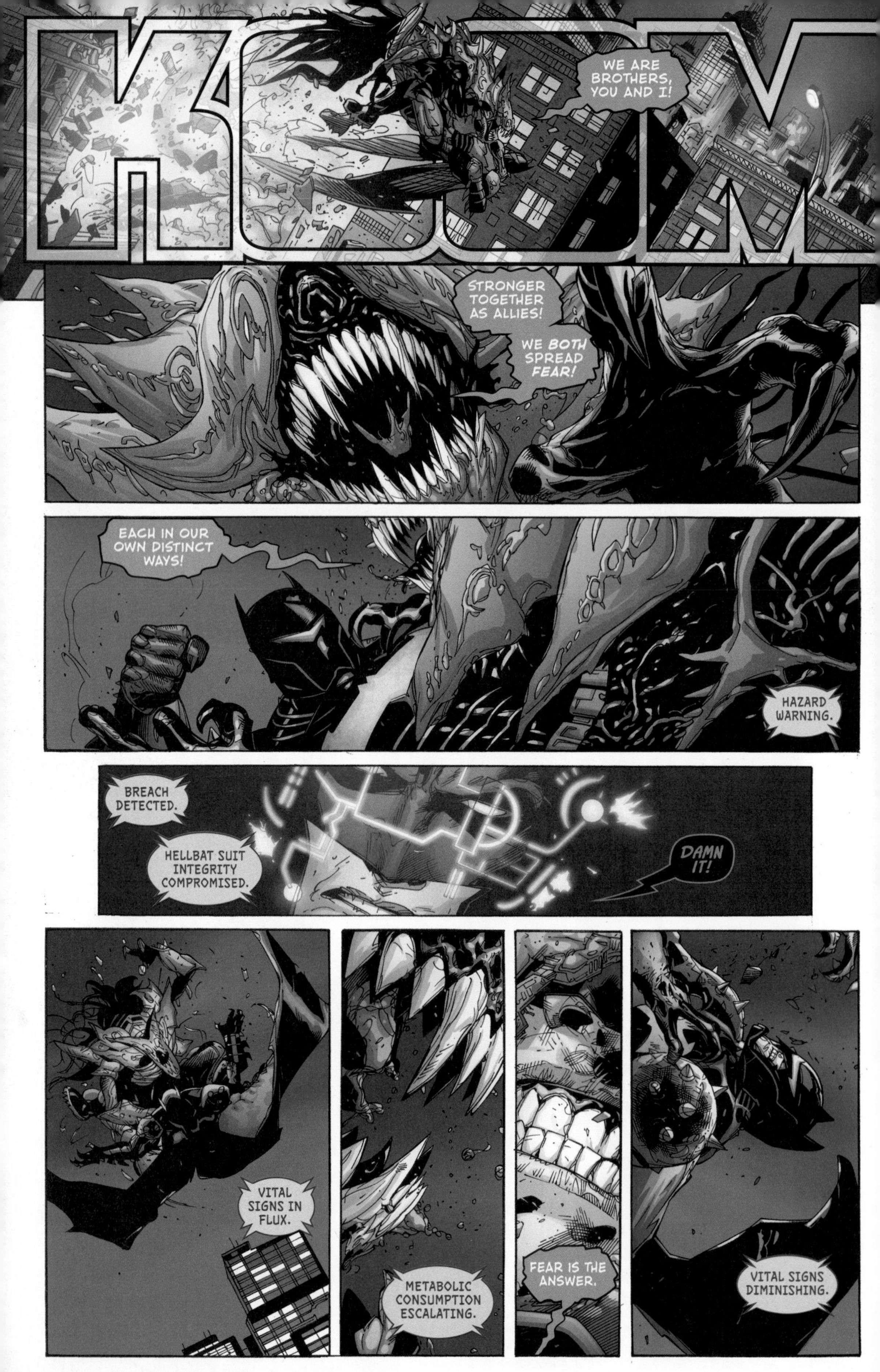
KROOM
WE ARE BROTHERS, YOU AND I!
STRONGER TOGETHER AS ALLIES!
WE BOTH SPREAD FEAR!
EACH IN OUR OWN DISTINCT WAYS!
HAZARD WARNING.
BREACH DETECTED.
HELLBAT SUIT INTEGRITY COMPROMISED.
DAMN IT!
VITAL SIGNS IN FLUX.
METABOLIC CONSUMPTION ESCALATING.
FEAR IS THE ANSWER.
VITAL SIGNS DIMINISHING.

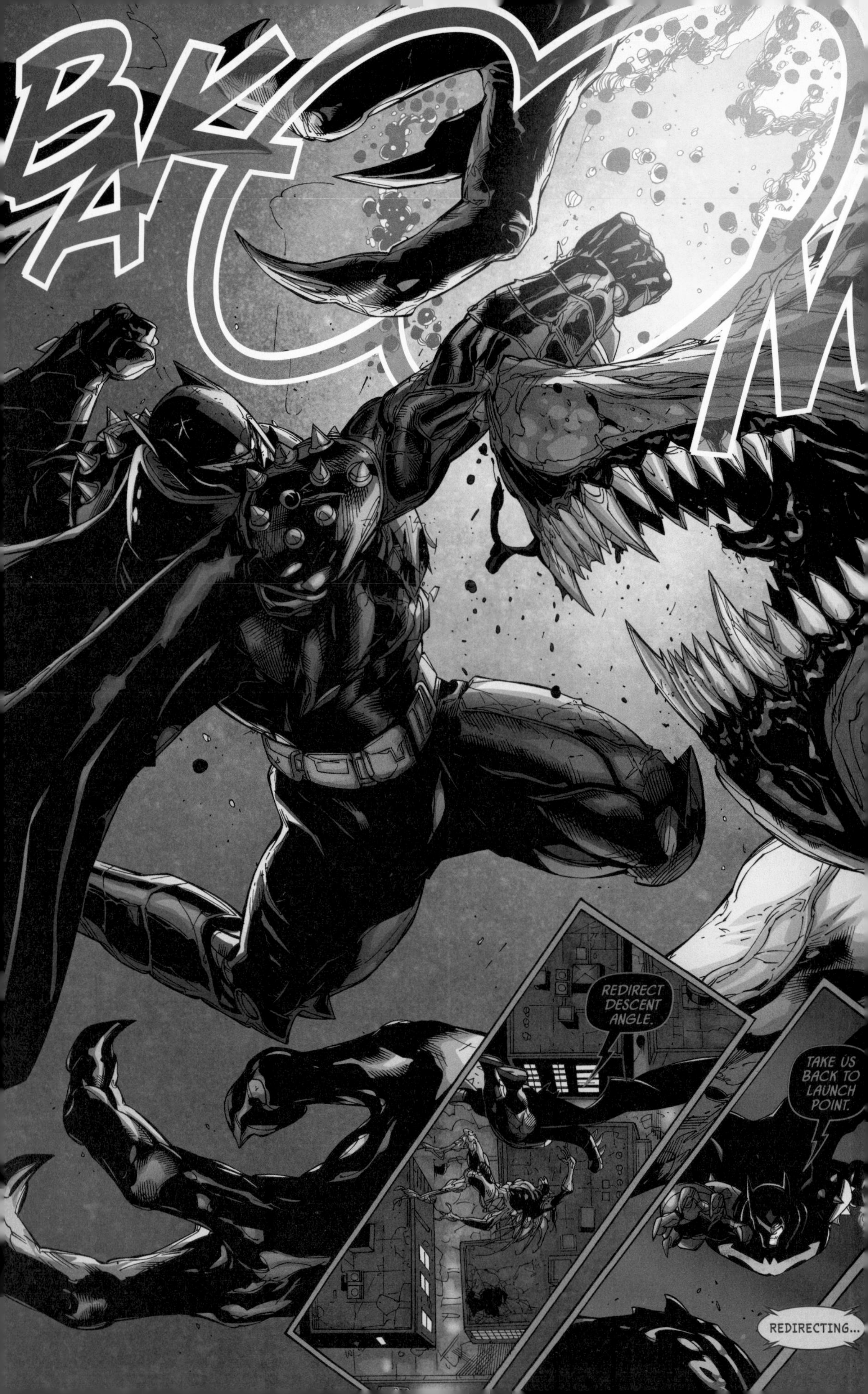
BKATOOM
REDIRECT DESCENT ANGLE.
TAKE US BACK TO LAUNCH POINT.
REDIRECTING...

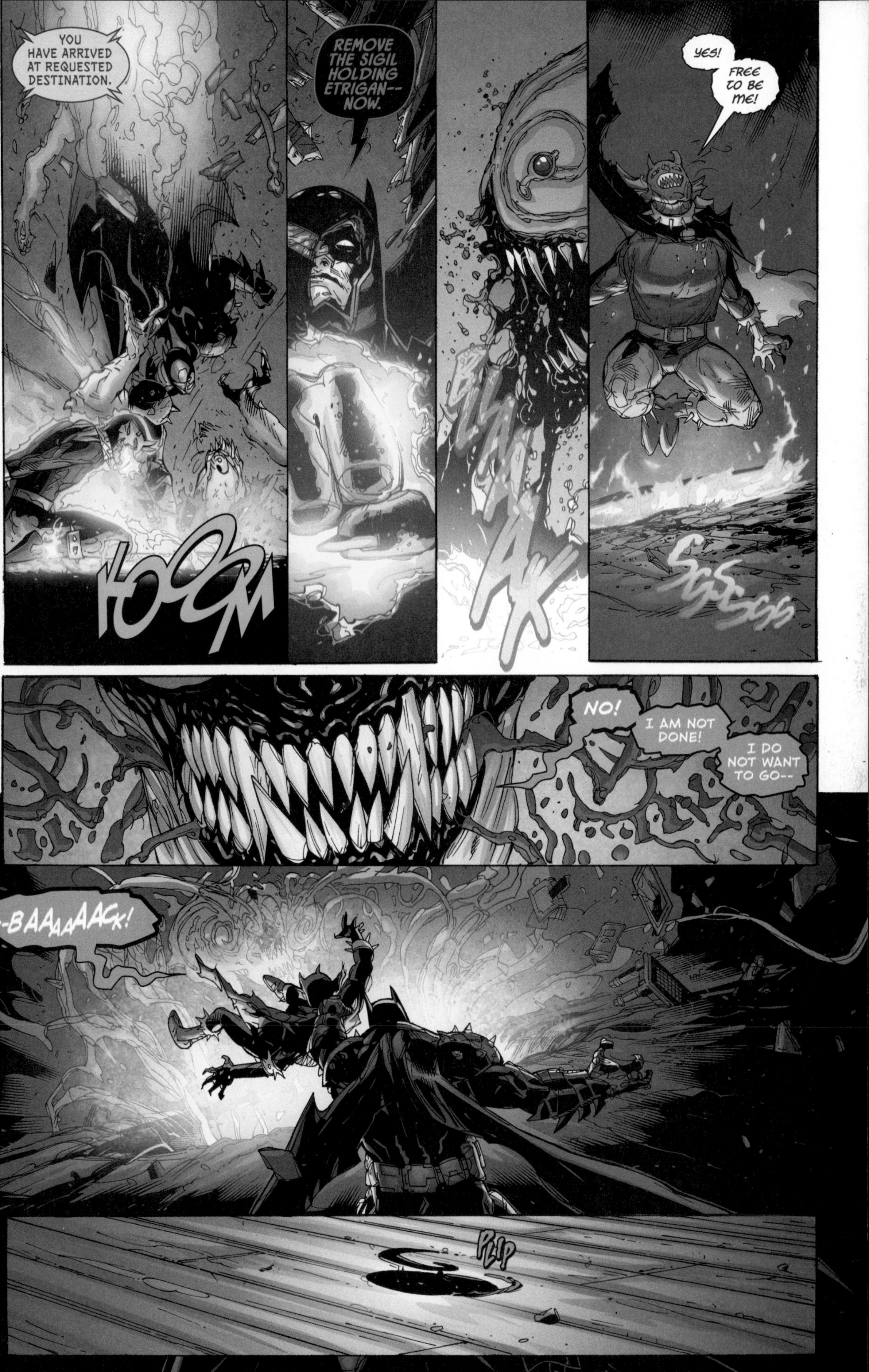
YOU HAVE ARRIVED AT REQUESTED DESTINATION.
REMOVE THE SIGIL HOLDING ETRIGAN-- NOW.
YES!
FREE TO BE ME!
BLAM
SSSSSSS
NO!
I AM NOT DONE!
I DO NOT WANT TO GO--
--BAAAAAACK!
PLIP

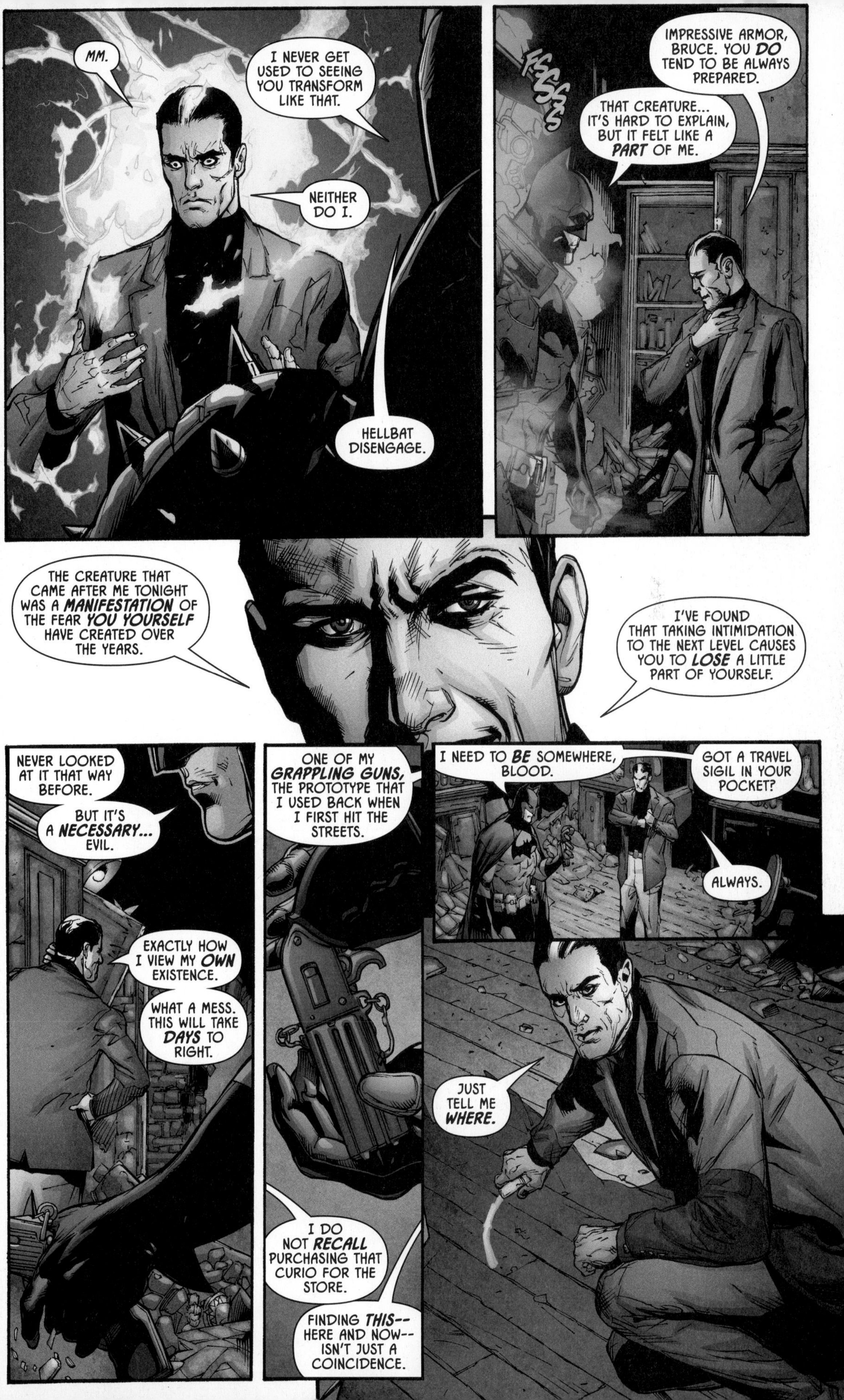
MM.
I NEVER GET USED TO SEEING YOU TRANSFORM LIKE THAT.
NEITHER DO I.
HELLBAT DISENGAGE.
FSSSS
IMPRESSIVE ARMOR, BRUCE. YOU DO TEND TO BE ALWAYS PREPARED.
THAT CREATURE... IT'S HARD TO EXPLAIN, BUT IT FELT LIKE A PART OF ME.
THE CREATURE THAT CAME AFTER ME TONIGHT WAS A MANIFESTATION OF THE FEAR YOU YOURSELF HAVE CREATED OVER THE YEARS.
I'VE FOUND THAT TAKING INTIMIDATION TO THE NEXT LEVEL CAUSES YOU TO LOSE A LITTLE PART OF YOURSELF.
NEVER LOOKED AT IT THAT WAY BEFORE.
BUT IT'S A NECESSARY... EVIL.
EXACTLY HOW I VIEW MY OWN EXISTENCE.
WHAT A MESS. THIS WILL TAKE DAYS TO RIGHT.
ONE OF MY GRAPPLING GUNS, THE PROTOTYPE THAT I USED BACK WHEN I FIRST HIT THE STREETS.
I DO NOT RECALL PURCHASING THAT CURIO FOR THE STORE.
FINDING THIS-- HERE AND NOW-- ISN'T JUST A COINCIDENCE.
I NEED TO BE SOMEWHERE, BLOOD.
GOT A TRAVEL SIGIL IN YOUR POCKET?
ALWAYS.
JUST TELL ME WHERE.

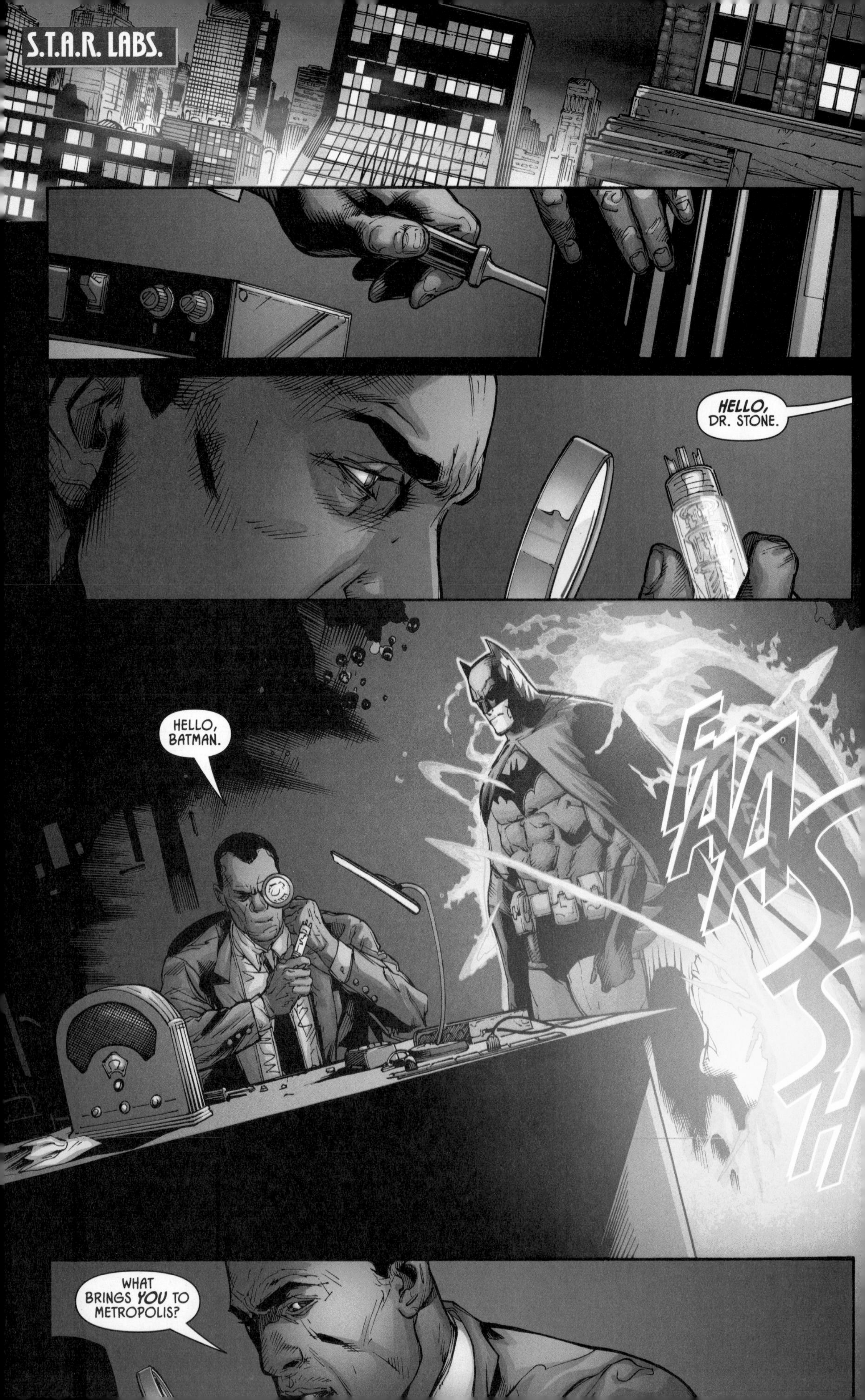
S.T.A.R. LABS.
HELLO, DR. STONE.
HELLO, BATMAN.
WHAT BRINGS YOU TO METROPOLIS?

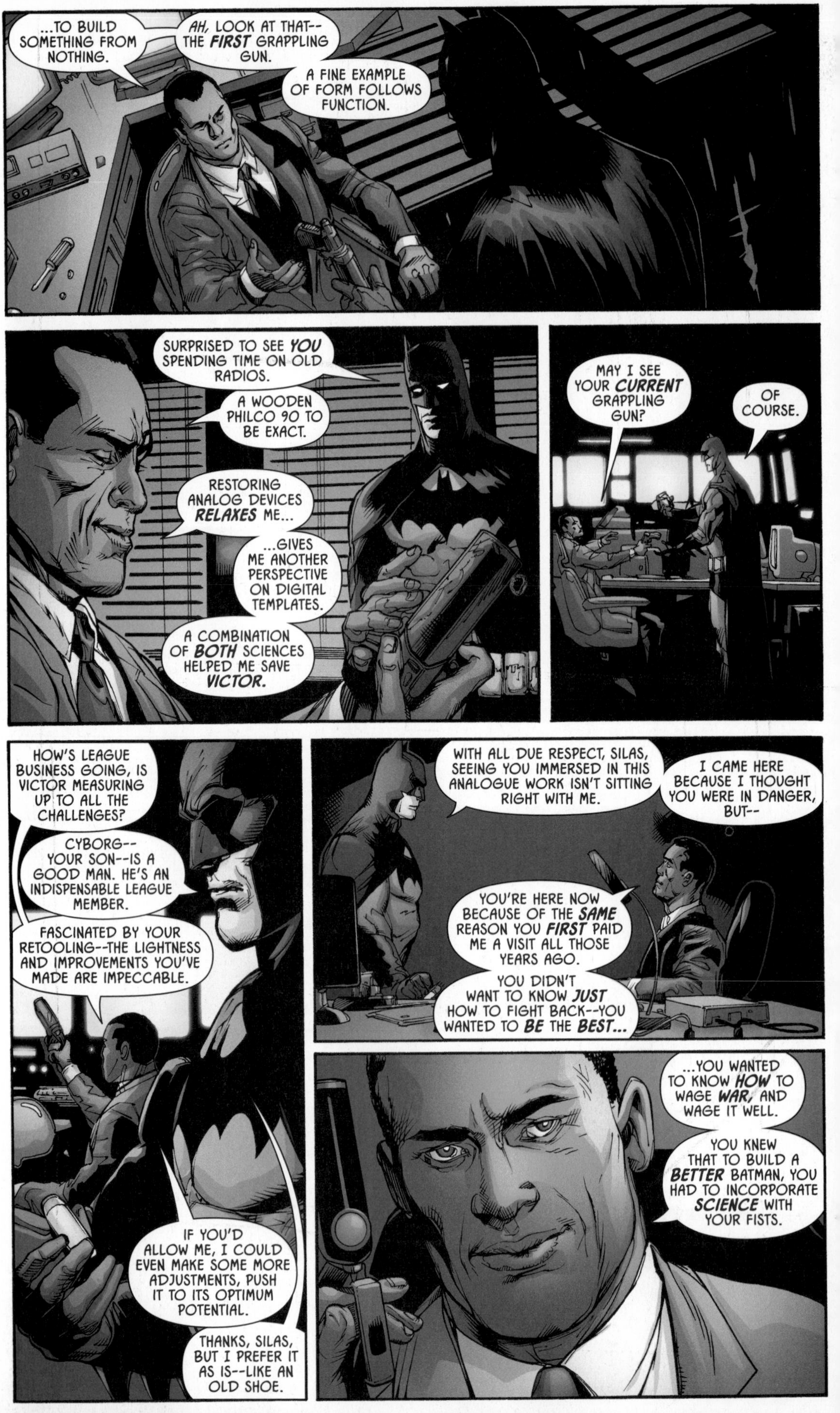
...TO BUILD SOMETHING FROM NOTHING.
AH, LOOK AT THAT-- THE FIRST GRAPPLING GUN.
A FINE EXAMPLE OF FORM FOLLOWS FUNCTION.
SURPRISED TO SEE YOU SPENDING TIME ON OLD RADIOS.
A WOODEN PHILCO 90 TO BE EXACT.
RESTORING ANALOG DEVICES RELAXES ME...
...GIVES ME ANOTHER PERSPECTIVE ON DIGITAL TEMPLATES.
A COMBINATION OF BOTH SCIENCES HELPED ME SAVE VICTOR.
MAY I SEE YOUR CURRENT GRAPPLING GUN?
OF COURSE.
HOW'S LEAGUE BUSINESS GOING, IS VICTOR MEASURING UP TO ALL THE CHALLENGES?
CYBORG-- YOUR SON--IS A GOOD MAN. HE'S AN INDISPENSABLE LEAGUE MEMBER.
FASCINATED BY YOUR RETOOLING--THE LIGHTNESS AND IMPROVEMENTS YOU'VE MADE ARE IMPECCABLE.
IF YOU'D ALLOW ME, I COULD EVEN MAKE SOME MORE ADJUSTMENTS, PUSH IT TO ITS OPTIMUM POTENTIAL.
THANKS, SILAS, BUT I PREFER IT AS IS--LIKE AN OLD SHOE.
WITH ALL DUE RESPECT, SILAS, SEEING YOU IMMERSED IN THIS ANALOGUE WORK ISN'T SITTING RIGHT WITH ME.
I CAME HERE BECAUSE I THOUGHT YOU WERE IN DANGER, BUT--
YOU'RE HERE NOW BECAUSE OF THE SAME REASON YOU FIRST PAID ME A VISIT ALL THOSE YEARS AGO.
YOU DIDN'T WANT TO KNOW JUST HOW TO FIGHT BACK--YOU WANTED TO BE THE BEST...
...YOU WANTED TO KNOW HOW TO WAGE WAR, AND WAGE IT WELL.
YOU KNEW THAT TO BUILD A BETTER BATMAN, YOU HAD TO INCORPORATE SCIENCE WITH YOUR FISTS.

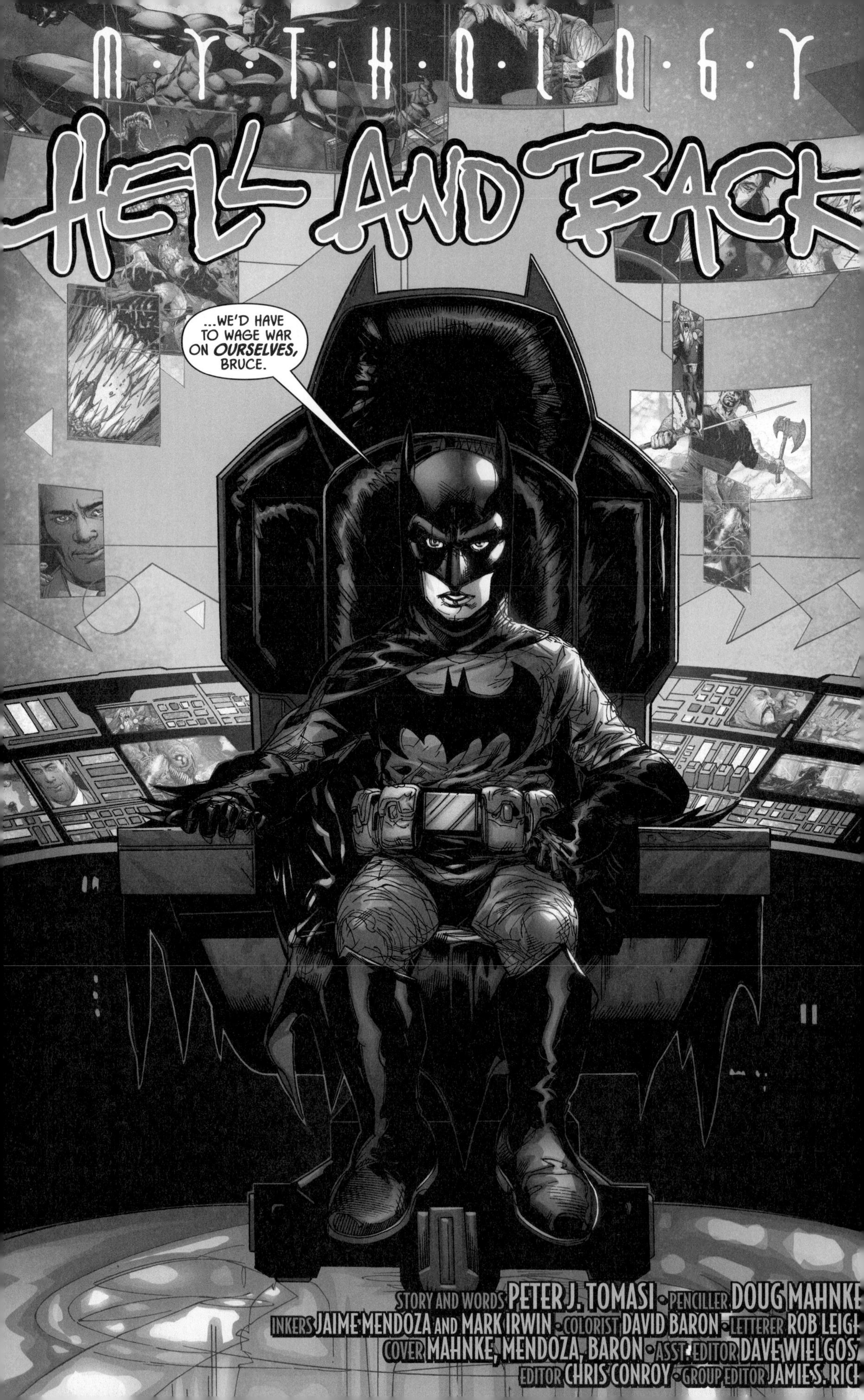

M·Y·T·H·O·L·O·G·Y
HELL AND BACK
...WE'D HAVE TO WAGE WAR ON *OURSELVES,* BRUCE.
STORY AND WORDS PETER J. TOMASI · PENCILLER DOUG MAHNK
INKERS JAIME MENDOZA AND MARK IRWIN · COLORIST DAVID BARON · LETTERER ROB LEIG
COVER MAHNKE, MENDOZA, BARON · ASST. EDITOR DAVE WIELGOS
EDITOR CHRIS CONROY · GROUP EDITOR JAMIE S. RIC

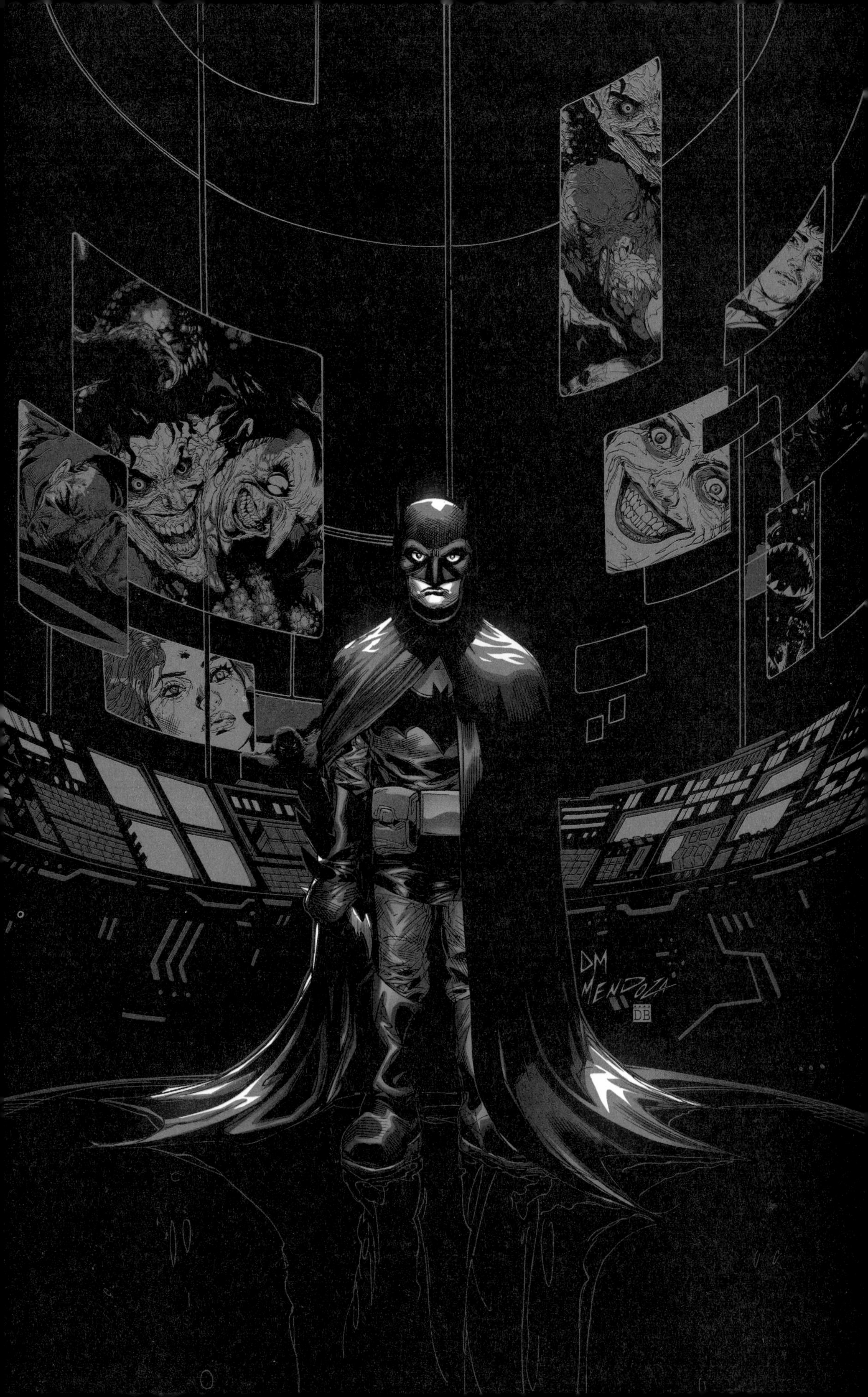
DM MENDOZA
DB

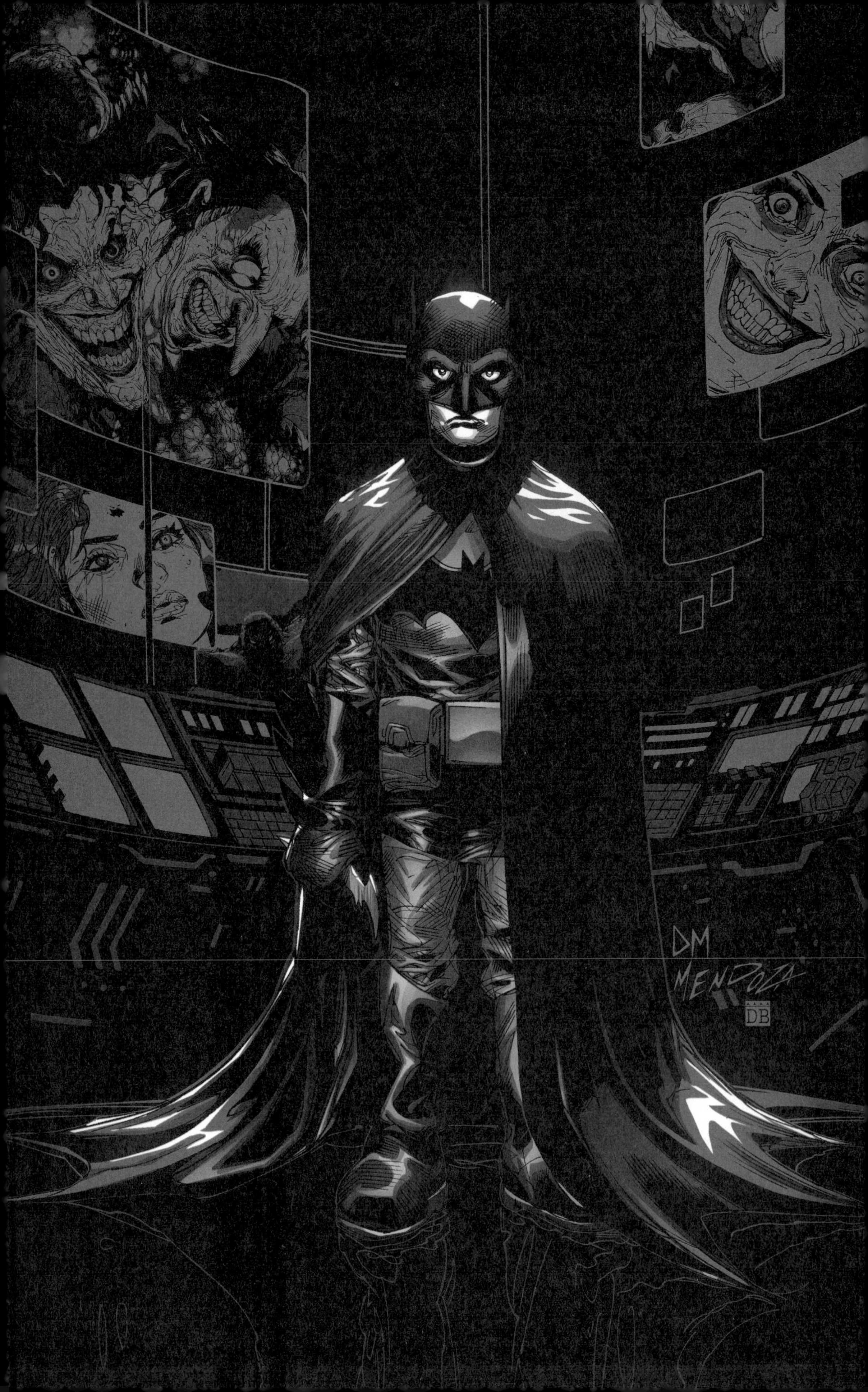
DM
MENDOZA
DB

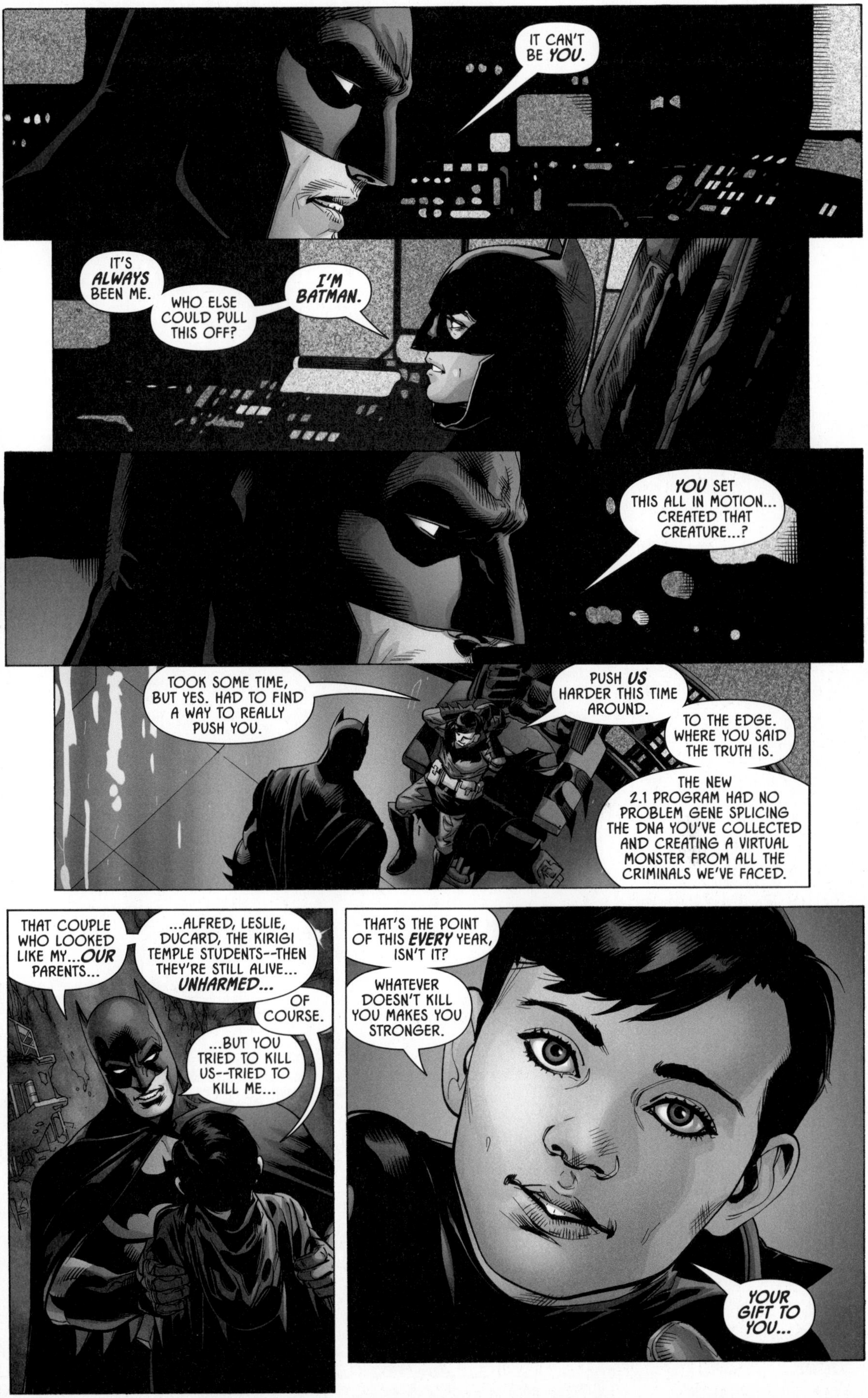

IT CAN'T BE *YOU.*
IT'S *ALWAYS* BEEN ME.
WHO ELSE COULD PULL THIS OFF?
I'M BATMAN.
YOU SET THIS ALL IN MOTION... CREATED THAT CREATURE...?
TOOK SOME TIME, BUT YES. HAD TO FIND A WAY TO REALLY PUSH YOU.
PUSH *US* HARDER THIS TIME AROUND.
TO THE EDGE. WHERE YOU SAID THE TRUTH IS.
THE NEW 2.1 PROGRAM HAD NO PROBLEM GENE SPLICING THE DNA YOU'VE COLLECTED AND CREATING A VIRTUAL MONSTER FROM ALL THE CRIMINALS WE'VE FACED.
THAT COUPLE WHO LOOKED LIKE MY...*OUR* PARENTS...
...ALFRED, LESLIE, DUCARD, THE KIRIGI TEMPLE STUDENTS--THEN THEY'RE STILL ALIVE... *UNHARMED...*
OF COURSE.
...BUT YOU TRIED TO KILL US--TRIED TO KILL ME...
THAT'S THE POINT OF THIS *EVERY* YEAR, ISN'T IT?
WHATEVER DOESN'T KILL YOU MAKES YOU STRONGER.
YOUR GIFT TO YOU...

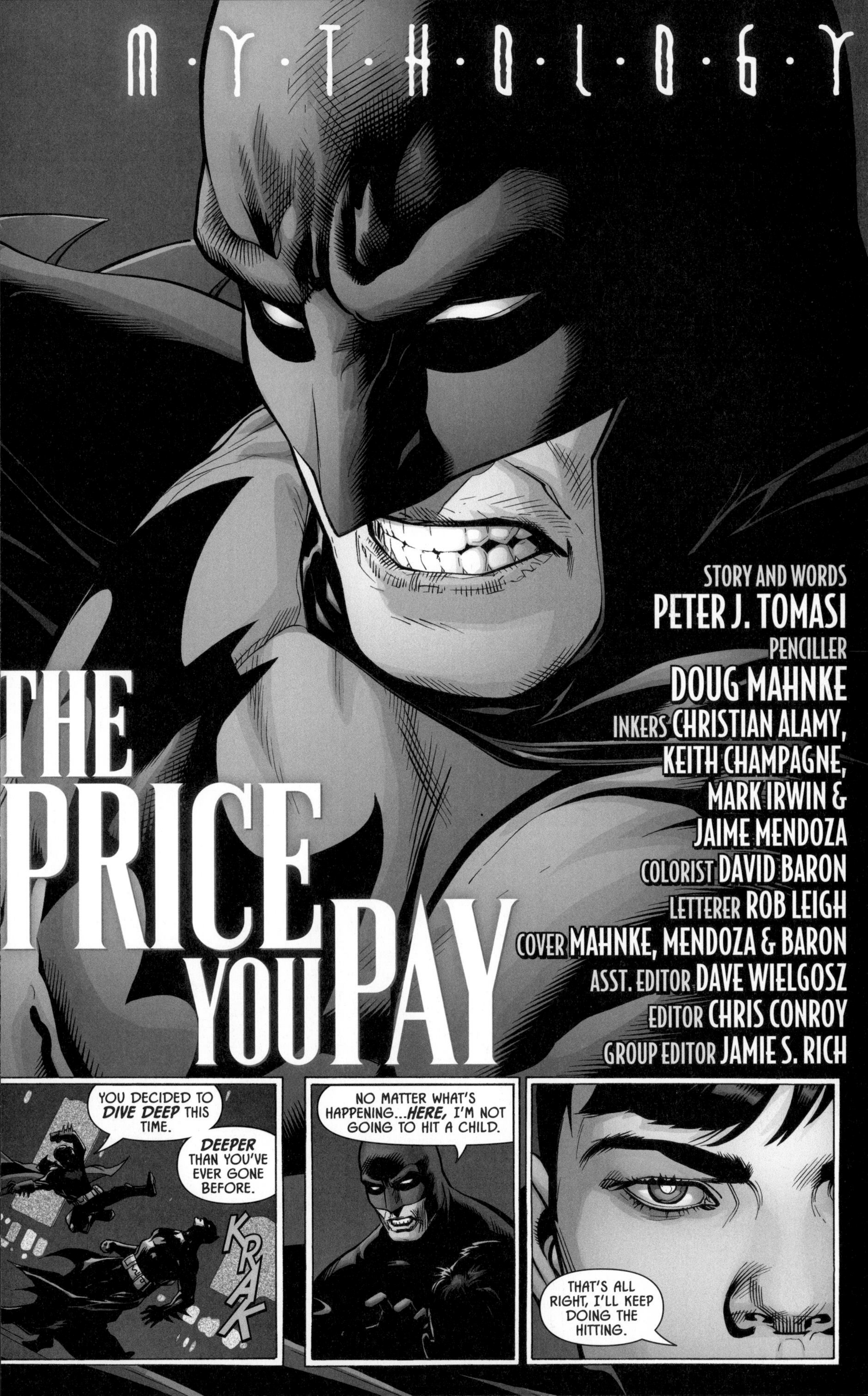
M·Y·T·H·O·L·O·G·Y
THE PRICE YOU PAY
STORY AND WORDS PETER J. TOMASI
PENCILLER DOUG MAHNKE
INKERS CHRISTIAN ALAMY, KEITH CHAMPAGNE, MARK IRWIN & JAIME MENDOZA
COLORIST DAVID BARON
LETTERER ROB LEIGH
COVER MAHNKE, MENDOZA & BARON
ASST. EDITOR DAVE WIELGOSZ
EDITOR CHRIS CONROY
GROUP EDITOR JAMIE S. RICH
YOU DECIDED TO DIVE DEEP THIS TIME.
DEEPER THAN YOU'VE EVER GONE BEFORE.
KRAK
NO MATTER WHAT'S HAPPENING...HERE, I'M NOT GOING TO HIT A CHILD.
THAT'S ALL RIGHT, I'LL KEEP DOING THE HITTING.

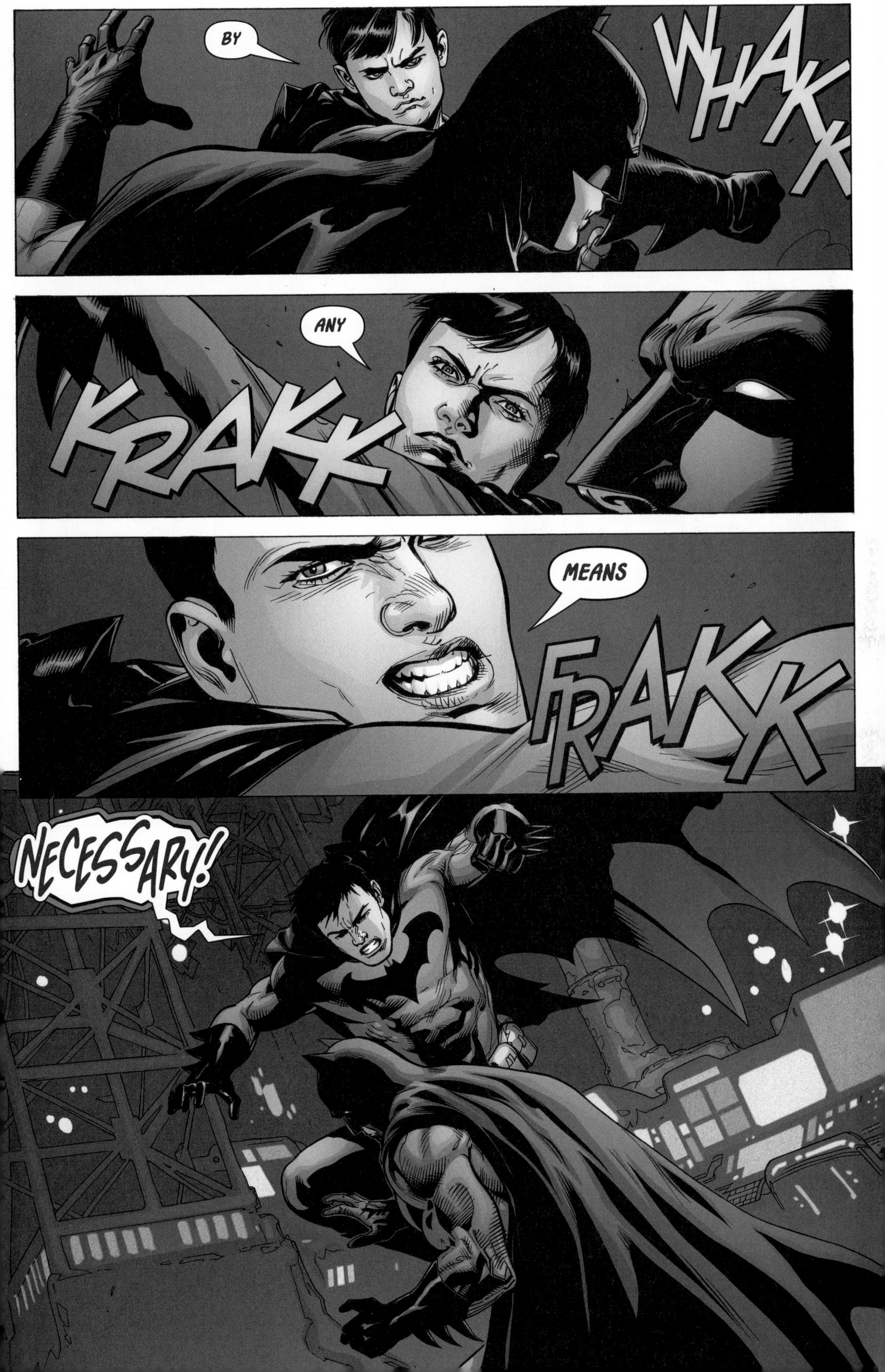
BY
WHAKK
ANY
KRAKK
MEANS
FRAKK
NECESSARY!

THAT'S ENOUGH!

WHOEVER OR WHATEVER YOU ARE--I SAID I'M NOT GOING TO HIT YOU AND I MEANT IT.

HOW ARE YOU *GROWING* EXPONENTIALLY WITH EACH PUNCH?

NNF

YOU STILL DON'T GET IT!

SKA SH

I'M YOU.

YOU'RE ME.

THIS IS US, AND WE'RE DROWNING.

WHO SENT YOU?!

YOU SENT ME, DAMN IT, AND I'M TRYING TO SAVE YOU!

GIVE US SOME PERSPECTIVE-- ILLUMINATION--

--TO WAKE YOU THE HELL UP!

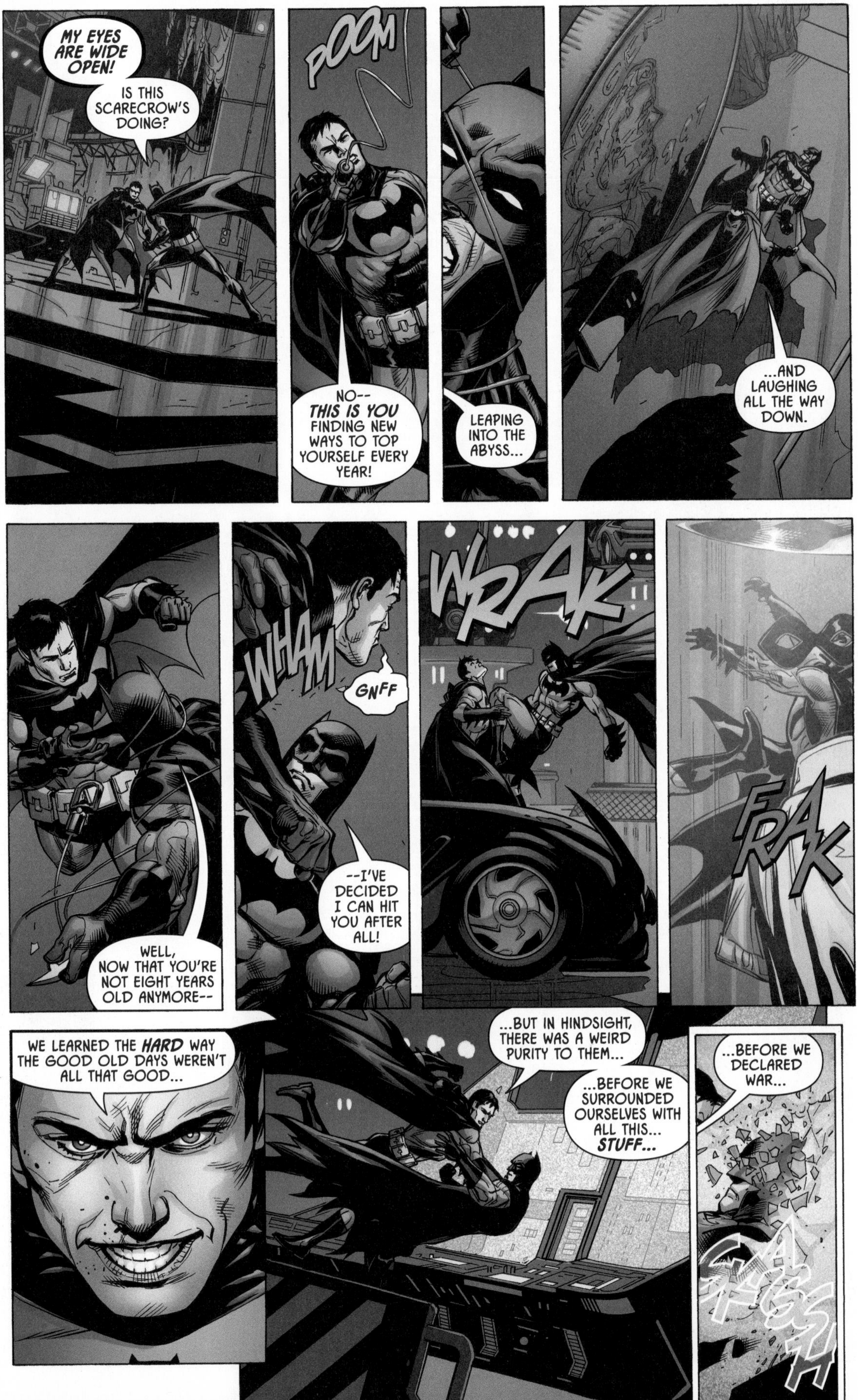
MY EYES ARE WIDE OPEN!
IS THIS SCARECROW'S DOING?
POOM
NO-- THIS IS YOU FINDING NEW WAYS TO TOP YOURSELF EVERY YEAR!
LEAPING INTO THE ABYSS...
...AND LAUGHING ALL THE WAY DOWN.
WELL, NOW THAT YOU'RE NOT EIGHT YEARS OLD ANYMORE--
WHAM
GNFF
--I'VE DECIDED I CAN HIT YOU AFTER ALL!
WRAK
FRAK
WE LEARNED THE HARD WAY THE GOOD OLD DAYS WEREN'T ALL THAT GOOD...
...BUT IN HINDSIGHT, THERE WAS A WEIRD PURITY TO THEM...
...BEFORE WE SURROUNDED OURSELVES WITH ALL THIS... STUFF...
...BEFORE WE DECLARED WAR...

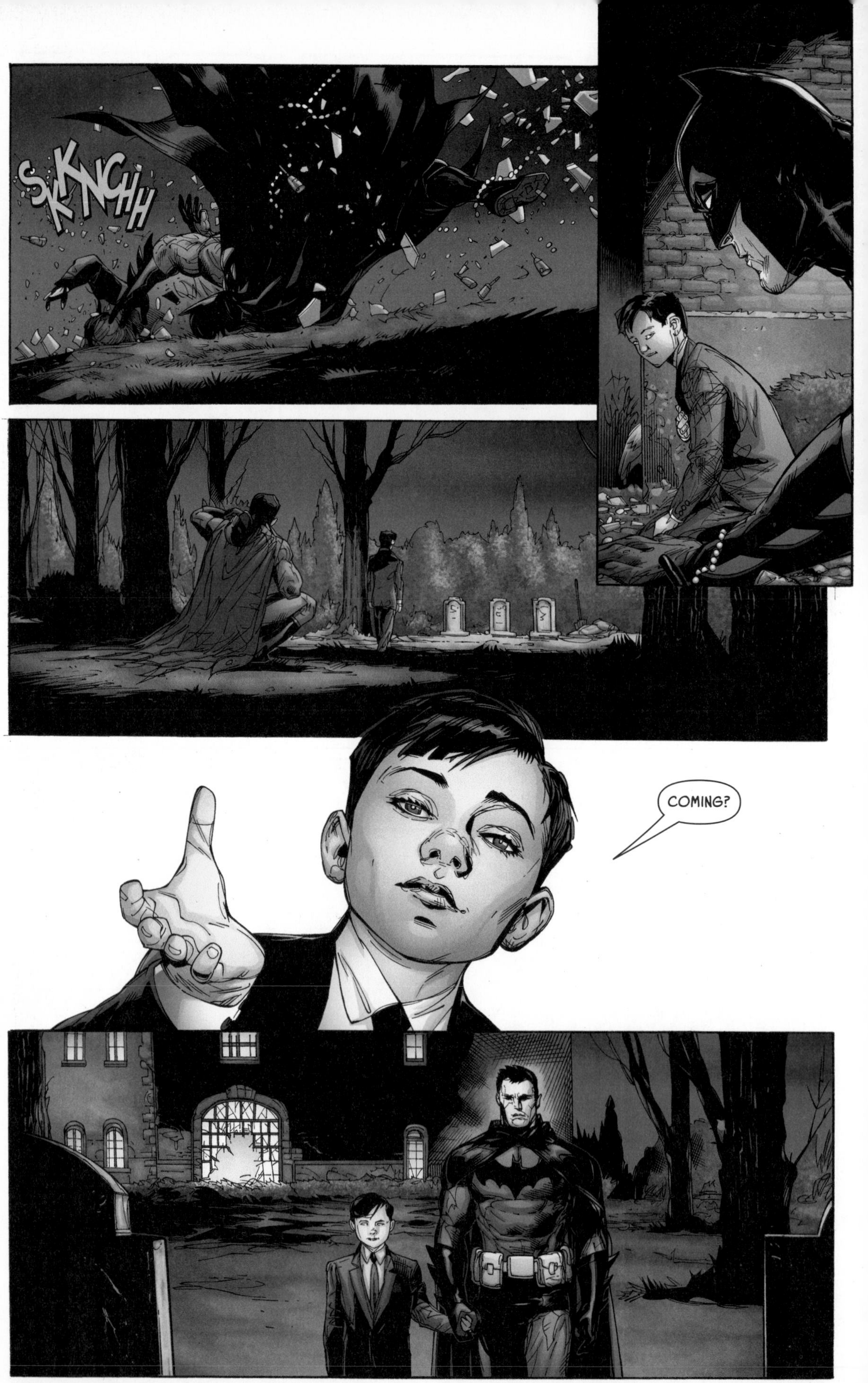
SKKNCHH
COMING?

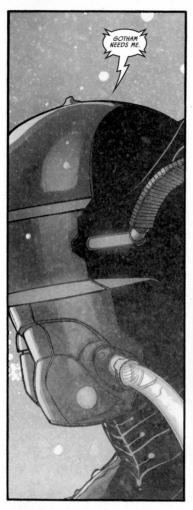

GOTHAM NEEDS ME.

GOTHAM NEEDS ME.

GOTHAM NEEDS ME!

CALM DOWN, BRUCE...

...THE WATER IS DRAINING.

I'VE HACKED IN-- THE PROGRAM'S ALREADY CYCLING DOWN--IT'S COME TO AN END.

GOTHAM NEEDS ME!

SK KRK

HOW LONG'S HE BEEN IN THAT THING, ALFRED?

SK KRK

GOTHAM NEEDS ME!

I DON'T KNOW, DAMIAN...

...SEEMS HE INITIATED THIS...STEALTH SEQUENCE HIMSELF.

SKRANKK

GOTHAM NEEDS ME!

STEALTH. ≥TT≤ YOU MEAN SECRET, DON'T YOU?

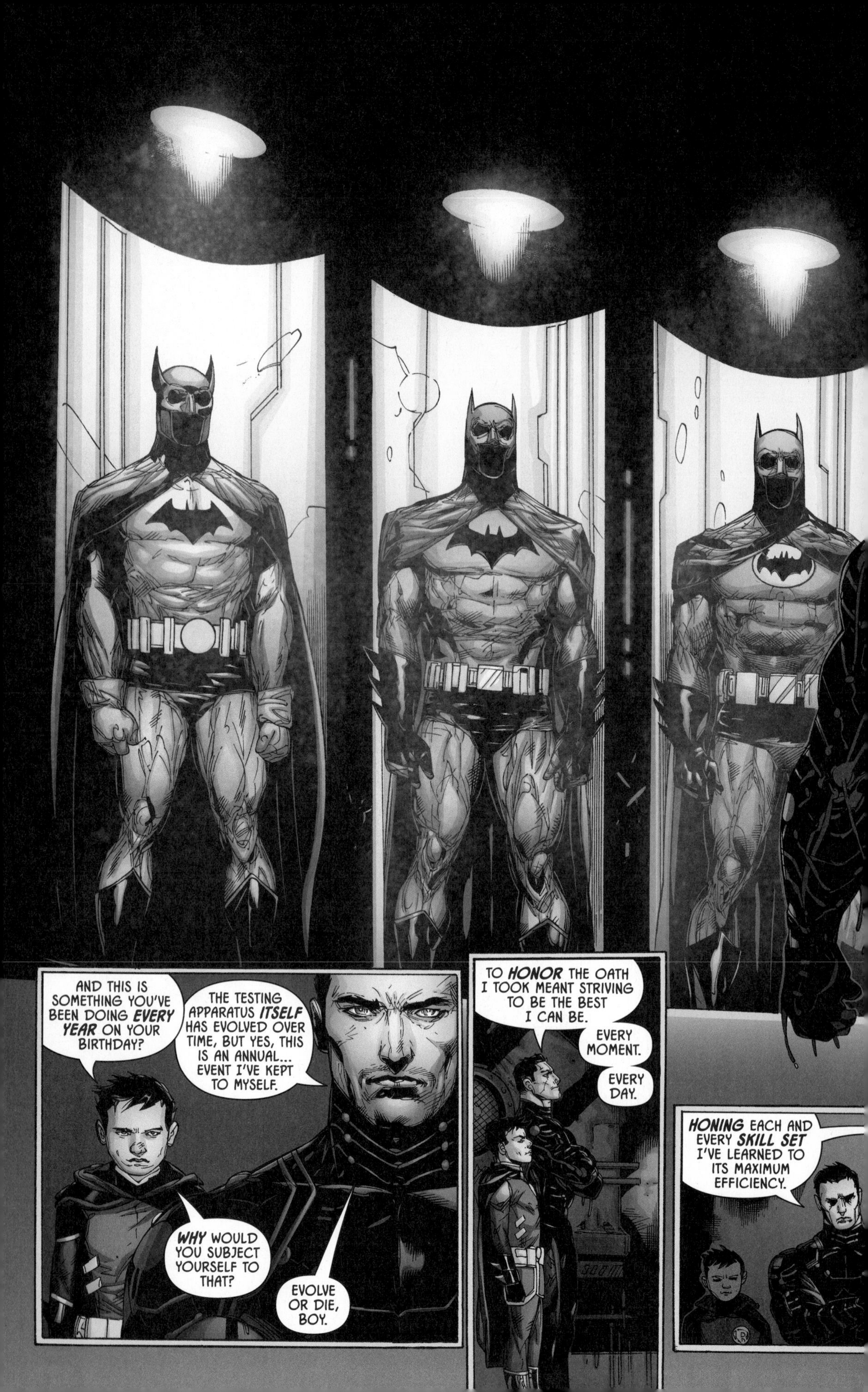
AND THIS IS SOMETHING YOU'VE BEEN DOING EVERY YEAR ON YOUR BIRTHDAY?
THE TESTING APPARATUS ITSELF HAS EVOLVED OVER TIME, BUT YES, THIS IS AN ANNUAL... EVENT I'VE KEPT TO MYSELF.
WHY WOULD YOU SUBJECT YOURSELF TO THAT?
EVOLVE OR DIE, BOY.
TO HONOR THE OATH I TOOK MEANT STRIVING TO BE THE BEST I CAN BE.
EVERY MOMENT.
EVERY DAY.
HONING EACH AND EVERY SKILL SET I'VE LEARNED TO ITS MAXIMUM EFFICIENCY.

"There is not one among us in whom a devil does not dwell; at some time, on some point, that devil masters each of us...It is not having been in the dark house, but having left it, that counts."
—*Theodore Roosevelt*

VARIANT COVER GALLERY

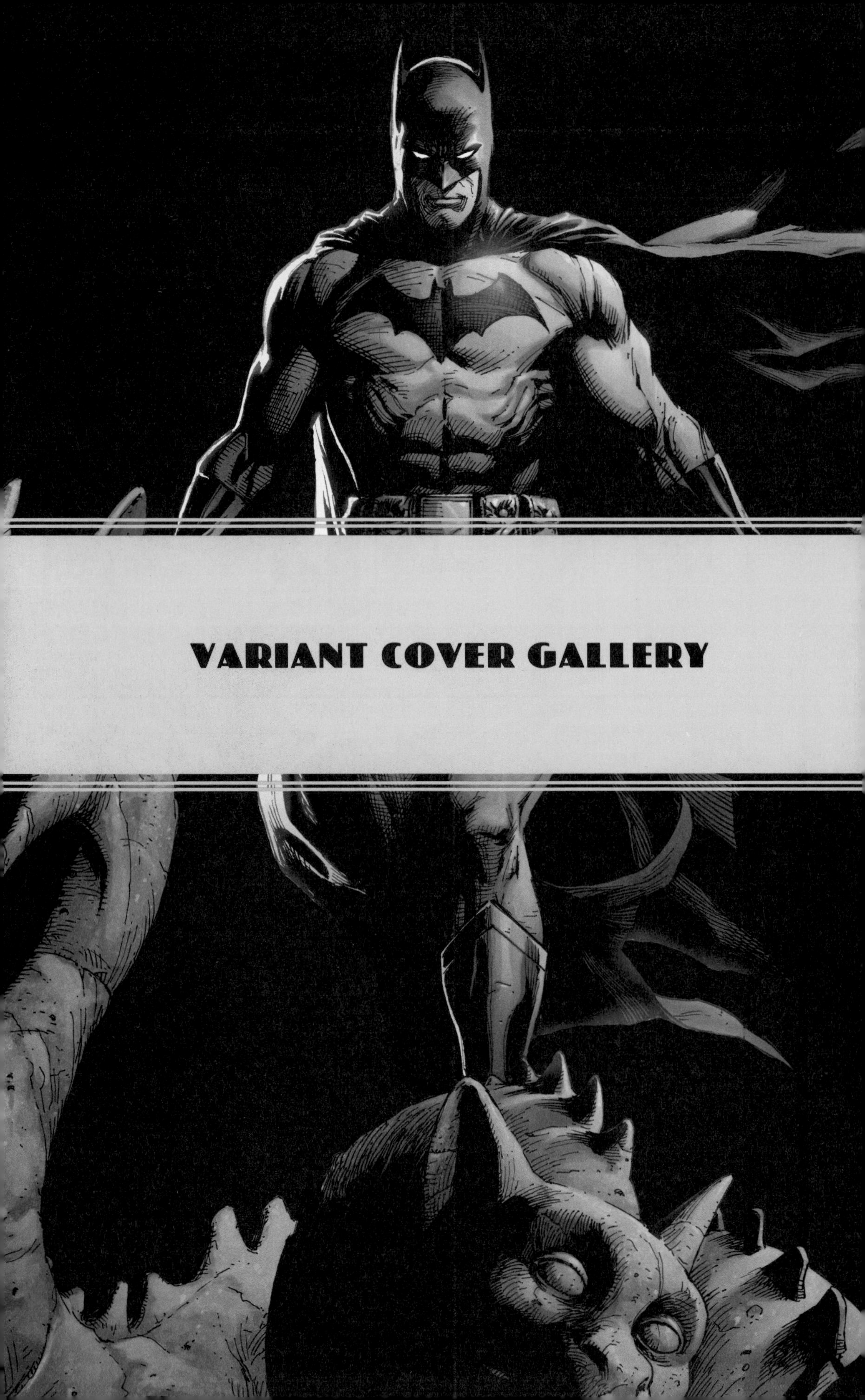

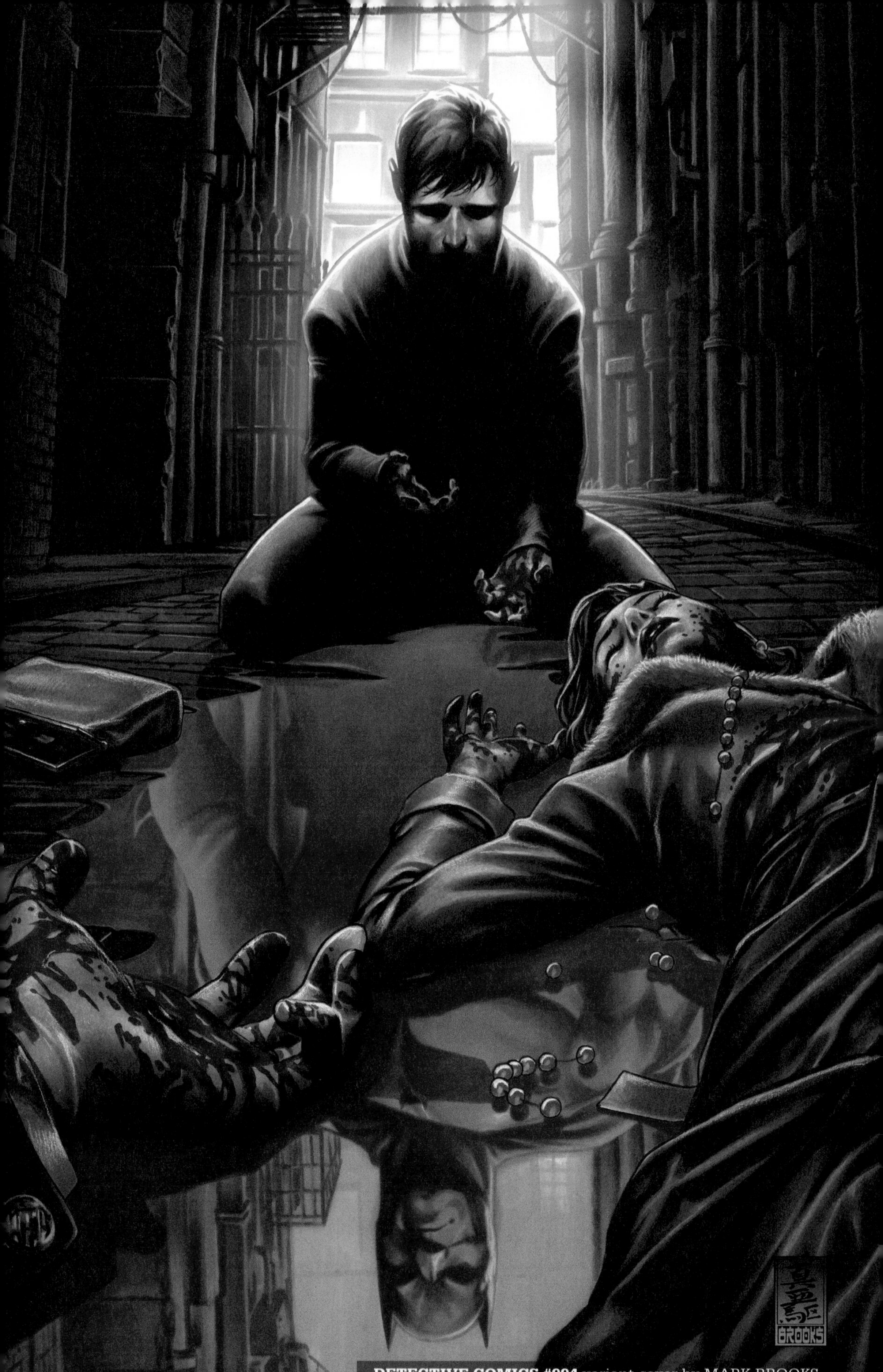
BROOKS

DETECTIVE COMICS #994 variant cover by MARK BROOKS

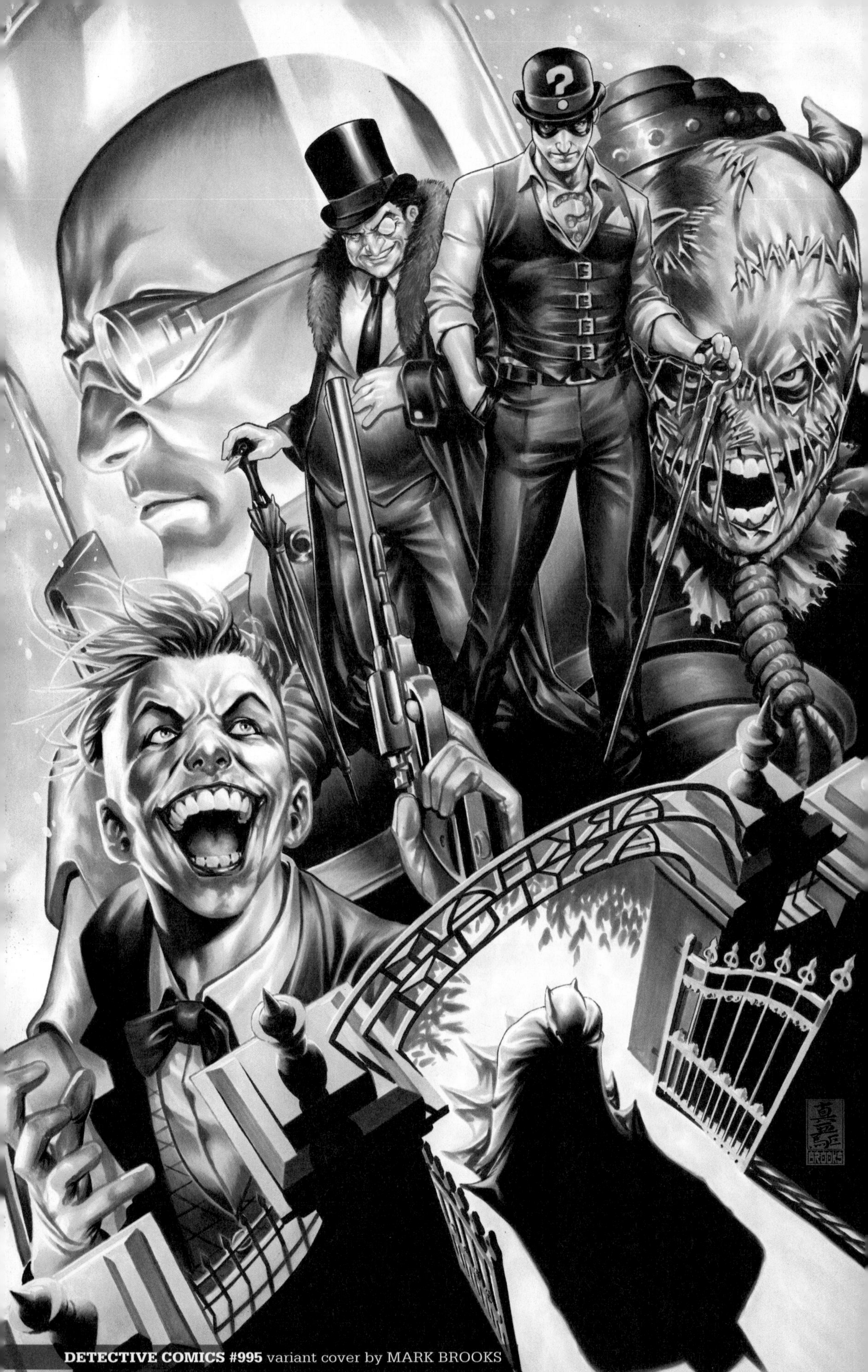
BROOKS

DETECTIVE COMICS #995 variant cover by MARK BROOKS

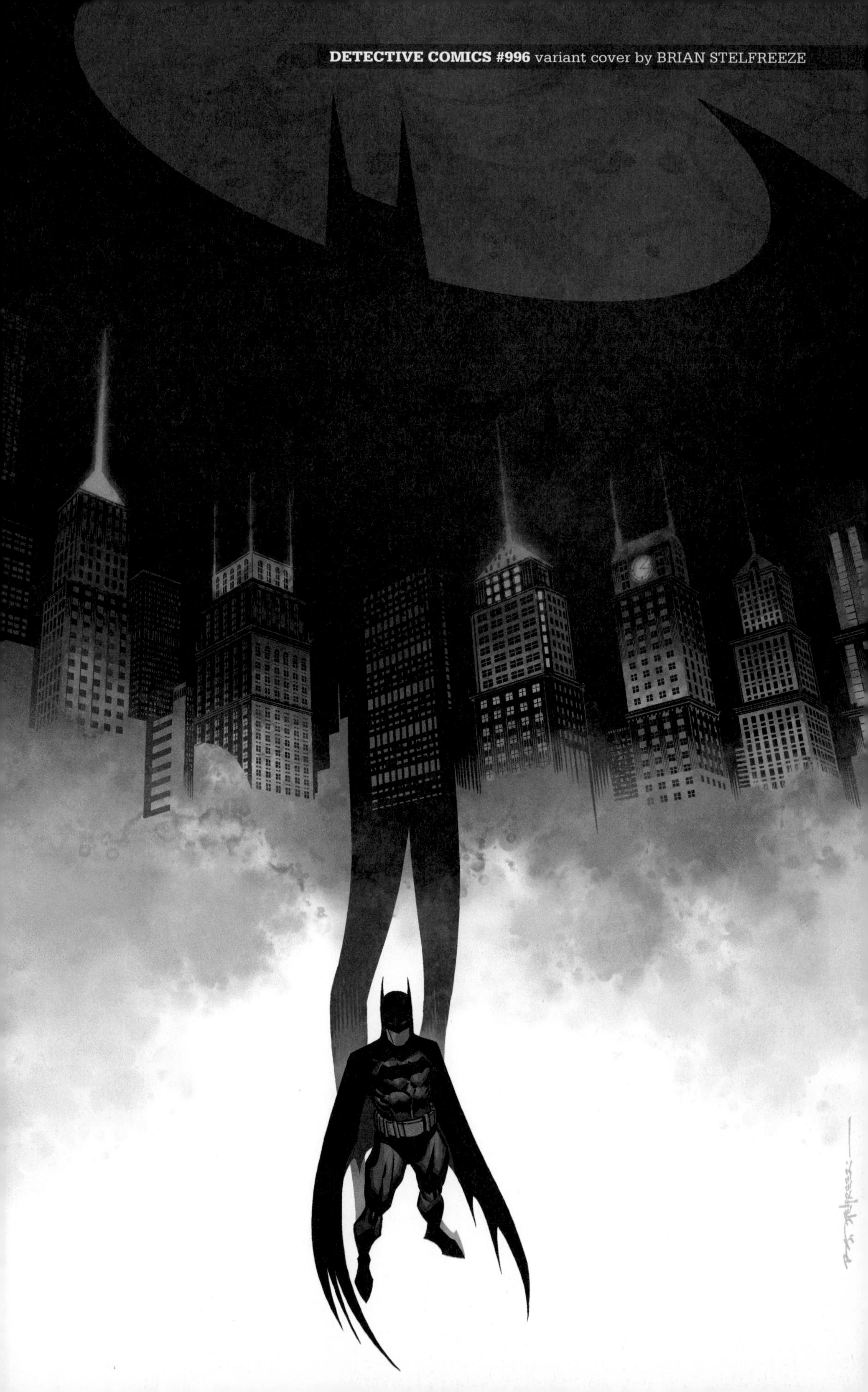

DETECTIVE COMICS #996 variant cover by BRIAN STELFREEZE